The *Economies* of
Central-*City* Neighborhoods

The *Economies of Central-City Neighborhoods*

Richard D. Bingham

*Levin College of Urban Affairs,
Cleveland State University*

Zhongcai Zhang

Ohio Savings Bank

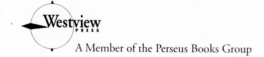
Westview
PRESS

A Member of the Perseus Books Group

Copyright © 2001 by Westview Press, A Member of the Perseus Books Group

Published in 2001 in the United States of America by Westview Press, 5500 Central Avenue, Boulder,
Colorado 80301–2877, and in the United Kingdom by Westview Press, 12 Hid's Copse Road, Cumnor
Hill, Oxford OX2 9JJ

Find us on the World Wide Web at www.westviewpress.com

Library of Congress Cataloging-in-Publication Data

Bingham, Richard D.
 The economies of central-city neighborhoods / Richard D. Bingham and Zhongcai Zhang.
  p. cm.
 Includes bibliographical references and index.
 ISBN 0-8133-9771-5
 1. Urban economics. 2. Inner cities—Economic aspects—Ohio. 3. Neighborhood—Economic
aspects—Ohio. 4. Industrial location—Ohio. 5. Ohio—Economic conditions. I. Zhang,
Zhongcai. II. Title.

HT321 .B55 2001
330.9173'2—dc21
                                                                                        00-065427

The paper used in this publication meets the requirements of the American National Standard for
Permanence of Paper for Printed Library Materials Z39.48–1984.

PERSEUS
POD
ON DEMAND   10   9   8   7   6   5   4   3   2   1

Contents

Illustrations

Acknowledgments

The authors are grateful for support provided for this research by the U.S. Department of Housing and Urban Development (Grant H–21112RG), the Graduate College of Cleveland State University, and the Urban Center of the Maxine Goodman Levin College of Urban Affairs, Cleveland State University. Without this support, this project would not have been possible. We thank Leo Wiegman, executive editor at Westview Press, whose suggestions significantly improved the book. Our thanks also go to our fine copy editor, Ida May Norton, who made this book infinitely more readable. We are indebted to our friends and colleagues who graciously assisted us with the case studies in Chapter 8—Jane Dockery, Donna Johnson, Jesse Marquette, Brian Mikelbank, Gil Peterson, and Howard Stafford.

Richard D. Bingham
Zhongcai Zhang

1

Neighborhoods and Neighborhood Economies in a Central-City Context

The central purpose of this book is to explain central-city neighborhood economies. This is a wide-ranging exploration because neighborhoods and neighborhood economies in the central city are by no means homogeneous. A neighborhood's heterogeneity may be embodied by locational attributes, such as proximity to urban and regional nodes, or by the various characteristics of residents in the neighborhood. Because of this wide array of variables, studies and analysis of central-city economies that treat the city as an aggregate are less insightful and meaningful.

A 1992 American Housing Survey shows that some two-thirds of Americans are more concerned with the quality of neighborhoods than with the quality of the physical structures. The reason may be that people feel they have more control over making improvements to their homes, whereas they are less confident about their ability to fix up the community (Apfel 1996). This perception may be particularly true in central-city neighborhoods. Negative spillover effects are observable in both intra- and interneighborhood contexts and have been detrimental to the health of the neighborhood as well as the health of the cluster of neighborhoods. This spillover also explains why piecemeal and isolated neighborhood redevelopment efforts have so far reaped little sustainable development across long-plagued central-city neighborhoods.

Neighborhood is defined as "a district or an area with distinctive characteristics" (*American Heritage Dictionary of the English Language,* 1992). Several studies (Teitz 1989; Wiewel et al. 1989; Wiewel et al. 1993) in the past decade have developed a framework to understand and study neighborhoods and neighborhood economies. From these studies, two main generalizations can be made: (1) Neighborhoods are contiguous subareas within a city or region that are seen by their inhabitants and others as possessing internal coherence and social meaning. On the side of culture and social relations, they are places where people live, sleep in relative security, and carry on the ordinary business of life with its need for both privacy and social contact. From an economic perspective, neighborhoods are places where both consumption and production take place. (2) A neighborhood economy not only includes the economic structure and process within geographic boundaries but also implies the labor force participation, occupational distribution, and earning power of neighborhood residents. In general, neighborhoods bring to the regional economies four major assets: the human and other capital resources of the residents; the physical stock of buildings, infrastructure, and amenities; the location within the region that creates economic rental value of the land; and the political strength of residents in larger formal and informal governmental systems.

Neighborhoods are building blocks of regional economies. At the metropolitan level, regional economy encompasses the functional labor market as well as the housing market, but the intraregional segmentation of such markets is related more to growth and decline in urban neighborhoods. Just as the national economy is viewed as a system of highly integrated regional economies, a regional economy is also composed of clusters of interconnected neighborhood economies. The literature on regional economies is rich, but there have been few efforts conceptualizing neighborhood and neighborhood economies. Decade after decade, urban and regional scholars have been preoccupied with studying the restructuring and development of regional economies in the context of national and global economic changes. In addition, many grassroots development efforts have been vigorously pursued even without a clear understanding of neighborhood economies that shape and are shaped by neighborhood characteristics. As pointed out by Wiewel et al. (1989, 94):

> There has been relatively little serious theoretical thinking about neighborhood economic development. Regional economic theorists rarely focus on how regional changes play out at the level where people actually experience them. This gap is particularly glaring because hundreds, if not thousands, of neighborhood organizations are presently involved in neighborhood development projects. Such projects are typically conceived and implemented without consideration of the economic trajectory of the region in which a neighborhood is located.

A neighborhood economy consists of clusters of firms that provide not only services but also neighborhood jobs for residents. One study has found that in the Chicago area, physical job proximity is the principal determinant of local working—the proportion of residents of a neighborhood who work near the neighborhood (Immergluck 1998a). Further, both the supply of and demand for labor in retail and neighborhood-oriented service industries are quite localized, and such firms tend to employ many neighborhood residents (Theodore and Carlson 1996). For example, a commercial bank branch would provide not only financial services but also service-sector jobs to the neighborhood. The presence of a supermarket is especially important to poor neighborhoods because it provides not only low-priced foods but also low-skill jobs for neighborhood residents.

More broadly defined, a neighborhood economy contains another two essential components: (1) the labor market characteristics of the residents and (2) the social, economic, demographic, and physical characteristics of the neighborhood. The first component directly concerns the earning power of the residents when they participate in the regional labor market and also attracts certain firms that prefer a neighborhood labor force. The second factor pertains to firms' decisions about location, as they choose the neighborhood in order to have proximity to their customers or to convey positive images to their clients. On one hand, neighborhood characteristics affect businesses' choice of location. On the other hand, business location strengthens a neighborhood.

Economic restructuring in the late 1970s and 1980s resulted in a decline in the manufacturing sector in many manufacturing-dependent regional economies and a consequent surge in services industries. The neighborhood economies in aged central cities like Ohio's have evolved over an entire century. Their past economic prosperity and their center position in regional economies were built around their strengths in manufacturing industries, and their economic deterioration in the 1980s and 1990s were partly the result of their reliance on manufacturing. Both industry activities and neighborhood characteristics have shaped and reshaped each other. First, the restructuring displaced countless workers in many urban neighborhoods who once earned a living wage from traditional factory jobs and now have been driven to low-paying service jobs. Second, manufacturing industries have become more technology-intensive, and the increased automation has reduced demand for low-skilled workers, even if these firms remain in the central city. Meanwhile, today's technology-driven new economy has left many already distressed urban neighborhoods further behind, as the residents in these neighborhoods are rarely able to ride with the new economy because of their human-capital deficit. The majority of various services industries seem unable to sustain and improve the living standards of many inner-city residents, especially when workers with these service jobs are the primary wage earners in the household. These are often called "dead-end" jobs that offer no employment security, few fringe benefits, and little possibility of career advancement (Bates 1997; Reichert 1997; Blakely and Small 1997).

Well-documented job decentralization (Wilson 1987, 1996; Kasarda 1989) has produced significant adverse effects on the economic fortunes of central-city neighborhoods and their residents. Job decentralization and population decentralization are two mutually reinforcing spatial flows within a regional economic space. Job decentralization has been triggered by a variety of factors, such as increasing urbanization diseconomies (e.g., crime, high land cost, congestion, and pollution), changes in manufacturing production technology, an increase in footloose industries due to rapid changes in transportation and telecommunications, and other policy factors (Bingham et al. 1997; Warf 1995; Mieszkowski and Mills 1993; Blair and Premus 1987). For example, public policy has been recently criticized for its anti-central-city and prosuburban orientation in the past decades in the form of major roadways and subsidies to buyers of newer and larger suburban homes (Ohio Urban University Program 1997; Szatan and Testa 1994). As firms suburbanize, their workforce typically follows. This trend is also partly the result of spatial shift of demand in many consumer-oriented industries (Zhang and Bingham 2000). Nevertheless, job decentralization not only eroded neighborhood job access in central cities but also further induced the exodus of middle-class families; these factors created a shortage of positive role models and job networks that are of fundamental importance to neighborhood stability and vitality.

One common accusation is that many poor urban neighborhoods lack and are underserved by a sufficient variety of neighborhood-oriented industries. For example, formal financial institutions (e.g., banks) that once served households of all income levels all but withdrew from low-income neighborhoods in the 1980s. Households in these areas now have to turn to a growing second-tier financial sector, such as check-cashing outlets and money orders, in order to meet their financial needs (Dymski and Veitch 1996). This informal financial sector provides not only more costly transaction services but also no adequate credit and savings mechanism (Dymski 1997). Vaughn (1989, 40) describes neighborhood disinvestment by banks:

A community bank is the primary financial service in any neighborhood for housing rehabilitation and commercial development, automobile purchases, and college tuition. . . . Unfortunately, most banks have pulled away from this ideal. Local branches are in reality depositories for money that banks invest elsewhere . . . in communities where there are several banks, the ones with the most resources are leaving. Though these banks proclaim their commitment to the community, they provide only token grants and loans, so as to meet their Community Reinvestment Act responsibilities. . . . In areas where all the banks have gone, the neighborhood faces economic strangulation. Businesses that depend on community banking services cannot survive, leaving the area ripe for further abandonment.

In the case of grocery industries, residents in many poor central-city neighborhoods still pay more for basic foods than do nearby urban and suburban residents (Bell 1993; Porter 1997). This is not because poor central-city neighborhoods seem to have fewer grocery stores but because they are served by a different type of store—mom-and-pop stores and convenience stores—whereas better-off central-city neighborhoods more frequently have supermarkets (Bingham and Zhang 1997). Other studies (e.g., Chung and Myers 1999) have also found that the major factor contributing to higher grocery costs in poor neighborhoods is that large chain stores, where prices tend to be lower, are not located in these neighborhoods. Alwitt and Donley in a study of Chicago neighborhoods (1997) also found that residents of poor neighborhoods must travel more than two miles to have access to the same numbers of supermarkets, large drug stores, banks, and other types of stores available to residents of non-poor areas.

Another commonly held view is that industries discriminate against racially mixed neighborhoods and their residents have fewer job opportunities. For example, a recent study (Immergluck 1998b, 12) found that low- and moderate-skilled jobs are significantly fewer in predominantly black neighborhoods (two-mile-radius zone) than the average. Others have also asserted that race and space remain deeply intertwined in the American political economy, and ghetto locations are simply not desirable space for most enterprises, irrespective of the economic fillips government offers (Blakely and Small 1997).

Although there have been long-standing efforts for redevelopment, revitalization, and rehabilitation of declining urban areas, little attention has been given to any serious understanding of central-city neighborhoods in both economic and social terms. It seems that, to some degree, central-city neighborhoods have been implicitly or explicitly assumed to be homogeneous. The seven Ohio central cities discussed in this book (Akron, Cincinnati, Cleveland, Columbus, Dayton, Toledo, and Youngstown) have historically been manufacturing centers and are still specialized in durable manufacturing. Each of these cities still has a larger population than most metropolitan areas, and it stands to reason that there must be healthy subareas as well as decayed ones in such central cities.

Economic forces that shape neighborhood fate do operate in a larger context. Studying central-city neighborhood economies, however, is vital because an understanding of intraneighborhood relationships between various industrial activities and neighborhood characteristics can shed light on the dynamics of urban neighborhood change and the interconnection among neighborhoods. Such understanding would, accordingly, be illuminating to central-city economic development policy.

References

Alwitt, Linda A., and Thomas D. Donley. 1997. "Retail Stores in Poor Urban Neighborhoods." *Journal of Consumer Affairs* 31(1) Summer: 139–164.

Apfel, Ira. 1996. "A Beautiful Day in the Neighborhood." *American Demographics* 18(3): 20–22.

Bates, Timothy. 1997. "Political Economy of Urban Poverty in the 21st Century: How Progress and Public Policy Generate Rising Poverty." In Thomas D. Boston and Catherine L. Ross (eds.), *The Inner City: Urban Poverty and Economic Development in the Next Century*, pp. 111–122. New Brunswick, NJ: Transaction Publishers.

Bell, Judith, and Bonnie Maria Burlin. 1993. "In Urban Areas: Many of the Poor Still Pay More for Food." *Journal of Public Policy and Marketing* 12(2) Fall: 268–270.

Bingham, Richard D., William M. Bowen, Yosra A. Amara, Lynn W. Bachelor, Jane Dockery, Jack Dustin, Deborah Kimble, Thomas Maraffa, David L. McKee, Kent P. Schwirian, Gail Gordon Sommers, and Howard A. Stafford. 1997. *Beyond Edge Cities*. New York: Garland.

Bingham, Richard D., and Zhongcai Zhang. 1997. "Poverty and Economic Morphology of Ohio Central-City Neighborhoods." *Urban Affairs Review* 32(6) July: 766–796.

Blair, John P., and Robert Premus. 1987. "Major Factors in Industrial Location: A Review." *Economic Development Quarterly* 1: 72–85.

_____. 1993. "Location Theory." In R. D. Bingham and R. Mier (eds.), *Theories of Local Economic Development*, pp. 3–26. Newbury Park, CA: Sage Publications.

Blakely, Edward J., and Leslie Small. 1997. "Michael Porter: New Gilder of Ghettos." In Thomas D. Boston and Catherine L. Ross (eds.), *The Inner City: Urban Poverty and Economic Development in the Next Century*, pp. 181–183. New Brunswick, NJ: Transaction Publishers.

Chung, Chanjin, and Samuel L Myers Jr. 1999. "Do the Poor Pay More for Food? An Analysis of Grocery Store Availability and Food Price Disparities." *Journal of Consumer Affairs* 33(2) Winter: 276–296.

Dymski, Gary A. 1997. "Business Strategy and Access to Capital in Inner-City Revitalization." In Thomas D. Boston and Catherine L. Ross (eds.), *The Inner City: Urban Poverty and Economic Development in the Next Century,* pp. 51–65. New Brunswick, NJ: Transaction Publishers.

Dymski, Gary, and John Veitch. 1996. "Credit Flows to Cities." In Todd Schafer and Jeff Faux (eds.), *Reclaiming Prosperity: A Blueprint for Progressive Economic Reform.* New York: M. E. Sharpe.

Immergluck, Daniel. 1998a. "Neighborhood Economic Development and Local Working: The Effects of Nearby Jobs on Where Residents Work." *Economic Geography* (April): 170–187.

———. 1998b. "Job Proximity and the Urban Employment Problem: Do Suitable Nearby Jobs Improve Neighborhood Employment Rates?" *Urban Studies* 35(1): 7–23.

Kasarda, J. D. 1989. "Urban Industrial Transition and the Underclass." *Annals of the American Academy of Political and Social Science* (501): 26–47.

———. 1993. "Urban Industrial Transition and the Underclass." In W. J. Wilson (ed.), *The Ghetto Underclass: Social Science Perspectives,* pp. 43–64. Newbury Park, CA: Sage Publications.

Mieszkowski, P., and Edwin S. Mills. 1993. "The Causes of Metropolitan Suburbanization." *Journal of Economic Perspectives* 7(3) Summer: 135–147.

Ohio Urban University Program. 1997. *The Creation and Movement of Community Wealth: The Shifting Resource Base.* Prepared for the fall forum of the Ohio Urban University Program, October 9, 1997.

Porter, Michael E. 1997. "An Economic Strategy for America's Inner Cities: Addressing the Controversy." In Thomas D. Boston and Catherine L. Ross (eds.), *The Inner City: Urban Poverty and Economic Development in the Next Century,* pp. 304–336. New Brunswick, NJ: Transaction Publishers.

Reichert, Usha Nair. 1997. "Revitalizing the Inner City: A Holistic Approach." In Thomas D. Boston and Catherine L. Ross (eds.), *The Inner City: Urban Poverty and Economic Development in the Next Century,* pp. 185–192. New Brunswick, NJ: Transaction Publishers.

Szatan, Jerry W., and William A. Testa. 1994. "Metropolitan Areas Spread Out." *Chicago Fed Letter* 83 (July): 1–3.

Teitz, Michael B. 1989. "Neighborhood Economics: Local Communities and Regional Markets." *Economic Development Quarterly* 3(2): 111–122.

Vaughn, John. 1989. "Banks Cash Out of the Ghetto." *Business and Society Review* 70 (Summer): 40–42.

Warf, B. 1995 "Telecommunications and the Changing Geographies of Knowledge Transmission in the Late 20th Century." *Urban Studies* 32(2): 361–378.

Wiewel, Wim, Bridget Brown, and Marya Morris. 1989. "The Linkage Between Regional and Neighborhood Development." *Economic Development Quarterly* 3(2): 94–110.

Wiewel, Wim, Michael Teitz, and Robert Giloth. 1993. "The Economic Development of Neighborhoods and Localities." In R. D. Bingham and R. Mier (eds.), *Theories of Local Economic Development: Perspectives from Across the Disciplines.* Newbury Park, CA: Sage Publications.

Wilson, W. J. 1987. *The Truly Disadvantaged*. Chicago, IL: University of Chicago Press.
_____. 1996. *When Work Disappears: The World of the New Urban Poor*. New York: Knopf.
Zhang, Zhongcai, and Richard D. Bingham. 2000. "Metropolitan Employment Growth and Neighborhood Job Access in Spatial and Skills Perspectives: Empirical Evidence from Seven Ohio Metropolitan Regions." *Urban Affairs Review* 35(3) January: 390–421.

2

Ohio's Central Cities[*]

Ohio is one of the more urban states in the union. Over 80 percent of the population—more than 8.5 million people—live in metropolitan areas. The state ranks eighth in the number of people living in urban areas. This study covers the seven central cities of the major metropolitan areas in the state: Akron, Cincinnati, Cleveland, Columbus, Dayton, Toledo, and Youngstown (see Figure 2.1). These cities are very different from one other in terms of the development of their local economies. It is therefore useful to describe briefly the economic histories of each city.

Historical Overview

Manufacturing is at the core of Ohio's economic history. The state is part of the industrial heartland of the nation. One perceived image of Ohio's early industrial history is a scene of ethnic workers passing through factory gates, smokestacks belching clouds of smoke, and massive industrial complexes. And much of that picture was true. Ohio's original industries included milling, cereals, clay products, foundries, matches, and farm machinery. But by 1890 these industries had all but vanished and been replaced by oil, steel, tires, automobiles, glass, and the cash register.

Youngstown was a steel empire. People called Akron the tire capital. John Patterson, president of National Cash Register (NCR), dominated business, social, and political life in Dayton to such a degree that the city was known as the "Cash." Toledo made glass. Cincinnati manufactured machinery and cleaning products for the nation. Cleveland's Standard Oil

---

[*]This chapter was coauthored with Abdelaziz El Jaouhari, whose contribution is greatly appreciated.

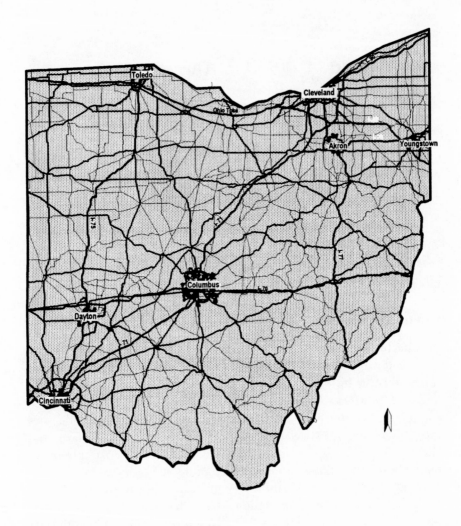

Figure 2.1   Ohio Central Cities

controlled the petroleum refining industry worldwide, and its steel mills stretched out from the central city, cutting deep into the Ohio landscape.

Automobile parts and assembly plants increased throughout the twentieth century and came to dominate directly the economic health of . Cleveland, Dayton, and Toledo and, indirectly, Akron (tires) and Youngstown (sheet metal) as well as scores of smaller cities. In the shadows of large manufacturing plants, thousands of smaller manufacturing companies fabricated metal, rubber, plastic, and fiber products needed by industry and consumers in the region, the state, and throughout the nation (Dockery et al. 1997, 46).

During the first half of the century, the economies of Ohio's cities ebbed and flowed with the times. World War I secured Ohio's dominance in manufacturing, but it also meant disaster in the Great Depression as thousands of factories shut their gates. The coming of World War II rescued Ohio's cities, and they reached their peaks of prosperity in the postwar period.

However, by the mid-1970s, all that had changed. Ohio's image became one of crumbling smokestacks, chained factory gates, deteriorating neighborhoods, and a burning Cuyahoga River in Cleveland. Between 1972 and 1994, manufacturing employment in Cleveland fell by 192,000, and as jobs declined, so too did population. Between 1960 and 1990, the population of Akron dropped by 23 percent, Cincinnati by 28 percent, Cleveland by 42 percent, and Dayton by 31 percent. Only Toledo and Columbus avoided the population loss. Population grew in Toledo by 5 percent and in Columbus by 34 percent (Dockery et al. 1997, 47).

Akron

Akron's economic claim to fame was rubber. Known as the rubber capital of the world, Akron was once home to the nation's leading rubber companies: Goodyear, Firestone, and General Tire. Today, rubber no longer plays the dominant role in Akron's economy. With the decline of the rubber industry locally, Akron has shifted its focus to a related and growing industry—polymers. In addition, the economy has broadened its linkages to Cleveland and northeast Ohio and is developing specializations in health services and medical products.

Akron's specialization in rubber began in 1870 when Goodrich opened a rubber hose and rain-gear factory. Soon a large rubber industry cluster developed to supply nearby Midwestern automakers and other local industries. A machinery and tool supplier base emerged to support rubber fabrication and industrial manufacturing. New immigrants and labor from the neighboring states settled in Akron, drawn to the opportunity of well-paying jobs. In 1910, Akron's population was 69,000. A decade later the city's population had tripled to more than 208,000. By 1930, Akron was supplying 40 percent of the nation's demand for tires. The Great Depression slowed the growth of the city, which lost 4 percent of its population, but the effect was only temporary as World War II demand for rubber and industrial products enabled Akron to regain its full productive capacity.

Beginning in the late 1960s, the rubber industry in Akron entered a period of slow but steady decline. A number of factories closed their facilities. Others began to organize and merge with firms headquartered outside the region or moved their production facilities. This restructuring occurred largely for two reasons—to reduce labor costs and to modernize production facilities. The result was that between 1950 and 1990, Akron lost 41,000 rubber jobs, and the local economy was thrown into a recession.

This crisis was difficult for Akron, but the region developed new sources of economic growth that are creating higher-skilled jobs and new economic opportunities. During the 1950s and 1960s, the Institute of Rubber Research at the University of Akron expanded its research activities into polymer materials such as synthetic rubber and plastics. The institute was joined in these efforts by the research divisions of the tire companies. Spin-off enterprises from these research efforts contributed to the beginnings of an advanced polymers industry cluster.

Today, Akron is home to some 400 firms involved in the research, development, and manufacture of synthetic polymers. These advanced materials are used in a wide range of industrial applications, including packaging, medical devices, auto components, household appliances, and construction processes. Recently, more than $1 billion in private capital for new plant expansion has flowed into the region. Akron's advanced polymers industry cluster now employs about 14,000 workers. The large polymer manufacturers such as Rubbermaid, Little Tikes (plastic toys), and Advanced Elastomer Systems LP (new synthetic rubber) make up the core of the cluster. The cluster draws strength from the support it receives from the College of Polymer Science and Engineering at the University of Akron and the Polymer Materials Department at Case Western Reserve University in Cleveland.

In addition to polymer production, the region has evolved into a leading international research center for related rubber and synthetic polymer sciences. Although the major tire companies have moved their production facilities elsewhere, their research divisions have stayed in Akron. In turn, this research complex has attracted the research and development branches of other firms, such as the Shanghai Tire and Rubber Company.

This brief survey is not to suggest that rubber production in Akron is entirely a thing of the past. Tire production is gone, but the fabrication of rubber components such as syringes and bags for medical and other industrial uses still exists. This industry cluster also includes aluminum and copper foundries and other manufacturers of machine parts. Rubber and machine parts manufacturing still employ about 15,000 people in the Akron area.

The health care system in Akron employs more than 29,000 workers. This cluster is centered on nine hospitals in the region, including the preeminent regional burn center at the Akron Children's Hospital. The industry is closely connected to the larger health care service cluster in Cleveland.

Finally, due to its location on a well-developed interstate highway system and three established rail lines, Akron has developed a significant transportation and warehousing industry. Fifty-seven percent of the U.S. population and 55 percent of the nation's manufacturing facilities are located within a 500-mile radius of Akron. Akron is headquarters for trucking giant Roadway Services Inc. The region has more than 159 trucking firms employing about 7,000 workers.

As with most older cities, much of the recent economic expansion in the region has been in the suburbs. Akron's downtown has witnessed a decline in businesses and employment over the past several decades. In addition, the city's population has been dropping at an annual rate of about 2.9 percent, whereas the remainder of the metropolitan area has been growing at a rate of about 3.8 percent (Dockery et al. 1997, 48–52).

Cincinnati

From its beginning in 1788, Cincinnati engaged in commerce as its main business activity. Early Cincinnati was a shipping center on the Ohio River, the major transportation route in the region, but the city quickly developed a significant manufacturing presence. The first decade of the nineteenth century marked the beginning of manufacturing with a few shops producing wood and iron objects, several breweries, a glass-making shop, a foundry, and a steam mill. By 1826 the city's population was more than 16,000, up from only 750 at the turn of the century. An estimated

500 people were employed in water transportation, 800 in trade and mercantile pursuits, and 3,000 in manufacturing. By the 1840s, Cincinnati had become a major meat-packing center and was nicknamed "Porkopolis" by virtue of its being the largest pork-packing center in the world. That legacy continues today (although the meat-packing industry is almost gone). Over the entrance to a new city park along the reviving waterfront are two "Flying Pig" sculptures (Dockery et al. 1997, 52–53).

Commerce remained the leading sector of Cincinnati's economy during the mid-1800s. The city imported more than $11 million in food products and exported approximately $9 million—largely in processed foods. Manufacturing also started to diversify and gain in importance. In the same period, Cincinnati had 1,594 manufacturing establishments that provided work to approximately 10,600 workers. The leading activities in manufacturing were the pork-packing houses, rolling mills, shipbuilding, foundries, and a number of small shops. Banks also were considered stable and played an important role in Cincinnati's economy (Glazer 1968).

Cincinnati's central location led to its development as a railroad center. The first railroad line to serve the city, the Little Miami Railroad, was chartered in 1836; by 1846 the company connected Cincinnati with Springfield. In 1851 another railroad line, CH&D (Cincinnati, Hamilton, and Dayton), connected Cincinnati with Hamilton and Dayton. By 1862, Cincinnati was connected to Dayton, Toledo, Cleveland, Pittsburgh, Wheeling, Lexington, St. Louis, and Chicago. The railroad enterprise proved to be profitable, and it contributed substantially to the expansion of Cincinnati's economy. About 44 trains were operated daily to ensure connection with major cities (Condit 1977).

The development of the transportation network attracted more immigrants to Cincinnati. By 1850 the population was 115,435, and in two decades it grew by more than 100,000, resulting in rapid urbanization that accompanied economic prosperity.

In 1900 the population of Cincinnati was 325,902, growing to 503,998 in 1950. The region has maintained a steady rate of growth. Many of the older industries, such as meat packing, are no longer part of Cincinnati's industrial life. However, the city was able to maintain a diversified economic base, which enabled it to avoid the economic downturns experienced by other Ohio cities such as Cleveland and Akron.

Today, there are more than 3,000 manufacturing plants in the eight-county Cincinnati Consolidated Metropolitan Statistical Area (CMSA). Major companies with 1,000 or more employees include General Electric (aircraft engines), Procter and Gamble (soaps, food, toiletries), Kroger (food stores and processing), Armco (steel), Cincinnati Milicron (machine tools), Ford Motor Company (automatic transmissions), Kenner Products (toys), Avon Products (cosmetics), U.S. Shoe Corporation (apparel, etc.), Merrell Dow Pharmaceutical, Gibson Greetings (greeting cards), Monsanto (plastics), and Steelcraft (metal doors). However, manufacturing accounts for only 20 percent of the region's employment. One-quarter of Cincinnati's labor force is in services, 12 percent in government and education, and 23 percent in construction, transportation, utilities, wholesale, finance, insurance, and real estate. The regional economy is diverse and is in good condition. It is expected to continue its steady growth. The city of Cincinnati, like most of its sister cities in Ohio, has not shared in that growth. The central city grew until the mid-1950s, but since then the population has declined by about 30 percent (Dockery et al. 1997, 53–56).

Cleveland

Modern Cleveland was born during the Civil War, the event that transformed Cleveland from a commercial city to an industrial city. Between 1860 and 1870, its population more than doubled from 43,400 to 92,800, making Cleveland the fifteenth-largest city in the nation. By 1870 fourteen rolling mills were operating in the city, and more than 1,100 factories were producing everything from railroad equipment to industrial machinery to stoves. There were also more than twenty oil refineries operating in the Cuyahoga Valley (Miller et al. 1990, 70).

By the late 1800s, Cleveland had become a classic "break-in-bulk" shipping point, with lake freighters meeting the east-west railroad running from New York to Chicago and the north-south line running through southern Ohio. The steel industry was fed by ore carriers bringing ore from the Upper Peninsula of Michigan and later from the Mesabi Range in Minnesota. The steel industry was fueled by coal hauled by rail car from southern Ohio and West Virginia. Transportation was also vital to the development of the oil industry. Crude oil was shipped by rail to Cleveland, processed into kerosene, and shipped by boat to Buffalo, Chicago, and various Canadian cities. John D. Rockefeller organized Cleveland's oil industry as the foundation of one of the nation's largest industrial monopolies. The city also became a shipbuilding center. Production of lake freighters boomed, and Cleveland became one of the largest shipbuilding centers in the country.

Each of these activities formed the core of clusters of major industrial complexes. The steel industry produced wire and rails for the opening of the west and flat-rolled steel for automobiles and appliances. The combination of steel and shipbuilding led to companies producing machine tools, industrial fittings, and, later, automobiles and automobile parts. The oil industry became the foundation of a large industrial complex producing chemicals, paints, and coatings.

The period from 1870 to the late 1920s produced an unprecedented entrepreneurialism and economic growth in the region that, by 1930, had made Cleveland the sixth-largest city in the United States. The lighting industry, which depended upon inventive genius and not transportation, took root. In 1878, Charles Brush invented the arc light. His company was absorbed by General Electric in 1891 and later became its lamp division. Westinghouse was founded in Cleveland in 1886. Cleveland also specialized in electric motors, which led to the development of a machine tool industry. Lincoln Electric, founded in 1895, produced motors, and Reliance Electric, established in 1905, produced variable-speed motors.

The major change in the Cleveland economy between 1905 and the end of World War II was the development of the auto industry. By 1930 the industry was well-established, and the region had become a major supplier of automotive parts and accessories.

In the 1950s and 1960s, the economy flourished, driven largely by steel and automotive production. The end of the Vietnam War brought the beginning of a serious decline in Cleveland's manufacturing economy that worsened throughout the late 1970s and early 1980s. Employment in the four-county Cleveland Primary Metropolitan Statistical Area (PMSA) peaked in 1979 at 903,000. By 1983 the region had lost 30 percent of its total employment and 14 percent of its annualized earnings. The list of plant closures was striking. Westinghouse, which had operated in a lakeside manufacturing plant since 1890, closed the facility in 1979 and ceased the manufacturing of lighting products in the region entirely in 1982. General Electric kept its lamp division headquarters in East Cleveland but closed six factories that manufactured bulbs and components and moved these operations offshore.

There was no visible improvement in the economy until 1993, and then the structure of the economy was very different from what it had been. Manufacturing employment accounted for 30.3 percent of employment in 1979 but only 19.9 percent by 1993. During this same period, employment in services increased from 18.6 percent to 29.2 percent. In short, the economy has undergone a major restructuring and become much more diversified. But, paradoxically, the durable-goods sector is much more dependent on the automotive industry than it was before 1979. However, most of the major decisions made in this sector are not made in the region. At the same time, services have strengthened to the point that this sector's proportion of employment in the region exceeds the national average. Social services have become an important part of the region's economic base, as have producer and business services (Hill 1990; Dockery et al. 1997, 56–61).

Columbus

Columbus is unlike any other city in Ohio, and unlike most cities anywhere, in that it was created for a specific purpose—to become the state capital. The site was chosen in 1812 because of its central location within the state. Ever since then, the activities, offices, and employees of the state government have been highly concentrated in the area. As a result, government workers constitute a significant part of local employment. In addition, other businesses that depend upon state government or state government regulation (e.g., banking, insurance) have made Columbus their home. For example, Bank One, State Savings, Nationwide Insurance, Aetna, Allstate, CIGNA, Farmers, and State Auto have national or regional headquarters in the city. Other corporate headquarters or regional centers include Bordens, Abbott Laboratories, Federal Express, Ford, General Electric, Honeywell, The Limited, and Battelle Memorial Institute. Thus the city has a distinctly white-collar flavor.

Between 1830 and 1880, the growth of the city was fostered by the establishment of a transportation network. The National Road and the Ohio-Erie Canal remarkably stimulated the growth of Columbus, as did the coming of the railroads in 1850. The transportation network spurred development of the city as a commercial center. Government, commerce, transportation, and education were predominant until the end of the nineteenth century, when Columbus started diversifying its economic base. Although industry played a small role in the early development of Columbus, the city had twenty-three malleable iron companies, foundries, and machine shops in 1887 (Blackford 1982). The economic progress was accompanied by an intensified urbanization.

As World War II neared, a significant manufacturing presence developed in Columbus. The city became the home of Curtis Aviation, and the company's aircraft plant employed 12,000 workers by 1940. This new investment had the effect of attracting other well-established companies. Between 1940 and 1950, the city added two new General Motors and Westinghouse plants. Even with these significant additions to the city's economic base, manufacturing still did not dominate the other sectors of the economy. The city continued its reliance on governmental services, education, and other commercial and financial institutions. The offices and stores in the downtown area continued to dominate the central-city economy. Employment in state government was still a large part of the picture, but so too was retailing. Major department and specialty stores included Lazarus, the Union Company, and Montaldo's. Several hotels and dining, recreation, and entertainment establishments gave the urban core a vital ambience. Old, well-established residential neighborhoods ringed the central business district (CBD) and added 40,000 residents to the downtown scene.

But downtown Columbus began to decay in the same manner as many of the older cities of the industrial Midwest. First came the suburbanization of shopping in the 1960s and 1970s with a ring of peripheral shopping centers. Then came an outward rush of the population to the new suburbs. With this loss of population, the inner city experienced a significant decline in shopping and business. The completion of the freeway system drew more employees and residential developments to the periphery. By 1980 the downtown was fighting a losing battle. The residential base declined from 40,000 to only 7,200, and the city was emblematic of many Midwestern downtowns.

However, Columbus has been relatively lucky. The city's population has increased dramatically in recent years because Columbus has pursued a vigorous policy of annexation. As the population moved out, so did the city's boundaries.

Also, since the mid-1980s, downtown Columbus has experienced a major turnaround. With the leadership of a joint public- and private-sector development corporation, Downtown Columbus, Inc., major projects have been completed in the CBD. These include a regional shopping mall, a convention center, major hotels, new office complexes, and housing. More than 80,000 people work in the downtown area, a number expected to increase to 120,000 by the early years of the twenty-first century. These jobs are heavily concentrated in producer and social services.

Residential development has accompanied commercial development. New upscale downtown housing projects include the Waterford and the Market-Mohawk. Old inner-city neighborhoods such as German Village, Victorian Village, Italian Village, and the Brewery District have been rehabilitated. The size of these residential developments is such that they now constitute the critical mass needed for further development of retail and entertainment activities in the core. A number of new projects for the downtown are on the drawing board, including a new hotel for the CBD and additional expensive residential developments. In sum, Columbus is relatively healthy and expanding. It is expanding both on its edges and in its core (Dockery et al. 1997, 61–64).

Dayton

The initial settlement of Dayton occurred around 1796 when a group of settlers purchased land at the confluence of three rivers: the Stillwater, Great Miami, and Mad. Dayton was the center of commerce, agricultural processing, and producer services throughout the nineteenth century. Because Dayton sits atop a large aquifer, the city had a natural advantage in its early development. Also, like Cleveland and Columbus, Dayton built upon its assets by supporting the construction of the Dayton-Cincinnati Canal and roads connecting the city to other markets and distribution points. Early commercial activities included firms specializing in farm machinery, wood products, and food processing.

By 1850, Dayton's population was more than 10,000, and manufacturing was on the rise. The first entrepreneurial attempt to provide the city with a solid industrial base was made possible by Barney and Thresher, a company that manufactured railroad cars in Dayton even before any railroad lines reached the city. This company was able to prosper despite numerous problems such as the lack of skilled labor and capital. By 1857 the company employed 150 workers. Most important, the new industry allowed the establishment of backward linkages with existing sectors such as foundries and the paint industry.

Between 1850 and 1860, fifty-six new manufacturing establishments opened in Dayton, creating 800 new jobs. The Civil War also had a positive impact on Dayton's economy. The main beneficiary was railroad car manufacturing, which experienced a remarkable expansion during the war period and gained a national reputation. The industrial profile of Dayton was approximately the same after the war. The car works, the agricultural implements factories, the foundries and machine shops, and the paper mills remained the leading industries that expanded and were able to attract other industries. These industries provided Dayton with a solid manufacturing base through the turn of the century (Becker 1971).

During the late nineteenth century and early twentieth century, entrepreneurialism fostered much of Dayton's growth. John H. Patterson founded National Cash Register (NCR) in 1883. In 1909, Charles F. Kettering left NCR to establish his own company, Dayton Engineering Laboratories Corporation (DELCO). DELCO was purchased by General Motors (GM) in 1916 but is still a permanent anchor in Dayton's industrial base (renamed Delphi in 1995). Today, Dayton is home to ten GM plants and is second only to Detroit in GM employment. Other manufacturing plants established in Dayton during these years included the Mead Corporation, Standard Register Company, Reynolds & Reynolds, and Phillips Industries.

The other pillar supporting Dayton's economy was the military. The federal government established Patterson Field as a supply depot during World War I. Dayton later gave land to the federal government to open Wright Field in 1927. The two were combined into Wright-Patterson Air Force Base (WPAFB) in 1948. Today, Wright-Patterson is the Dayton area's largest employer with 22,700 workers.

The post–World War II era was kind to Dayton. The city's manufacturing mix was uniquely poised to meet the demands of worldwide markets, but the shifts in the global economy during the 1970s greatly affected its economy. High labor costs and new technology led to downsizing, firm relocations, and shutdowns. By 1979, for example, NCR had relocated its production facilities and reduced employment from 20,000 to 5,000. Frigidaire closed all of its plants in the region, costing the area 20,000 jobs.

From 1970 to 1990, Dayton's population declined from 243,000 to 182,000, a drop of slightly more than 25 percent. Once an engine of growth, the city now specializes in government, legal affairs, headquarters functions, and human services. Yet Dayton is still unique. It is unlike most other central cities in the state in that its downtown still has a major concentration of manufacturing firms. More than 30 percent of downtown Dayton's employment is in manufacturing (Dockery et al. 1997, 64–69).

Toledo

Settlement of the Toledo area began in the early 1800s as farms and trading posts were established along the Maumee River. The city of Toledo was created in 1837 with the merger of two villages—Vistula and Port Lawrence. When Toledo was incorporated, some 2,000 people lived in the city and surrounding area. A significant downtown was slow to develop because of the low, wet ground. But construction of canals, the drainage of marshes, and the coming of the railroad led to Toledo's development as a shipping center for agricultural products. By 1860, Toledo's population exceeded 13,000.

Early industrial development was related to supporting residences: sawmills, a foundry, brickyards, and carriage makers. But Toledo essentially remained a small rural town until 1875 when the Milburn Wagon Works relocated from Mishawaka, Indiana. However, it was not wagons that made Toledo, but glass. Development of the glass industry was made possible by the presence of high-silica sandstone in the area. In 1888, Toledo officials convinced Edward Drummond Libbey to relocate his glass factory from Massachusetts to Toledo. Toledoans provided the factory site and fifty building lots for Libbey's workers. Libbey's operation was a success, and other glass makers followed. Michael Owens, with financial assistance from Edward Libbey, founded the Owens Bottle Company in 1907. Edward Ford, one of the founders of Pittsburgh Plate Glass, built a completely mechanized glass factory just outside Toledo's city limits. Other major factories established at the time were the Toledo Scale Company, foundries, refineries, and a bicycle factory.

By 1900, Toledo had a population of more than 125,000. Twenty-seven percent of the residents were foreign-born, and many others had foreign-born parents. The largest numbers of immigrants were from Poland and Hungary, with substantial numbers also from Germany, Ireland, and Russia.

In the early 1900s, Toledo entered the automobile era. Automobile production began at the Pope Motor Car Company in 1903. Pope employed about 1,600 workers. The company failed and went into receivership in 1907. However, the plant was purchased two years later by Willys-Overland, which moved its operations from Indianapolis to Toledo in 1911. By 1915 the company was the second-largest automobile manufacturing company in the United States—second only to Ford. Willys-Overland was followed to Toledo by parts suppliers, which produced sheet metal, gears, carburetors, starters, and springs, and later by Champion Spark Plugs. By 1916 one-third of Toledo's workforce was employed in the auto industry. Willys-Overland was the largest auto factory in the world, and in its peak year employed 23,000 workers.

Toledo's glass industry also prospered. The Owens Bottle Company acquired the Illinois Glass Company to become Owens-Illinois, and the Libbey-Owens Glass Company merged with Ford Plate Glass to become Libbey-Owens-Ford.

Toledo was hit hard by the Great Depression primarily because of its reliance on the auto industry. Willys-Overland laid off thousands of workers, and by 1930 the city had 18,000 unemployed. By 1931 the unemployment rate had reached 50 percent. The city was saved only because of the depression-era employment programs—the Works Progress Administration, Civil Works Administration, and the Federal Emergency Relief Administration. With the hiring of unemployed workers, these agencies built schools, a new public library, additions to the zoo, parks, sewer and water lines, and the city's first public housing project.

Defense contracts in the early 1940s brought Toledo out of the depression. Willys-Overland received a contract for an all-purpose military vehicle—the Jeep—and produced more than 300,000 for the war effort. After the war, a "peacetime Jeep" was developed, with Willys-Overland employing about 7,500 workers.

The return of more than 16,000 veterans to Lucas County and a heavy increase in automobiles stressed downtown Toledo. More than 60,000 vehicles entered the central business district each day, and an estimated four cars competed for each parking space in 1950. Traffic congestion thus stimulated the development of shopping centers in the suburbs. Toledo responded with aggressive annexation. There were fourteen annexations in 1950 and 1951 that added more than 10,500 residents to the city. Between 1960 and 1965, Toledo's land area nearly doubled, and its population increased by 22 percent.

Throughout the 1970s and 1980s, the city's major industries (glass, automobiles, and refining) continued to prosper. Downtown development included a new federal building, a Holiday Inn, and a seventeen-story Toledo Edison office building. In 1982, Owens-Illinois moved its headquarters into the new SeaGate Building. Government Center, housing city and state offices, opened in 1983. A convention center and festival marketplace were constructed as a major part of the economic landscape (although Portside, the festival marketplace, later closed). As in so many of Ohio's cities, manufacturing declined in Toledo. Although Jeep still remains a major employer, the major employers are government, education, and hospitals (Dockery et al. 1997, 69–75).

Youngstown

In the early phase of its history, Youngstown was an outfitting point for settlers moving into the Western Reserve, but it soon progressed into iron and steel. A blast furnace using local resources began operating in 1803 on Yellow Creek, a tributary of the Mahoning River. However, the region's iron industry did not at first thrive because of limited access to markets and fuel and shrinking ore resources. The market-access problem was solved with the construction of the Pennsylvania and Ohio Canal through Youngstown in 1841 and the arrival of a railroad in 1856. The problem of fuel was solved when it was discovered that local coals could be used in place of charcoal, and the shortage of iron was overcome by importing ores.

The combination of improved transportation, a location between coking coals of Pennsylvania and West Virginia, and iron ore from the upper Great Lakes made Youngstown an important iron center. The first steel mill was located in the Mahoning Valley in 1895. Steel soon became the most important industrial product of the region.

As the iron and steel industry expanded, the valley location proved providential for industrial development. The flood plain provided sites for plants and railroad yards and afforded space to store raw materials and finished products, and the river supplied the requisite water for processing and cooling as well as a place to discharge industrial wastes. By 1930 there was a nearly continuous string of iron and steel works and related metal-working industries in a twenty-five-mile stretch along the Mahoning River from Warren through Youngstown to the Pennsylvania border. The Youngstown district ranked as the third-leading steel-producing center in the world (Dockery et al. 1997, 76–77).

In a sense, 1930 was Youngstown's high point. The depression ended Youngstown's population growth and brought on substantial unemployment. World War II brought a temporary recovery in the area's economy, but in the postwar period, Youngstown's fate was tied to the ups and downs of the steel industry. As markets changed and sources of raw materials shifted, Youngstown's comparative advantage became a comparative disadvantage. Land transportation was the only way for steel-making inputs to reach Youngstown and for its products to reach market. Tidewater locations, newer and more efficient plants, high labor costs, lack of reinvestment, and absentee ownership all proved economic handicaps. By the 1970s, Youngstown's economic base of more than 150 years was in serious trouble.

In fall 1977, the Lykes Corporation, owner of Youngstown Sheet and Tube, announced the closing of its Campbell Works, laying off 4,100 workers. In 1980 both U.S. Steel and Jones and Laughlin announced the closing of plants and layoffs affecting almost 5,000 workers. By 1982 the unemployment rate in the Mahoning Valley was almost 20 percent. In 1968 there were 50,000 people employed in primary metals industries in the Youngstown-Warren Standard Metropolitan Statistical Area. By 1993 this number had dropped to fewer than 18,000.

The changes in Youngstown's CBD have mirrored the changes in the steel industry. Until about 1930 the CBD was a vibrant and growing commercial center, but the depression brought development to a halt. Since 1929 only three structures having more than five stories have been constructed in downtown Youngstown: a nine-story glass and steel office building, a sixteen-story high-rise for the elderly, and the seven-story county jail. All of these required substantial public funding. The post–World War II years brought a substantial decline in the CBD as many retail and commercial establishments moved to the suburbs or went out of business. Between 1963 and 1982, the number of retail businesses in the downtown declined from 319 to 88. A study of Federal Street, Youngstown's major east-west artery in the CBD, showed a 62 percent decline in retail establishments along the street from 1950 to 1980. This was accompanied by a 53 percent decline in the number of office functions.

Today, Youngstown is only a shadow of its former self. The city has lost population, manufacturing jobs, and most of its downtown. The CBD is almost exclusively populated by financial and governmental institutions. Nearly 75 percent of the workers remaining in the downtown are in information, producer, and social services. In fact, the social services sector (government workers) accounts for more than 55 percent of the downtown employment (Dockery et al. 1997, 75–81).

Conclusion

Virtually all of Ohio's central cities grew and developed because they had locational advantages. All (except Columbus) grew and developed because of what is now called the "old economy" but have since had to endure major economic restructuring. The cities and their downtowns are not what they once were. Neither are their neighborhoods. It is within this context that we examine the social and economic characteristics of Ohio's central-city neighborhoods.

References

Becker, Carl M. 1971. *Mill, Shop, and Factory: The Industrial Life of Dayton, Ohio, 1830–1900.* Madison: University of Wisconsin Press.

Bingham, Richard D., William M. Bowen, Yosra A. Amara, Lynn W. Bachelor, Jane Dockery, Jack Dustin, Deborah Kimble, Thomas Maraffa, David L. McKee, Kent P. Schwirian, Gail Gordon Sommers, and Howard A. Stafford. 1997. *Beyond Edge Cities.* New York: Garland.

Blackford, G. Mansel. 1982. *A Portrait Cast in Steel: Buckeye International and Columbus, Ohio, 1881–1980.* Westport, CT: Greenwood Press.

Campbell, F. Thomas, and Edward M. Miggins. 1988. *The Birth of Modern Cleveland, 1865–1930.* 1988. London and Toronto: Associated University Press.

Condit, W. Carl. 1977. *The Railroad and the City: A Technological and Urbanistic History of Cincinnati*. Columbus: Ohio State University Press.

Dockery, Jane, Jack Dustin, Gary Gappert, Edward W. Hill, Kent P. Schwirian, Howard A. Stafford, and David Stephens. 1997. "Metropolitan Ohio." In Richard D. Bingham et al., *Beyond Edge Cities*, pp. 45–82. New York: Garland.

Glazer, W. Stix. 1968. *Cincinnati in 1840: A Community Profile*. Ann Arbor: University of Michigan Press.

Hill, Edward W. 1990. "Cleveland, Ohio: Manufacturing Matters, Services Are Strengthened but Earnings Erode." In Richard D. Bingham and Randall W. Eberts, *Economic Restructuring of the American Midwest*, pp. 103–140. Norwell, MA: Kluwer.

Love, Steve, and David Giffels. 1998. *Wheels of Fortune: The Story of Rubber in Akron*. Akron, OH: University of Akron Press.

Miller, C. Poh, and Robert Wheeler. 1990. *Cleveland: A Concise History, 1796–1990*. Bloomington and Indianapolis: Indiana University Press.

Porter, M. Tana. 1987. *Toledo Profile: A Sesquicentennial History*. Toledo, OH: Buettner Toledo, Inc.

Stanback, Thomas M., and Thierry J. Noyelle, Jr. 1982. *Cities in Transition: Changing Job Structures in Atlanta, Denver, Buffalo, Phoenix, Columbus (Ohio), Nashville, Charlotte*. Totowa: NJ: Allanheld, Osmun.

Vexler, I. Robert. 1975. *Cincinnati: A Chronological and Documentary History, 1676–1970*. New York: Oceana Publications.

Wade, C. Richard. 1959. *The Urban Frontier: The Rise of Western Cities, 1790–1830*. Cambridge: Harvard University Press.

3

Research Design and Methodology

Neighborhood Definition, Characteristics, and Categorization

In our examination of central-city neighborhood economies, we analyzed the location patterns of various industries in response to neighborhood demographic, socioeconomic, labor force, and housing (including federally assisted housing) variables. Throughout the analysis, we used postal zip codes as proxies for urban neighborhoods in the seven Ohio central cities (Akron, Cincinnati, Cleveland, Columbus, Dayton, Toledo, and Youngstown). Industry-by-industry employment data by zip code were available to us only for the state of Ohio, and thus the study is limited to Ohio central cities. The findings cannot in a true sense be generalized, but there is a strong likelihood that they are common to other similar regions of the Northeast and Midwest, if not beyond.

In the study of urban neighborhood economies in relation to poverty, analysis at the zip code level has advantages over conventional analysis at the census tract level. First, this procedure permits use of the most recently available and most accurate information regarding employment, earnings, and establishments. Second, zip codes are much larger than census tracts and thus more appropriate for the analysis of many industrial activities, particularly various service industries, because such activities are largely dictated by density of demand, which is determined by population and level of income and wealth. On average, a census tract contains about 4,000 residents, whereas a zip code is approximately six times larger. In addition, it has been increasingly acknowledged that postal zip codes are the best proxies for communities in marketing (Weiss 1988).

To determine whether to include zip codes that straddle city borders, we used one of two criteria: A border zip code is included (1) if its centroid falls in the central-city boundary or (2) if more than 50 percent of the border zip code's population resides in the central city. The latter was determined by summing the population by census tract that has its centroid in the zip code and in the city as well. The analysis was executed with the help of MapInfo—a geographic information system. The first criterion alone would not suffice because several zip codes have unusual geography. For instance, the centroid of a Cleveland zip code (44114) is in Lake Erie, and one Columbus zip code (43228) has its majority of area, but not its centroid, in the city.

There are 120 zip code–defined neighborhoods in the seven Ohio central cities. We excluded 22 central business district (CBD) zip codes because few people live in them, and company headquarters and the concentration of business services firms would skew the analysis. Accordingly, our sample includes 98 non-CBD central-city zip codes.

Central-city neighborhoods are very diverse in terms of demographics, socioeconomic levels, housing, industry, and other variables. For example, each of these neighborhoods is, on average, home to 24,505 persons, ranging from a maximum of 56,272 to a minimum of 571, with a standard deviation of 12,074. For every 100 residents, about 22 lived in poverty in a typical neighborhood; about 63 lived in poverty in the poorest neighborhood; only 2 lived in poverty in the wealthiest neighborhood. In terms of racial composition, an average neighborhood had 32 percent nonwhite population. This percentage ranged from 1.2 percent (predominantly white) to 97.9 percent (predominantly nonwhite).

To facilitate the analysis, central-city neighborhoods were divided into five categories based on their poverty rates. Instead of using thresholds of 20 percent and 40 percent to determine poverty rates as has been used in the literature (Jargowsky and Bane 1990; Jargowsky 1994), we used smaller intervals to provide more detailed information about neighborhood economic transformation and disintegration. Also, to discuss these neighborhoods without constantly referring to percentage of poverty, we used the following poverty-rate definitions of neighborhoods, generally taken from the literature, throughout the study: less than 10 percent, middle-class neighborhoods; 10–19.99 percent, working-class neighborhoods; 20–29.99 percent, moderate-poverty neighborhoods; 30–39.99 percent, severe-poverty neighborhoods; and 40 percent and above, extreme-poverty neighborhoods.

Central-city neighborhoods with poverty rates below 10 percent constitute the wealthiest among neighborhoods in the sample. There are 26 neighborhoods in the seven central cities with this classification, with an average population of 27,109 and average poverty rate of 6.1 percent.

TABLE 3.1   Ohio Central-City Neighborhood Categorization and Characteristics

Poverty Category	Neighborhood Type	Number of Neighborhoods	Average Population	Average Poverty %
<10%	Middle-class neighborhood	26	27,109	6.1
10–19.99%	Working-class neighborhood	27	25,987	14.6
20–29.99%	Moderate-poverty neighborhood	18	26,925	23.9
30–39.99%	Severe-poverty neighborhood	13	22,730	32.8
>=40%	Extreme-poverty neighborhood	14	15,346	50.1
Total		98	24,505	21.5

Whereas Jargowsky and Bane (1990) classify those neighborhoods between ghetto (extreme-poverty) neighborhoods (40 percent and above poverty) and nonpoor neighborhoods (below 20 percent poverty) as mixed-income neighborhoods, we define mixed-income neighborhoods—working-class neighborhoods—as those between middle-class (less than 10 percent poverty) and moderate-poverty neighborhoods (20–29.99 percent poverty). The working-class category has 27 neighborhoods and constitutes the largest in the sample (more than one-fourth). A typical working-class neighborhood had a population of 25,987 and 14.6 percent poverty in 1990. We designate severe-poverty neighborhoods as those with poverty rates between 30 percent and 39.99 percent, and extreme-poverty neighborhoods as those with a poverty rate of 40 percent or above. Slightly less than one-half of the neighborhoods are classified as moderate-poverty, severe-poverty, or extreme-poverty neighborhoods. Nearly 1 million people (40 percent of the total population of the seven central cities) live in poverty-stricken neighborhoods. The classification and characteristics of each type of neighborhood are presented in Table 3.1.

Industry Groupings

The U.S. government's standard industrial classification (SIC) is the statistical classification standard underlying all establishment-based federal economic statistics, by industry. The classification covers the entire field of U.S. economic activity and consists of four levels. Ten major industry divisions are conventionally used: agriculture, mining, construction, manufacturing, TCPU (transportation, communication, and public utilities), retail, wholesale, FIRE (finance, insurance, and real estate), services, and government. Within each division are major groups of industries (two-digit SIC level). Within each major group are industry groups (three-digit SIC) and then individual industries (four-digit SIC). Excluding agriculture and mining, there are about 70 industries at the two-digit SIC level, about 360 industries at the three-digit SIC level, and more than one thousand industries at the four-digit SIC level.

We elected to examine central-city neighborhood economic transformation primarily at the two-digit SIC level, as examining industries at the three- or four-digit level would make the study cumbersome. The industries that we believe are of great importance to neighborhood vitality are analyzed at the three-digit level. Examples of these industries include grocery stores (SIC 541), commercial banks (SIC 602), hospitals (SIC 806), individual and family services (SIC 832), and child day care services (SIC 835). In addition, the increasing role of producer services and information service industries in today's urban economies has rendered the conventional classification of service industries of little use in producing meaningful analysis. We find the industry grouping scheme developed by Harley Browning and Joachim Singlemann (1978) and modified by Edward Hill to be useful in studying Ohio central-city neighborhood economic change. This industrial grouping scheme was used in this study and is shown in Table 3.2.

Industries are important to urban neighborhoods, as they provide not only various services but also job opportunities to residents. Table 3.3 presents an informal industry profile of Ohio central-city neighborhoods. Note that about 45 percent of all jobs in Ohio central cities are derived from industries in construction (4 percent), manufacturing (16.6 percent), transportation (3.2 percent), wholesale (5.8 percent), information (3.6 percent), and producer services (10.8 percent). The other 55 percent of jobs are in retail (13.6), social services (including government) (29.2), and personal service industries (13.1). Industries in the former group are sources of relatively higher-paying jobs and exist largely for other industries in the region or merely for the external market. However, industries in the latter group are not only major job providers but also residential service providers in the neighborhood. The availability of neighborhood jobs is crucial to low-wage earners due to commuting costs and the job market information asymmetry.

Data and Variables

The major data source for this research is the Ohio Economic Development Database (ES-202). ES-202 is the employment security form num-

TABLE 3.2   Industries Included in This Study

Industry Sector	SIC Code
Mining	
Construction	15
General contractors	16
Heavy contractors	17
Special trade	
Manufacturing	
Durable manufacturing	
Lumber and wood products	24
Furniture and fixtures	25
Stone, clay, and glass products	32
Primary metals	33
Fabricated metal products	34
Industrial machinery and equipment	35
Electronic and other electric equipment	36
Transportation equipment	37
Instruments and related products	38
Miscellaneous manufacturing industries	39
Nondurable manufacturing	
Food and kindred products	20
Tobacco products	21
Textiles mills products	22
Apparel and other textile products	23
Paper and allied products	26
Chemicals and allied products	28
Petroleum and coal products	29
Rubber and miscellaneous plastic products	30
Leather and leather products	31
Transportation services	40–42, 44–47
Wholesale and retail services	
Wholesale	50–51
Retail	52–57, 59
Information	
Printing and publishing	27
Communications	48
Advertising	731
Credit reporting and collection	732
Motion picture and allied services	781
Engineering and management services	87

(continues)

TABLE 3.2   *(Continued)*

Industry Sector	SIC Code
Producer services	
Electric, gas, and sanitary	49
Banking	60–62
Insurance	63–64
Real estate	65–66
Engineering and architecture	871
Accounting	872
Miscellaneous business	67, 73 (except 731–732), 892, 899
Legal services	81
Social services	
Medical services	801–805, 807–809
Hospitals	806
Education	82
Welfare	832
Nonprofit	86
Postal services	43
Government	91–97
Miscellaneous social services	833–839
Personal services	
Domestic services	88
Hotels	70
Eating and drinking establishments	58
Repair	725, 753, 76
Laundry	721
Barber and beauty shop	723, 724
Entertainment	78–79 (except 781), 84
Miscellaneous personal services	722, 726–729, 751, 752, 754

ber used by the government to collect employment and earnings data for the unemployment insurance system. The analysis is based on employment, earnings, and establishment data for the first quarter of 1993. Data for other neighborhood characteristics are drawn from the *1990 Census of Population and Housing* (U.S. Bureau of the Census 1990). The database allows researchers to study the most recent economic growth at a disaggregated level—zip codes. ES-202 is the most reliable governmental source for employment and earnings data (Galster et al. 1997).

To examine the relationship between central-city neighborhood economic activities and poverty level, we constructed four economic indica-

TABLE 3.3   Importance of Major Industries to Ohio Central-City Neighborhoods

Industry	Employment (1st quarter 1993)	Percent of Total Employment	Workers' Average Earnings (1st quarter 1993, $)	Average Establishment Size
Construction	31,059	4.0	6,930	8.1
Manufacturing	130,740	16.6	8,565	44.5
Transportation	25,003	3.2	6,589	23.3
Wholesale	45,346	5.8	7,336	12.9
Retail	107,196	13.6	3,747	15.4
Information	28,628	3.6	7,939	29.5
Producer services	85,120	10.8	5,916	11.2
Social services	229,747	29.2	6,063	38.3
Personal services	103,151	13.1	2,609	11.2
Total	785,990	100.0	5,887	18.7

tors: average earnings, average size of establishment, employment per 1,000 residents, and residents per establishment. These indicators were created on the basis of industry-specific employment, establishments, and earnings data for the first quarter of 1993. In the study, we provide an industry-by-industry examination of neighborhood economies in terms of both number and size of establishments. For example, earlier studies (e.g., Bingham and Zhang 1997) found that a grocery store in the poorest neighborhoods serves as many residents as one in the wealthiest neighborhoods. However, in the wealthier neighborhoods, grocery stores average 50 employees, and in the poorest, they average 4. Thus, we rely on the population-weighted industry employment in studying general patterns of neighborhood economic activity (number of jobs per 1,000 residents).

We initially selected 41 variables from the census and 2 crime indicators[1] as our independent variables.[2] These variables represented four significant characteristics of neighborhoods (beyond industrial). They are demographic characteristics, socioeconomic characteristics, labor market characteristics, and housing characteristics.

---

[1]Two measures of neighborhood crime risk were obtained from "Find a Neighborhood" (2000): violent- and nonviolent-crime indexes. The index numbers show the zip code's crime rate relative to all zip codes in the country, with a value of 100 being the average. A value of 200 means that the zip code has twice the crime rate as the average zip code. A value of 50 means that the zip code has half the crime rate as the average.

[2]We intended to use a dummy variable, the presence of an enterprise zone in the zip code, as an indicator of government support for economic development of the neighborhood. However, for Ohio's central cities, enterprise zones cover the entire central cities, so all neighborhoods are covered by enterprise zones (thus there is no variation in the distribution).

To reduce the number of independent variables to a more manageable number, we made a few adjustments. Some highly interrelated variables were removed. Eight housing-age variables defined by the census were collapsed into one: percentage of housing units built before 1950. Four employment-rate variables (male, female, white male, and nonwhite male) were discarded in favor of a single employment-rate variable. The number of independent variables was thus reduced to 22. The variables are shown in Table 3.4, and their frequencies are shown in Table 3.5.

The first vector of independent variables includes four neighborhood demographic characteristics: percentage nonwhite population in 1990 (PTNWITE); percentage Hispanic population (PTHISPAN); percentage foreign-born population (PTFBALL); and percentage of female-headed households (PTFEMHOS). The nonwhite and Hispanic variables are included to test the usual hypothesis that minority populations adversely affect industry location and, thus, neighborhood job opportunities. The foreign-born variable is intended to capture any impact of the proportion of the foreign-born population on industry activities. We also believe it likely that a high percentage of female-headed households will be negatively related to employment in the community, as it may be linked to a low demand for retail services (due to its relationship to income).

The second vector of independent variables includes six socioeconomic characteristics: per capita income (PCI90); percentage of the population in poverty in 1989 (POVRAT90); percent households with public assistance (PTPAHSHD); employment rate (EMPRATE); and indexes of violent crimes (CRIMVIO) and nonviolent crimes (CRIMNVI). Whereas the poverty and crime measures are expected to have a negative impact on neighborhood job opportunities, employment rate should positively affect industry activities in a neighborhood.

Neighborhood labor force characteristics affect industry location through the level of participation in the labor market and human capital and occupational mixes. The vector of labor force variables in the model includes seven characteristics: civilian labor force participation rate (CIVLFPR); percentage of the population (18 years old and above) with less than a high school education (PTNOHISC); percentage of the population with a high school diploma (PTHISCOL); percentage of the population with a college education (PTCOLEGE); percentage of workers in management and the professions (PTMGTPRF); percentage of workers in labor occupations (PTLABOR); and percentage of workers in service occupations (PTSERVIS). The labor force participation rate variable is a measure of the working-age population's willingness or ability to partici-

TABLE 3.4   Definitions of Demographic, Socioeconomic, Labor Force, Housing, and Industrial Variables

Demographic
    Percent nonwhite population (PTNWITE)
    Percent Hispanic population (PTHISPAN)
    Percent foreign-born population (PTFBALL)
    Percent female-headed households (PTFEMHOS)

Socioeconomic
    Per capita income (PCI90)
    Percent population below poverty (POVRAT90)
    Percent households with public assistance (PTPAHSHD)
    Employment rate (EMPRATE)
    Violent-crime index (U.S. average = 100) (CRIMVIO)
    Nonviolent-crime index (U.S. average = 100) (CRIMNVI)

Labor Market
    Civilian labor force participation rate (CIVLFPR)
    Percent less than high school education (PTNOHISC)
    Percent high school education (PTHISCOL)
    Percent college and above education (PTCOLEGE)
    Percent management and professionals (PTMGTPRF)
    Percent labor occupation (PTLABOR)
    Percent service occupation (PTSERVIS)

Housing
    Percent owner-occupied housing units (PTOWNHS)
    Percent vacant housing units (PTVACHS)
    Median value of owner-occupied housing (MEDVOWHS)
    Percent housing built before 1950 (PTYH78)
    Percent federally subsidized housing units (PTPUBHOS)

Industrial
    All-industry jobs per 1,000 residents (ALLEMP)
    Construction jobs per 1,000 residents (CSTEMP)
    Manufacturing jobs per 1,000 residents (MFGEMP)
    Transportation jobs per 1,000 residents (TSPEMP)
    Wholesale jobs per 1,000 residents (WSLEMP)
    Retail jobs per 1,000 residents (RETEMP)
    Information jobs per 1,000 residents (INFEMP)
    Producer services jobs per 1,000 residents (PRDEMP)
    Social services jobs per 1,000 residents (SOCEMP)
    Personal services jobs per 1,000 residents (PSLEMP)

TABLE 3.5   Distribution of Characteristics in Ohio Central-City Neighborhoods

	Mean	Standard Deviation	Minimum	Maximum
Demographic				
Population	24,505	12,074	571	56,272
Percent nonwhite population	32.63	30.88	1.18	97.87
Percent Hispanic population	1.73	2.93	0.00	20.20
Percent foreign-born population	3.12	2.45	0.08	15.63
Percent female-headed households	18.00	9.91	0.87	51.56
Socioeconomic				
Per capita income ($)	12,351	5,223	3,712	30,415
Percent population below poverty	21.54	14.72	1.55	62.52
Percent households with public assistance	14.31	11.14	0.00	48.07
Employment rate	89.94	6.65	58.71	98.57
Violent-crime index (U.S. average = 100)	199.47	126.95	7.00	422.00
Nonviolent-crime index (U.S. average = 100)	118.16	75.66	5.00	432.00
Labor Force				
Civilian labor force participation rate	60.91	9.31	39.72	79.94
Percent less than high school education	28.73	13.39	0.12	57.22
Percent high school education	28.62	9.95	0.30	42.40
Percent college and above education	16.02	13.15	2.07	57.80
Percent management and professionals	23.99	10.92	8.50	52.52
Percent labor occupation	16.87	7.01	2.99	38.04
Percent service occupation	16.92	6.14	5.06	32.65
Housing				
Percent owner-occupied housing units	53.07	14.93	1.55	76.52
Percent vacant housing units	9.93	10.64	2.42	68.96
Median value of owner-occupied housing ($)	67,682	28,319	50,000	208,353
Percent housing built before 1950	49.30	23.41	0.66	85.35
Percent federally subsidized housing units	6.28	8.74	0.00	47.79
Industrial				
All-industry jobs per 1,000 residents	344.9	271.4	53.0	1,997.4
Construction jobs per 1,000 residents	14.0	12.2	0.8	75.8
Manufacturing jobs per 1,000 residents	63.6	98.9	0.0	741.3
Transportation jobs per 1,000 residents	11.8	23.7	0.0	157.1
Wholesale jobs per 1,000 residents	19.6	18.4	0.0	96.4
Retail jobs per 1,000 residents	41.5	37.4	0.0	198.8
Information jobs per 1,000 residents	13.8	28.2	0.0	194.0
Producer services jobs per 1,000 residents	34.3	38.4	0.0	188.4
Social services jobs per 1,000 residents	106.1	214.1	5.2	1,832.5
Personal services jobs per 1,000 residents	40.2	31.3	0.0	141.0

SOURCES: The U.S. Bureau of Census, *1990 Census of Population and Housing;* Ohio Economic Development Database (ES-202); "Find a Neighborhood," 2000, at http://www.realtor.com.

pate in the labor market. Differing neighborhood job opportunities might partially reflect the variation of this labor force participation rate. Higher labor force participation rates should be associated with higher neighborhood job opportunities. The education variables are three variables that would approximate the human-capital mix of workers in each neighborhood. The occupational variables are included to determine the types of skills available in the neighborhood.

Housing is another important aspect of neighborhood economic health. A sound housing stock provides development and growth opportunities for a variety of consumer-oriented and other industries and thus has a stabilizing effect on a neighborhood. The housing stock also helps producer-oriented firms enhance their image by locating in the neighborhood. Factors that determine the quality of housing stock include tenure, represented by the percentage of owner-occupied housing units (PTOWNHS); occupancy, represented by the percentage of vacant housing units (PTVACHS); market value of owner-occupied housing, represented by the median value of owner-occupied housing units (MEDVOWHS); and age, represented by the percentage of housing units built before 1950 (PTYH78). We also include the percentage of housing units that are federally assisted (PTPUBHOS) to measure the impact of assisted housing on neighborhood industry location. It is expected that the impacts of MEDVOWHS and PTOWNHS on economic activities in many industries are positive and that impacts of PTVACHS, PTYH78, and PTPUBHOS are negative.

Research Hypotheses

According to the basics of urban economics, various factors influence industry location to differing degrees. Among the major industry location factors are transportation cost, labor supply, amenities, infrastructure, and interindustry linkages. At the neighborhood level, additional factors such as density of demand, safety, and the soundness of the housing stock may play a more pronounced role in retaining and attracting industrial firms. These factors constitute the pull force for various consumer-oriented industries.

We recognize the conventional hypothesis that both consumer and business services decline as neighborhoods become poorer. This premise probably holds true in general but not necessarily for all types of activities. For example, whereas banks and savings and loans institutions are found less frequently in poverty-stricken neighborhoods, the presence of other services, such as nondepository banking institutions, appliance repair shops, and used merchandise stores, might actually increase in these neighborhoods. Also, a positive correlation between poverty and welfare services (SIC 832) is anticipated.

We hypothesize that many firms in retail industries would be more likely to be located in neighborhoods where the demand for these services is relatively higher. Demand for retail services is dependent on both quantitative factors (population counts) and qualitative factors (income and wealth effect). On the quantitative side, for example, although a more populous neighborhood may have more retail activities than a less populated one, we would expect the spatial differences in population-weighted industry employment across urban neighborhoods to be minimal in many retail activities. On the other hand, the quality of demand matters. This may lead to a finding that poorer neighborhoods are indeed underserved. Poorer neighborhoods may have lower population-weighted service activities and, at the same time, have different types of services by industry. For example, poorer neighborhoods not only have less grocery store employment but also are served by a different type of grocery store (mom-and-pop stores and convenience stores) from the type serving wealthier neighborhoods (supermarkets).

The location of firms in many social service and personal service industries is hypothesized to follow a pattern similar to that of retail industry firms. For example, medical services, such as offices of medical doctors (SIC 801) and dentists (SIC 802), would be more frequently found in wealthier neighborhoods, whereas welfare offices (SIC 832) and repair shops (SIC 725, 753, and 76) would be more readily available in poorer neighborhoods. On the other hand, the location pattern of many social and personal service industries, such as education institutions and area hospitals, is expected to be less tied to neighborhood income and wealth because those establishments have a much higher threshold of population than an ordinary retail establishment.

For industries such as manufacturing, producer services, information services, and wholesale, we hypothesize that interindustry clustering, proximity to transportation nodes, and inertia are more important determinants of their locations. The presence of firms in these industries may accordingly be less related to major neighborhood characteristics, such as poverty, than would be found for firms in other industries previously discussed.

Model and Methodology

For this study, we employed three levels of analysis: descriptive analysis, a regression model, and a two-stage least square equation with a spatial lag specification. For each industry listed in Table 3.2, we first compared industry activities across the five types of neighborhoods using four indicators: employment per 1,000 population, mean wages, average establishment size, and number of residents served per establishment. For each industry, we also performed a zero-order correlation analysis between the population-weighted industry employment and neighborhood demographic, socioeconomic, labor force, and housing characteristics.

As a supplement to the descriptive analysis, we used a regression model to explain the variation of industry employment across neighborhoods by neighborhood characteristics. Mathematically, the model is expressed as follows:

$$\text{EMPPOP}_{ij} = \acute{a}_j + \hat{a}_{j1} \ (\text{poverty})$$
$$+ \hat{a}_{j2} \ (\text{working-class})$$
$$+ \hat{a}_{j3} \ (\text{crime})$$
$$+ \hat{a}_{j4} \ (\text{ethnic})$$
$$+ \hat{a}_{jp} \ (\text{city dummy vector})$$
$$+ \varsigma_j \quad (3.1)$$

where i = neighborhood defined by zip code; j = industry; EMPPOP_{ij}—the dependent variable—represents total employment in industry j per 1,000 population in neighborhood i (the weighting would remove any biases of measure against smaller neighborhoods); p = a vector of city dummies to account for intercity variations (e.g., Akron, Cincinnati, Cleveland, Columbus, Dayton, and Toledo, with Youngstown left in the constant); $\hat{a}_{j1}$, $\hat{a}_{j2}$, $\hat{a}_{j3}$, and $\hat{a}_{j4}$ are vectors of coefficients to be estimated; and ς represents the stochastic error term.

The four independent variables—poverty neighborhood, working-class neighborhood, high-crime neighborhood, and ethnic neighborhood—are factor scores resulting from a factor analysis of the 22 demographic, socioeconomic, labor market, and housing variables shown in Table 3.4. The factor analysis is discussed in the next chapter.

We further explore neighborhood effect—how industries in adjoining neighborhoods impact the location of the same types of industries in the primary neighborhood. We accomplish this by testing a simultaneous equation with a spatially lagged dependent variable included on the right-hand side of the equation. The equation was estimated by the two-stage least square procedure. Spatial lags of the independent variables—the four neighborhood characteristic factors—were used as instruments. The equation is specified as follows:

Industry factor dimension $_{ij}$ = f (neighborhood socioeconomic dimension $_{ik}$,
                                                   Spatial lag of industry factor dimension $_{ij}$,
                                                   City dummy vector $_n$)   (3.2)

where i = industry factor (producer/personal services, strip shopping, neighborhood retail, metal, public services I, public services II, low-income industries, or rubber industries); j = neighborhood; k = neighborhood socioeconomic factors (poverty neighborhood, working-class neighborhood, crime neighborhood, and ethnic neighborhood); and n = Akron, Cleveland, Cincinnati, Columbus, Dayton, and Toledo. Youngstown was to be captured in the intercept.

Finally, a second factor analysis performed is intended to identify types of neighborhoods with distinctive industrial and socioeconomic characteristics. With this exercise, we attempt to examine how industrial and socioeconomic characteristics interact to produce distinctive urban neighborhoods.

References

Bingham, Richard D., and Zhongcai Zhang. 1997. "Poverty and Economic Morphology of Ohio Central-City Neighborhoods." *Urban Affairs Review* 32(6): 766–796.

Browning, Harley L., and Joachim Singlemann. 1978. "The Transformation of the U.S. Labor Force: The Interaction of Industry and Occupation." *Politics and Society* 8 (3–4): 481–509.

"Find a Neighborhood." 2000. http://www.realtor.com/FindNeig.

Galster, George, Ronald Mincy, and Mitchell Tobin. 1997. "The Disparate Racial Neighborhood Impacts of Metropolitan Economic Restructuring." *Urban Affairs Review* 32(6): 797–824.

Jargowsky, P. A. 1994. "Ghetto Poverty Among Blacks in the 1980s." *Journal of Policy Analysis and Management* 13: 288–310.

Jargowsky, P. A., and M. J. Bane. 1990. "Ghetto Poverty: Basic Questions." In L. E. Lynn and M. G. H. McGeary (eds.), *Inner-City Poverty in the United States*, pp. 16–67. Washington, DC: National Academy Press.

Stanback, T. M., P. J. Bearse, T. J. Noyelle, and R. A. Karasek. 1981. *Services: The New Economy*. Totowa, NJ: Allanheld, Osmun.

U.S. Bureau of the Census. 1990. Summary Tape File 3A. *1990 Census of Population and Housing*. Washington, DC: Government Printing Office.

U.S. Office of Management and Budget. 1987. *Standard Industrial Classification Manual*. Washington, DC: Government Printing Office.

Weiss, Michael J. 1988. *The Clustering of America*. New York: Harper & Row.

4

Central-City Neighborhoods

This book is not only about neighborhood economies and employment but also about neighborhoods and their characteristics, because these often determine neighborhood employment. As stated earlier, Ohio central-city neighborhoods are defined by postal zip code. Because Ohio central cities are mostly older, this operational definition makes sense. The neighborhood post offices were built many years ago and are in the centers of neighborhood shopping and business areas. For example, in Cleveland, the post office for zip code 44119 is located on East 185th Street in the heart of the old ethnic North Collinwood neighborhood called Beachland. The shopping area along 185th Street surrounding the post office has recently been designated "Old World Plaza."

There are 98 neighborhoods in Ohio's central cities (excluding central business districts). On average they are home to 24,505 people, but this figure varies from 571 to 56,272 with a standard deviation of 12,074. These neighborhoods are quite diverse in terms of ethnicity, wealth, housing, and other such characteristics commonly used to describe neighborhoods.

Table 3.4 showed the variables used in this study to describe Ohio's central-city neighborhoods. These variables are classified into five groups: demographic characteristics, socioeconomic characteristics, labor market characteristics, housing characteristics, and industrial characteristics. Demographic characteristics include variables such as race, population size, and female-headed households. Socioeconomic variables include income and poverty variables. Labor market variables are those related to educational characteristics and labor force participation. Housing variables are those related to housing age, value, and condition. Industrial characteristics are variables showing employment within categories of industries.

The Primacy of Poverty

For descriptive purposes, we sought to use the variables in Table 3.4 to identify the underlying dimensions of neighborhoods. We thus subject the nonindustrial variables to factor analysis. Since the purpose of the factor analysis is both descriptive and explanatory, varimax rotation with Kaiser normalization was selected. The number of factors generated was limited to those with eigenvalues greater than 1.0. Table 4.1a shows the factors. (Note: Throughout the book, the names of factors are in italics; generic descriptions that happen to correspond to the factor names are in standard type.)

The factor analysis generated four factors that explain 80 percent of the variance (see Table 4.1b). The first factor generated, *poverty neighborhoods*, explains 32 percent of the variance and is a clear expression of neighborhood poverty. Twelve neighborhood characteristics (variables) had high loadings on this factor:

- Percent of the population below poverty level
- Percent nonwhite population
- Percent owner-occupied housing units (negative loading)
- Percent vacant housing units
- Percent of households receiving public assistance
- Percent of female-headed households
- Per capita income (negative loading)
- Percent of the population with less than a high school education
- Percent of the population in service occupations
- Civilian labor force participation rate (negative loading)
- Employment rate (negative loading)
- Percent federally subsidized housing units

These twelve variables are at the core of the factor *poverty neighborhoods*. They are also clearly interrelated, a feature that is at the heart of factor analysis.

The second factor explains 27 percent of the variance and has been labeled *working-class neighborhoods*. Seven variables had high loadings on this factor:

- Median value of owner-occupied housing (negative loading)
- Per capita income (negative loading, also high loading on *poverty neighborhoods*)

TABLE 4.1a   Rotated Component Matrix

	Factor			
Variable	Poverty Neighborhoods	Working-Class Neighborhoods	High-Crime Neighborhoods	Ethnic Neighborhoods
POVRAT90	**0.873**	0.333	0.000	0.207
PTNWITE	**0.845**	0.063	0.143	−0.181
PTHISPAN	−0.076	0.400	0.238	**0.561**
PTFBALL	−0.277	−0.260	−0.219	**0.716**
PTOWNHS	**−0.675**	0.149	0.284	−0.396
PTVACHS	**0.509**	0.066	0.184	0.436
MEDVOWHS	−0.399	**−0.827**	−0.131	−0.117
PTYH78	0.353	0.299	**0.604**	0.337
PTPAHSHD	**0.852**	0.420	0.133	−0.015
PTFEMHOS	**0.836**	0.374	0.144	−0.213
PCI90	**−0.566**	**−0.757**	0.014	−0.108
PTNOHISC	**0.546**	**0.665**	0.275	−0.054
PTHISCOL	−0.226	**0.624**	−0.119	**−0.546**
PTCOLEGE	−0.297	**−0.911**	−0.105	0.102
PTMGTPRF	−0.271	**−0.926**	−0.072	0.058
PTSERVIS	**0.791**	0.452	0.114	−0.012
PTLABOR	0.257	**0.854**	0.283	−0.027
CIVLFPR	**−0.685**	−0.445	−0.216	−0.137
EMPRATE	**−0.768**	−0.443	−0.203	−0.087
PTPUBHOS	**0.734**	0.154	−0.158	−0.272
CRIMVIO	0.054	0.088	**0.925**	−0.003
CRIMNVI	−0.005	0.096	**0.920**	−0.048

NOTES: Extraction method: principal component analysis. Rotation method: varimax with Kaiser normalization. Rotation converged in 10 iterations.
Numbers in bold indicate the neighborhood variables are loaded significantly on the extracted factor.

TABLE 4.1b   Total Variance Explained: The First Factor Analysis

		Rotation Sums of Squared Loadings	
Factor	Initial Eigenvalues	% of Variance Explained	Cumulative % Variance Explained
Poverty neighborhoods	10.9	32.3	32.3
Working-class neighborhoods	2.8	26.9	59.2
High-crime neighborhoods	2.2	12.2	71.4
Ethnic neighborhoods	1.6	8.4	79.8

- Percent of the population with less than a high school education (also high loading on *poverty neighborhoods*)
- Percent of the population with a high school education
- Percent of the population with a college education (negative loading)
- Percent of the population in management and the professions (negative loading)
- Percent of the population in labor occupations

The third factor explains 12 percent of the variance and, for obvious reasons, is labeled *high-crime neighborhoods.* Three variables had high loadings on this factor:

- Percent of housing built before 1950
- Violent-crime index
- Nonviolent-crime index

The final factor explains 8 percent of the variance. Three variables also have high loadings on this factor, which has been named *ethnic neighborhoods:*

- Percent Hispanic population
- Percent foreign-born population
- Percent high school education (also high loading on *working-class neighborhoods*)

The principal factor is, of course, *poverty neighborhoods.* This factor is headlined by the percent of population below the poverty level, a high unemployment rate, and a significant percent of the population receiving public assistance. The abundance of vacant housing units is the result of disinvestment in urban neighborhoods, which helps reinforce the poverty cycle. Public housing is also a symbol of neighborhood poverty. The percentages of nonwhite residents and of female-headed households also have high loadings on the neighborhood poverty factor because poverty is usually higher among minority populations and female-headed households. Other factors contributing to neighborhood poverty include a high percentage of high school dropouts, a high percentage of workers in services occupation, a low labor force participation rate, and a high unemployment rate. However, there is a two-way causal link. Neighborhood poverty tends to reinforce those unfavorable labor market and housing outcomes. Here the cumulative causation is in reverse, or the spiral growth is downward.

Poverty Neighborhoods

The overwhelming importance of neighborhood poverty to the description of central-city neighborhoods makes it logical to examine their poverty status in detail. Urban neighborhoods were classified into five categories (see chart) based upon the percentage of residents below the poverty level in 1989:

Type of Neighborhood	Poverty Rate	Average Population	Number of Neighborhoods
Middle-class	<10%	27,109	26
Working-class	10–19.99%	25,987	27
Moderate-poverty	20–29.99%	26,925	18
Severe-poverty	30–39.99%	22,731	13
Extreme-poverty	>=40%	15,346	14

Table 4.2 shows the relationships between the demographic variables and neighborhood poverty. Some of the relationships were expected, but some were not. First, there is little relationship between the percentage of foreign-born residents and neighborhood poverty. People not born in the United States are as likely to live in middle-class neighborhoods as they are anywhere else. The same is true of Hispanics.

On the other hand, there is a strong relationship between the percentage of nonwhite residents and poverty. Nonwhites constitute about 10 percent of the population in middle-class neighborhoods and over two-thirds of the population in the very poorest neighborhoods. And, as expected, the percentage of female-headed households is related to neighborhood type. About 10 percent of the total households in middle-class neighborhoods are headed by women, whereas in poorer neighborhoods the figure is slightly over 30 percent.

Table 4.3 shows the relationships between the socioeconomic variables and neighborhood poverty. As expected, per capita income declines almost linearly from just above $17,000 in the middle-income neighborhoods to about $6,000 in extreme-poverty neighborhoods. And, as income drops, the percentage of households receiving public assistance climbs. Only about 4 percent of the households in middle-income neigh-

TABLE 4.2   Relationship Between Demographic Characteristics and
Neighborhood Poverty

	Neighborhood Poverty				
	<10%	10–19.99%	20–29.99%	30–39.99%	>=40%
Percent nonwhite	9.6	23.6	42	51.3	69.6
Percent Hispanic	1.1	1.0	3.4	3.1	1.6
Percent foreign-born	3.9	2.9	3.0	3.3	3.0
Percent female-headed households (among all households)	9.4	15.0	20.5	24.3	31.3

TABLE 4.3   Relationship Between Socioeconomic Characteristics and
Neighborhood Poverty

	Neighborhood Poverty				
	<10%	10–19.99%	20–29.99%	30–39.99%	>=40%
Per capita income 1990	$17,256	$12,996	$10,318	$9,145	$6,248
Percent of population below poverty	6.2	14.6	23.9	32.8	50.0
Percent of households receiving public assistance	3.9	9.8	16.4	23.3	32.0
Employment rate	95.9	92.7	88.6	85.7	82.4
Violent crime index (U.S. average=100)	154.0	201.4	255.3	242.2	168.7
Nonviolent crime index (U.S. average=100)	94.9	121.3	154.2	133.7	94.6

borhoods receive public assistance. That number rises with each poverty
category to its highest rate in extreme-poverty neighborhoods, where
about one-third of the families receive public aid.

The employment rate follows this same trend. The employment rate declines from above 95 percent in middle-class neighborhoods to about 80
percent in extreme-poverty neighborhoods. At first glance, an employment rate of over 80 percent in an extreme-poverty neighborhood, one
with a poverty rate in excess of 40 percent, might not seem unduly serious.
However, this employment rate includes only those people working or ac-
tively looking for work; thus, the true unemployment rate is much higher.

TABLE 4.4   Relationship Between Labor Force Characteristics and
Neighborhood Poverty

	Neighborhood Poverty				
	< 10%	*10–19.99%*	*20–29.99%*	*30–39.99%*	*>=40%*
Civilian labor force					
participation rate	69.5	64.7	60.0	54.0	49.9
Percent less than high					
school education	16.1	25.7	35.0	37.8	36.8
Percent high school					
graduates	28.7	33.9	31.3	29.2	25.3
Percent college and					
above education	26.6	14.5	11.0	10.7	9.3
Percent management					
and professional					
specialty occupations	33.2	22.6	20.0	19.9	18.6
Percent services occupations	10.8	14.8	18.1	20.3	24.7
Percent operators,					
fabricators, and laborers	10.6	17.2	20.3	20.4	17.9

The crime indexes also increase until the neighborhood is in moderate poverty, then decline. This trend is primarily because five extreme-poverty neighborhoods in Columbus had fewer crimes than some middle-class neighborhoods in Columbus with higher crime indexes.

A more complete picture is shown by the labor market variables. Table 4.4 shows labor force participation rates for the various neighborhood categories. The participation rate drops steadily from about 70 percent in middle-class neighborhoods to less than 50 percent in extreme-poverty neighborhoods. Thus, about half of adults in extreme-poverty neighborhoods are not working (in fairness, some are elderly).

The types of jobs held by workers also vary by neighborhood, but not as much as might be expected. Over 30 percent of workers living in middle-class neighborhoods are managers or professionals, but almost 20 percent of workers in extreme-poverty neighborhoods are also in these occupations. Differences are most pronounced in the service occupations. Only 10 percent of the labor force living in middle-income neighborhoods work in service occupations, but that percentage rises linearly as poverty increases: In extreme-poverty neighborhoods, 25 percent of the employed residents work in service occupations.

The final variables in the labor market category are those related to education. The relationship between education and neighborhood poverty is somewhat predictable. The percentage of the population with less than a high school education is lowest in middle-class neighborhoods—16 percent. It increases to 35 percent in moderate-poverty neighborhoods and remains at that level in both severe-poverty and extreme-poverty neighborhoods. The same basic pattern is true for the percent of college graduates, only reversed. Over 25 percent of the residents of middle-class neighborhoods hold college degrees, whereas about 10 percent of those living in the three poverty neighborhoods are college graduates. There is virtually no relationship between education and neighborhood type concerning the percent of high school graduates.

The housing variables shown in Table 4.5 show a clear relationship between the housing in neighborhoods and neighborhood wealth. Most housing in better-off neighborhoods is owner-occupied; in poorer neighborhoods it is renter-occupied. In the wealthiest neighborhoods, the average value of housing units is just over $80,000; in extreme-poverty neighborhoods it is $30,000. Housing in the wealthiest neighborhoods is newer, and there are also fewer vacancies in the units that are for rent. Subsidized housing is overwhelmingly in the poorer neighborhoods.

Poverty and Industrial Location

Table 4.6 shows the relationships between neighborhood poverty and employment for the 55 industrial classifications discussed in Chapter 3. The employment and establishment variables are total employment, total establishments, employment per 1,000 residents (controlling for neighborhood size), average number of employees per establishment, and neighborhood residents per establishment.

Part A of the table is for overall employment. It is obvious from the data that jobs and businesses can be located in any neighborhood. The number of neighborhood jobs is fairly substantial in all economic categories of neighborhoods. There are as many jobs in the middle-class neighborhoods of Ohio's central cities as in extreme-poverty neighborhoods (over 380 jobs per 1,000 residents). However, closer inspection of the data shows that the heavy representation of industry jobs in extreme-poverty neighborhoods is caused by the above-average presence of a few industries, including manufacturing (16,039), printing (4,189), hospitals (15,027), and educational institutions (14,077).

TABLE 4.5 Relationship Between Housing Characteristics and Neighborhood Poverty

	Neighborhood Poverty				
	< 10%	*10–19.99%*	*20–29.99%*	*30–39.99%*	*>=40%*
Percent owner-occupied housing units	61.1	58.7	52.9	45.6	28.7
Percent vacant housing units	4.9	6.0	8.9	10.4	15.5
Median value of owner-occupied housing units	80,338	56,215	39,702	38,076	30,046
Percent housing units built before 1950	28.8	40.8	65.2	66.7	59.1
Percent subsidized housing units	1.5	4.1	4.6	11.6	19.5

Following is a breakdown for each major industry division (Parts B through J in Table 4.6) indicating the relationship between industry employment and neighborhood poverty, categorized according to the five employment and establishment variables previously discussed.

Construction. Part B shows the relationship between employment in the construction industry by neighborhood wealth. Most of the employment and most of the businesses are in middle- and working-class neighborhoods; however, the majority of the people also live in these neighborhoods. Once size is controlled (employment per 1,000 residents), it is clear that the location of construction companies is unrelated to the type of neighborhood. Construction firms are as likely to be located in the poorest neighborhoods as in the wealthiest. On the other hand, the construction industry is not a major job generator. It accounts for only about 4.3 percent of the employment in Ohio central-city neighborhoods. And these firms are small, with an average of five to ten employees. When the type of contractor is considered, it is clear that most of the employment is in specialty trades. Overall, there are fewer than 5 employees per 1,000 population working for either general or heavy contractors in any of the types of neighborhoods (except working-class). This figure compares to about 10 employees per 1,000 in the specialty trades, such as plumbing or electrical, except for severe-poverty neighborhoods, which have only 5 employees per 1,000.

Manufacturing.   In Part C of Table 4.6, manufacturing is broken down into two categories—durable and nondurable goods. As was the case with construction, employment in durable-goods manufacturing is spread throughout various types of neighborhoods. Furthermore, if there is any trend at all to the data, it is that middle-class neighborhoods are typically short of durable-goods manufacturing. There are only about 25 durable-goods manufacturing jobs per 1,000 residents in middle-class neighborhoods, compared with over 50 in the poorer neighborhoods. This fact should not be surprising, as the better-off neighborhoods in Ohio central cities tend to be more residential in character and much less mixed-use.

The same basic trends are apparent for nondurable-goods manufacturing. Middle-class neighborhoods also have a dearth of nondurable-manufacturing jobs.

The data for both durable- and nondurable-goods manufacturing exhibit another anomaly. Moderate-poverty neighborhoods (those with poverty rates between 20 and 30 percent) have substantially fewer manufacturing jobs per 1,000 residents than either the wealthier working-class neighborhoods or the poorer severe-poverty or extreme-poverty neighborhoods. There is no ready explanation for these findings.

Durable Goods.   The bigger job generators in central-city neighborhoods include the primary metals, fabricated metals, and industrial machinery and equipment industries. The primary metals industry (defined as SIC 33) averages 23 jobs per 1,000 population in severe-poverty neighborhoods, compared with 5 or fewer jobs in other neighborhoods. However, these numbers are slightly misleading because they are skewed by a few primary metals businesses that employ over 5,800 in a single severe-poverty neighborhood of Cleveland (zip code 44127). If these few establishments and this neighborhood are excluded, primary metals employment in severe-poverty neighborhoods is only 2.6 jobs per 1,000 population.

Part C of the table also shows that fabricated metal products and industrial machinery and equipment are significant job generators for central-city neighborhoods. In both cases, this is especially true for working-class and extreme-poverty neighborhoods.

Nondurable Goods.   The table shows no one or two nondurable-goods sectors standing out as particularly strong employment generators in urban neighborhoods. Extreme-poverty neighborhoods have a little more employment in food and kindred products and chemicals and allied products than do other neighborhoods, and severe-poverty neighborhoods are slightly advantaged in rubber and miscellaneous plastic products.

Transportation Services.   Part D of Table 4.6 shows that there is a moderate transportation presence almost everywhere in Ohio central cities. Working-class and moderate-poverty neighborhoods, however, have a few more jobs per 1,000 residents in transportation than do other neighborhoods.

Wholesale Services.   The distribution of wholesale services in central cities is fairly flat across the poverty topology (Part E). There are roughly 20 jobs per 1,000, on average, across the urban neighborhoods.

Retail Services.   Part F shows that retail services are an important employment generator and have a significant relationship to neighborhood wealth. There are almost 70 retail jobs per 1,000 population in middle-class neighborhoods, with that number declining linearly to only 16 jobs per 1,000 in extreme-poverty neighborhoods. Retail services seem to be clearly dependent on neighborhood wealth. When disaggregated, most retail industries primarily serve the better-off (middle- and working-class) neighborhoods; there is a significant drop in the presence of retail activities in a neighborhood once poverty reaches 20 percent. Primary retail activities include general merchandise stores (SIC 53), food stores (SIC 54), automotive dealers and gasoline service stations (SIC 55), apparel and accessories (SIC 56), furniture and home furnishings (SIC 57), and miscellaneous retail (SIC 59).

Information Services.   The data indicate that both the better-off and very poorest neighborhoods are the major locations for establishments in information services (Part G). This is largely due to the location of communications businesses in middle-class neighborhoods and printing and publishing and engineering and management services in both middle-class and (especially) extreme-poverty neighborhoods. However, extreme-poverty neighborhoods host a different type of printing and publishing firms. Several large establishments (employing more than 3,300 workers) in a few extreme-poverty neighborhoods are engaged in periodicals printing and publishing, manifold business form printing, and commercial printing. Once these establishments are excluded, information services are clearly clustered in middle- and working-class neighborhoods (see Chapter 6 for a detailed discussion of SIC 27—printing and publishing).

TABLE 4.6   Industry Employment Characteristics by Type of Neighborhood

Industry/Neighborhood	Employ- ment (1st quarter 1993)	Establish- ments (1st quarter 1993)	Employ- ment per 1,000 Residents	Size of Establish- ment (# of employees)	Resi- dents per Estab- lishment
A. All industries in the sample					
Middle-class	269,073	16,680	381.75	16.13	42
Working-class	225,406	12,437	321.25	18.12	56
Moderate-poverty	114,101	6,461	235.43	17.66	75
Severe-poverty	95,398	3,892	332.83	24.51	76
Extreme-poverty	82,264	2,756	382.91	29.85	78
B. Construction					
Middle-class	9,256	1,410	13.13	6.56	500
Working-class	10,713	1,199	15.27	8.93	585
Moderate-poverty	5,922	677	12.22	8.75	716
Severe-poverty	2,385	317	8.07	7.52	932
Extreme-poverty	2,783	237	12.95	11.74	906
General contractors					
Middle-class	2,086	435	2.96	4.80	1,620
Working-class	2,055	296	2.93	6.94	2,370
Moderate-poverty	1,135	149	2.34	7.62	3,253
Severe-poverty	693	85	2.35	8.15	3,476
Extreme-poverty	502	57	2.34	8.81	3,769
Heavy contractors					
Middle-class	574	40	0.81	14.35	17,621
Working-class	1,444	57	2.06	25.33	12,310
Moderate-poverty	470	39	0.97	12.05	12,427
Severe-poverty	132	8	0.45	16.50	36,938
Extreme-poverty	122	8	0.57	15.25	26,855
Special trade					
Middle-class	6,596	935	9.36	7.05	754
Working-class	7,213	846	10.28	8.53	829
Moderate-poverty	4,317	489	8.91	8.83	991
Severe-poverty	1,560	224	5.28	6.96	1,319
Extreme-poverty	2,159	172	10.05	12.55	1,249
C. Manufacturing					
Durable Manufacturing					
Middle-class	18,385	492	26.08	37.37	1,433
Working-class	34,278	710	48.85	48.28	988
Moderate-poverty	16,111	561	33.24	28.72	864
Severe-poverty	15,013	297	50.81	50.55	995
Extreme-poverty	11,390	220	53.02	51.77	977
Lumber and wood products					
Middle-class	295	16	0.42	18.44	44,052
Working-class	218	32	0.31	6.81	21,927
Moderate-poverty	382	25	0.79	15.28	19,386
Severe-poverty	166	19	0.56	8.74	15,553
Extreme-poverty	62	6	0.29	10.33	35,807

Funiture and fixtures					
Middle-class	312	14	0.44	22.29	50,345
Working-class	744	24	1.06	31.00	29,236
Moderate-poverty	156	12	0.32	13.00	40,388
Severe-poverty	165	11	0.56	15.00	26,864
Extreme-poverty	315	8	1.47	39.38	26,855
Stone, clay, and glass products					
Middle-class	1,232	20	1.75	61.60	35,242
Working-class	1,789	36	2.55	49.69	19,491
Moderate-poverty	1,021	34	2.11	30.03	14,255
Severe-poverty	161	10	0.54	16.10	29,550
Extreme-poverty	177	9	0.82	19.67	23,871
Primary metals					
Middle-class	896	15	1.27	59.73	46,989
Working-class	2,797	33	3.99	84.76	21,262
Moderate-poverty	1,700	40	3.51	42.50	12,116
Severe-poverty	6,627	24	22.43	276.13	12,313
Extreme-poverty	1,094	22	5.09	49.73	9,765
Fabricated metal products					
Middle-class	2,820	103	4.00	27.38	6,843
Working-class	7,061	160	10.06	44.13	4,385
Moderate-poverty	4,411	156	9.10	28.28	3,107
Severe-poverty	2,356	85	7.97	27.72	3,476
Extreme-poverty	2,270	71	10.57	31.97	3,026
Industrial machinery and equipment					
Middle-class	4,393	181	6.23	24.27	3,894
Working-class	9,096	281	12.96	32.37	2,497
Moderate-poverty	5,055	204	10.43	24.78	2,376
Severe-poverty	2,184	101	7.39	21.62	2,926
Extreme-poverty	2,643	62	12.30	42.63	3,465
Electronic and other electric equipment					
Middle-class	1,907	51	2.71	37.39	13,820
Working-class	7,975	39	11.37	204.49	17,991
Moderate-poverty	933	23	1.93	40.57	21,072
Severe-poverty	1,007	13	3.41	77.46	22,731
Extreme-poverty	1,101	16	5.12	68.81	13,428
Transportation equipment					
Middle-class	5,105	22	7.24	232.05	32,038
Working-class	1,560	29	2.22	53.79	24,195
Moderate-poverty	1,418	18	2.93	78.78	26,925
Severe-poverty	1,571	11	5.32	142.82	26,864
Extreme-poverty	3,382	9	15.74	375.78	23,871
Instruments and related products					
Middle-class	1,298	35	1.84	37.09	20,138
Working-class	2,482	39	3.54	63.64	17,991
Moderate-poverty	552	12	1.14	46.00	40,388
Severe-poverty	520	8	1.76	65.00	36,938
Extreme-poverty	57	3	0.27	19.00	71,613

(continues)

Miscellaneous manufacturing industries

Middle-class	126	35	0.18	3.60	20,138
Working-class	555	37	0.79	15.00	18,964
Moderate-poverty	483	37	1.00	13.05	13,099
Severe-poverty	256	15	0.87	17.07	19,700
Extreme-poverty	290	14	1.35	20.71	15,346

Nondurable manufacturing

Middle-class	6,675	144	9.47	46.35	4,895
Working-class	13,956	237	19.89	58.89	2,961
Moderate-poverty	4,891	117	10.09	41.80	4,142
Severe-poverty	5,393	86	18.25	62.71	3,436
Extreme-poverty	4,649	76	21.64	61.17	2,827

Food and kindred products

Middle-class	2,973	31	4.22	95.90	22,737
Working-class	3,009	44	4.29	68.39	15,947
Moderate-poverty	1,210	27	2.50	44.81	17,950
Severe-poverty	1,209	16	4.09	75.56	18,469
Extreme-poverty	1,962	19	9.13	103.26	11,307

Textiles mills products

Middle-class	3	2	0.00	1.50	352,418
Working-class	174	5	0.25	34.80	140,332
Moderate-poverty	11	1	0.02	11.00	484,658
Severe-poverty	0	1	0.00	0.00	295,501
Extreme-poverty	77	1	0.36	77.00	214,840

Apparel and other textile products

Middle-class	310	20	0.44	15.50	35,242
Working-class	1,289	38	1.84	33.92	18,465
Moderate-poverty	375	19	0.77	19.74	25,508
Severe-poverty	872	11	2.95	79.27	26,864
Extreme-poverty	214	12	1.00	17.83	17,903

Paper and allied products

Middle-class	366	20	0.52	18.30	35,242
Working-class	1,212	26	1.73	46.62	26,987
Moderate-poverty	215	7	0.44	30.71	69,237
Severe-poverty	919	18	3.11	51.06	16,417
Extreme-poverty	603	12	2.81	50.25	17,903

Chemicals and allied products

Middle-class	1,073	25	1.52	42.92	28,193
Working-class	3,365	43	4.80	78.26	16,318
Moderate-poverty	2,125	26	4.38	81.73	18,641
Severe-poverty	209	9	0.71	23.22	32,833
Extreme-poverty	1,549	17	7.21	91.12	12,638

Petroleum and coal products

Middle-class	68	6	0.10	11.33	117,473
Working-class	17	3	0.02	5.67	233,886
Moderate-poverty	145	6	0.30	24.17	80,776
Severe-poverty	75	6	0.25	12.50	49,250
Extreme-poverty	82	2	0.38	41.00	107,420

Rubber and miscellaneous plastic products

Middle-class	1,858	38	2.64	48.89	18,548
Working-class	3,869	74	5.51	52.28	9,482
Moderate-poverty	800	30	1.65	26.67	16,155
Severe-poverty	2,105	24	7.12	87.71	12,313
Extreme-poverty	162	13	0.75	12.46	16,526

Leather and leather products

Middle-class	23	2	0.03	11.50	352,418
Working-class	1,021	4	1.46	255.25	175,415
Moderate-poverty	8	1	0.02	8.00	484,658
Severe-poverty	3	1	0.01	3.00	295,501
Extreme-poverty			0.00	0.00	0

D. Transportation

Middle-class	6,019	330	8.54	18.24	2,136
Working-class	9,328	341	13.29	27.35	2,058
Moderate-poverty	6,200	204	12.79	30.39	2,376
Severe-poverty	1,886	117	6.38	16.12	2,526
Extreme-poverty	1,570	80	7.31	19.63	2,686

E. Wholesale services

Middle-class	13,151	1,198	18.66	10.98	588
Working-class	14,833	1,171	21.14	12.67	599
Moderate-poverty	8,665	577	17.88	15.02	840
Severe-poverty	4,179	333	14.14	12.55	887
Extreme-poverty	4,518	249	21.03	18.14	863

F. Retail services

Middle-class	46,899	2,707	66.54	17.33	260
Working-class	38,888	2,296	55.42	16.94	306
Moderate-poverty	11,935	956	24.63	12.48	507
Severe-poverty	6,030	624	20.41	9.66	474
Extreme-poverty	3,444	364	16.03	9.46	590

Building materials, hardware, and garden supplies (SIC 52)

Middle-class	2,450	158	3.48	15.51	4,461
Working-class	1,787	144	2.55	12.41	4,873
Moderate-poverty	1,011	79	2.09	12.80	6,135
Severe-poverty	407	35	1.38	11.64	8,443
Extreme-poverty	165	15	0.77	11.00	14,323

General merchandise stores (SIC 53)

Middle-class	9,090	91	12.90	99.89	7,745
Working-class	8,492	88	12.10	96.50	7,973
Moderate-poverty	946	28	1.95	33.78	17,309
Severe-poverty	676	22	2.29	30.74	13,432
Extreme-poverty	287	6	1.34	47.88	35,807

Variety stores (SIC 533)

Middle-class	599	25	0.85	23.96	28,193
Working-class	2,384	31	3.40	76.90	22,634
Moderate-poverty	138	15	0.29	9.22	32,311
Severe-poverty	141	13	0.48	10.82	22,731
Extreme-poverty	102	4	0.48	25.58	53,710

(continues)

Food stores (SIC 54)

Middle-class	12,392	411	17.58	30.15	1,715
Working-class	8,870	413	12.64	21.48	1,699
Moderate-poverty	3,266	283	6.74	11.54	1,713
Severe-poverty	2,418	196	8.18	12.34	1,508
Extreme-poverty	980	132	4.56	7.43	1,628

Grocery stores (SIC 541)

Middle-class	11,039	244	15.66	45.24	2,889
Working-class	7,769	309	11.07	25.14	2,271
Moderate-poverty	2,403	216	4.96	11.12	2,244
Severe-poverty	2,123	156	7.19	13.61	1,894
Extreme-poverty	797	118	3.71	6.75	1,821

Meat and fish markets (SIC 542)

Middle-class	250	28	0.35	8.93	25,173
Working-class	86	16	0.12	5.39	43,854
Moderate-poverty	121	15	0.25	8.09	32,311
Severe-poverty	106	13	0.36	8.18	22,731
Extreme-poverty	31	6	0.14	5.17	35,807

Dairy products stores (SIC 545)

Middle-class	30	5	0.04	6.06	140,967
Working-class	2	2	0.00	0.85	350,830
Moderate-poverty	0	0	0.00	0.00	0
Severe-poverty	0	0	0.00	0.00	0
Extreme-poverty	0	0	0.00	0.00	0

Retail bakeries (SIC 546)

Middle-class	633	73	0.90	8.68	9,655
Working-class	698	51	0.99	13.69	13,758
Moderate-poverty	636	41	1.31	15.52	11,821
Severe-poverty	150	21	0.51	7.16	14,071
Extreme-poverty	67	5	0.31	13.46	42,968

Automotive dealers and service stations (SIC 55)

Middle-class	7,455	431	10.58	17.30	1,635
Working-class	5,234	451	7.46	11.60	1,556
Moderate-poverty	1,922	207	3.97	9.28	2,341
Severe-poverty	1,020	122	3.45	8.36	2,422
Extreme-poverty	775	60	3.61	12.92	3,581

Car dealers (SICs 551 and 552)

Middle-class	4,725	125	6.70	37.80	5,639
Working-class	2,543	127	3.62	20.03	5,525
Moderate-poverty	580	51	1.20	11.37	9,503
Severe-poverty	392	23	1.33	17.06	12,848
Extreme-poverty	211	17	0.98	12.41	12,638

Gasoline service stations (SIC 554)

Middle-class	1,330	187	1.89	7.11	3,769
Working-class	1,339	199	1.91	6.73	3,526
Moderate-poverty	582	98	1.20	5.94	4,945
Severe-poverty	391	63	1.32	6.21	4,690
Extreme-poverty	121	23	0.56	5.25	9,341

Apparel and accessory stores (SIC 56)

Middle-class	3,038	330	4.31	9.21	2,136
Working-class	3,460	227	4.93	15.24	3,091
Moderate-poverty	385	55	0.79	7.00	8,812
Severe-poverty	206	43	0.70	4.78	6,872
Extreme-poverty	62	17	0.29	3.63	12,638

Furniture and home-furnishing stores (SIC 57)

Middle-class	2,761	381	3.92	7.25	1,850
Working-class	2,452	251	3.49	9.77	2,795
Moderate-poverty	740	60	1.53	12.33	8,078
Severe-poverty	302	51	1.02	5.92	5,794
Extreme-poverty	343	40	1.60	8.58	5,371

Miscellaneous retail (SIC 59)

Middle-class	9,713	905	13.78	10.73	779
Working-class	8,594	722	12.25	11.90	972
Moderate-poverty	3,666	244	7.56	15.02	1,986
Severe-poverty	1,000	155	3.39	6.45	1,906
Extreme-poverty	831	94	3.87	8.84	2,286

Drug stores and proprietary stores (SIC 591)

Middle-class	1,900	109	2.70	17.43	6,466
Working-class	1,605	110	2.29	14.59	6,379
Moderate-poverty	653	59	1.35	11.07	8,215
Severe-poverty	418	38	1.41	11.00	7,776
Extreme-poverty	135	21	0.63	6.41	10,230

Liquor stores (SIC 592)

Middle-class	286	78	0.41	3.66	9,036
Working-class	1,418	106	2.02	13.37	6,619
Moderate-poverty	150	31	0.31	4.85	15,634
Severe-poverty	83	26	0.28	3.19	11,365
Extreme-poverty	46	16	0.21	2.88	13,428

Used merchandise stores (SIC 593)

Middle-class	117	28	0.17	4.19	25,173
Working-class	317	35	0.45	9.06	20,047
Moderate-poverty	97	19	0.20	5.12	25,508
Severe-poverty	46	14	0.16	3.31	21,107
Extreme-poverty	101	13	0.47	7.79	16,526

G. Information

Middle-class	13,161	386	18.67	34.09	1,826
Working-class	7,792	283	11.11	27.53	2,479
Moderate-poverty	2,382	157	4.91	15.17	3,087
Severe-poverty	1,017	75	3.44	13.56	3,940
Extreme-poverty	4,275	71	19.90	60.21	3,026

Printing and publishing

Middle-class	7,669	200	10.88	38.35	3,524
Working-class	5,905	179	8.42	32.99	3,920
Moderate-poverty	1,502	104	3.10	14.44	4,660
Severe-poverty	807	47	2.73	17.17	6,287
Extreme-poverty	4,189	60	19.50	69.82	3,581

(continues)

Communications

Middle-class	4,208	67	5.97	62.81	10,520
Working-class	1,334	39	1.90	34.21	17,991
Moderate-poverty	781	25	1.61	31.24	19,386
Severe-poverty	128	13	0.43	9.85	22,731
Extreme-poverty	64	6	0.30	10.67	35,807

Advertising

Middle-class	647	72	0.92	8.99	9,789
Working-class	320	39	0.46	8.21	17,991
Moderate-poverty	41	16	0.08	2.56	30,291
Severe-poverty	45	10	0.15	4.50	29,550
Extreme-poverty	22	5	0.10	4.40	42,968

Credit reporting and collection

Middle-class	556	30	0.79	18.53	23,495
Working-class	171	16	0.24	10.69	43,854
Moderate-poverty	16	5	0.03	3.20	96,932
Severe-poverty	6	1	0.02	6.00	295,501
Extreme-poverty			0.00	0.00	0

Motion picture and allied services

Middle-class	81	17	0.11	4.76	41,461
Working-class	63	10	0.09	6.30	70,166
Moderate-poverty	43	7	0.09	6.14	69,237
Severe-poverty	32	4	0.11	8.00	73,875
Extreme-poverty	0	0	0.00	0.00	0

H. Producer Services

Middle-class	44,090	3,932	62.55	11.21	179
Working-class	21,975	1,980	31.32	11.10	354
Moderate-poverty	7,777	815	16.05	9.54	595
Severe-poverty	5,298	528	17.93	10.03	560
Extreme-poverty	5,980	372	27.83	16.07	578

Electric, gas, and sanitary

Middle-class	1,382	38	1.96	36.37	18,548
Working-class	1,240	23	1.77	53.91	30,507
Moderate-poverty	486	16	1.00	30.38	30,291
Severe-poverty	1,031	7	3.49	147.29	42,214
Extreme-poverty	284	7	1.32	40.57	30,691

Banking

Middle-class	4,956	396	7.03	12.52	1,780
Working-class	2,663	204	3.80	13.05	3,440
Moderate-poverty	920	73	1.90	12.60	6,639
Severe-poverty	439	54	1.49	8.13	5,472
Extreme-poverty	321	39	1.49	8.23	5,509

Insurance

Middle-class	6,809	631	9.66	10.79	1,117
Working-class	1,399	246	1.99	5.69	2,852
Moderate-poverty	246	47	0.51	5.23	10,312
Severe-poverty	185	47	0.63	3.94	6,287
Extreme-poverty	189	20	0.88	9.45	10,742

Real estate					
Middle-class	4,732	737	6.71	6.42	956
Working-class	2,321	382	3.31	6.08	1,837
Moderate-poverty	1,110	180	2.29	6.17	2,693
Severe-poverty	678	129	2.29	5.26	2,291
Extreme-poverty	475	84	2.21	5.65	2,558
Engineering and management services					
Middle-class	6,876	846	9.76	8.13	833
Working-class	3,739	398	5.33	9.39	1,763
Moderate-poverty	1,053	124	2.17	8.49	3,909
Severe-poverty	470	92	1.59	5.11	3,212
Extreme-poverty	2,729	68	12.70	40.13	3,159
Miscellaneous Business					
Middle-class	18,688	1,089	26.51	17.16	647
Working-class	10,169	616	14.49	16.51	1,139
Moderate-poverty	3,752	286	7.74	13.12	1,695
Severe-poverty	2,455	173	8.31	14.19	1,708
Extreme-poverty	1,846	124	8.59	14.89	1,733
Legal services					
Middle-class	646	195	0.92	3.31	3,615
Working-class	445	111	0.63	4.01	6,321
Moderate-poverty	210	89	0.43	2.36	5,446
Severe-poverty	40	26	0.14	1.54	11,365
Extreme-poverty	135	30	0.63	4.50	7,161
I. Social services					
Middle-class	66,264	2,471	94.01	26.82	285
Working-class	41,936	1,497	59.77	28.01	469
Moderate-poverty	37,577	847	77.53	44.36	572
Severe-poverty	44,850	638	151.78	70.30	463
Extreme-poverty	39,121	553	182.09	70.74	388
Medical services					
Middle-class	18,081	1,687	25.65	10.72	418
Working-class	9,572	866	13.64	11.05	810
Moderate-poverty	5,405	454	11.15	11.91	1,068
Severe-poverty	6,278	356	21.25	17.63	830
Extreme-poverty	4,643	255	21.61	18.21	843
Hospitals					
Middle-class	11,076	7	15.71	1,582.29	100,691
Working-class	12,974	8	18.49	1,621.75	87,707
Moderate-poverty	18,194	10	37.54	1,819.40	48,466
Severe-poverty	29,263	11	99.03	2,660.27	26,864
Extreme-poverty	15,027	7	69.95	2,146.71	30,691
Education					
Middle-class	21,668	134	30.74	161.70	5,260
Working-class	7,092	53	10.11	133.81	13,239
Moderate-poverty	8,301	24	17.13	345.88	20,194
Severe-poverty	5,313	25	17.98	212.52	11,820
Extreme-poverty	14,077	9	65.52	1,564.11	23,871

(continues)

Welfare

Middle-class	2,542	78	3.61	32.59	9,036
Working-class	1,505	47	2.14	32.02	14,929
Moderate-poverty	1,272	64	2.62	19.88	7,573
Severe-poverty	901	49	3.05	18.39	6,031
Extreme-poverty	984	51	4.58	19.29	4,213

Nonprofit

Middle-class	2,567	220	3.64	11.67	3,204
Working-class	2,022	227	2.88	8.91	3,091
Moderate-poverty	927	129	1.91	7.19	3,757
Severe-poverty	821	77	2.78	10.66	3,838
Extreme-poverty	936	75	4.36	12.48	2,865

Government

Middle-class	5,207	114	7.39	45.68	6,183
Working-class	5,723	94	8.16	60.88	7,464
Moderate-poverty	415	15	0.86	27.67	32,311
Severe-poverty	442	5	1.50	88.40	59,100
Extreme-poverty	1,009	32	4.70	31.53	6,714

Miscellaneous social services

Middle-class	5,123	231	7.27	22.18	3,051
Working-class	3,048	202	4.34	15.09	3,474
Moderate-poverty	3,063	151	6.32	20.28	3,210
Severe-poverty	1,832	115	6.20	15.93	2,570
Extreme-poverty	2,446	124	11.39	19.73	1,733

J. Personal services

Middle-class	45,075	3,570	63.95	12.63	197
Working-class	31,642	2,696	45.10	11.74	260
Moderate-poverty	12,588	1,539	25.97	8.18	315
Severe-poverty	9,313	865	31.52	10.77	342
Extreme-poverty	4,533	530	21.10	8.55	405

Domestic services

Middle-class	580	458	0.82	1.27	1,539
Working-class	406	295	0.58	1.38	2,379
Moderate-poverty	223	188	0.46	1.19	2,578
Severe-poverty	143	114	0.48	1.25	2,592
Extreme-poverty	130	58	0.61	2.24	3,704

Hotels

Middle-class	1,968	59	2.79	33.36	11,946
Working-class	1,151	50	1.64	23.02	14,033
Moderate-poverty	303	17	0.63	17.82	28,509
Severe-poverty	541	14	1.83	38.64	21,107
Extreme-poverty	249	12	1.16	20.75	17,903

Eating and drinking places

Middle-class	27,816	1,389	39.46	20.03	507
Working-class	21,037	1,130	29.98	18.62	621
Moderate-poverty	7,283	654	15.03	11.14	741
Severe-poverty	4,736	370	16.03	12.80	799
Extreme-poverty	2,641	249	12.29	10.61	863

Repair

Middle-class	2,289	479	3.25	4.78	1,471
Working-class	2,544	472	3.63	5.39	1,487
Moderate-poverty	1,416	336	2.92	4.21	1,442
Severe-poverty	678	148	2.29	4.58	1,997
Extreme-poverty	601	112	2.80	5.37	1,918

Laundry

Middle-class	2,261	180	3.21	12.56	3,916
Working-class	1,412	122	2.01	11.57	5,751
Moderate-poverty	1,099	100	2.27	10.99	4,847
Severe-poverty	415	55	1.40	7.55	5,373
Extreme-poverty	270	22	1.26	12.27	9,765

Barber and beauty shops

Middle-class	2,562	356	3.63	7.20	1,980
Working-class	618	167	0.88	3.70	4,202
Moderate-poverty	136	62	0.28	2.19	7,817
Severe-poverty	160	34	0.54	4.71	8,691
Extreme-poverty	68	18	0.32	3.78	11,936

Entertainment

Middle-class	4,472	348	6.34	12.85	2,025
Working-class	2,120	204	3.02	10.39	3,440
Moderate-poverty	1,148	65	2.37	17.66	7,456
Severe-poverty	1,787	53	6.05	33.72	5,575
Extreme-poverty	269	23	1.25	11.70	9,341

Miscellaneous personal services

Middle-class	3,126	301	4.44	10.39	2,342
Working-class	2,355	256	3.36	9.20	2,741
Moderate-poverty	981	117	2.02	8.38	4,142
Severe-poverty	853	77	2.89	11.08	3,838
Extreme-poverty	304	36	1.42	8.44	5,968

Producer Services.   As might be expected, the employment pattern in producer services (Part H) mirrors the retail sector. There are almost 63 jobs per 1,000 in this sector in middle-class neighborhoods but only 17 or so such jobs in moderate- and severe-poverty neighborhoods. The higher industry employment in extreme-poverty neighborhoods is caused by a cluster of engineering and management firms (14) in a Columbus extreme-poverty neighborhood (with more than 2,300 employees). If this neighborhood is excluded, the extreme-poverty neighborhoods are as disadvantaged as other poverty neighborhoods in producer services. The two low-poverty neighborhoods are particularly advantaged by banking, insurance, real estate, and miscellaneous business services (e.g., detective and armored car services, security systems services, news syndicates, and photo-finishing laboratories).

Social Services.   Part I shows that all neighborhoods benefit from social services activities, but this is particularly true of the poorest neighborhoods. This finding stems primarily from the huge presence of hospitals and educational institutions in severe- and extreme-poverty
neighborhoods. For example, two educational establishments in a single
Columbus extreme-poverty neighborhood provide nearly 14,000 jobs. A
Cleveland severe-poverty neighborhood is home to over 18,000 hospital
jobs (discussed in detail in Chapter 8).

The pattern of hospital location deserves more explanation. At first
glance, hospitals seem to be positively related to neighborhood poverty.
However, there is no causal link for such correlation. Among 98 central-
city neighborhoods, fewer than one-third (29) have at least one hospital
establishment. Several severe- and extreme-poverty neighborhoods in
Cincinnati, Cleveland, Columbus, and Dayton host 15 large hospitals
with a total of 44,000 employees, over 51 percent of all hospital employment in the seven central cities. This locational pattern can be best explained by inertia (Blair 1995). The hospital presence existed long before
the host neighborhoods started to decline. The second explanation can be
found in the competitive advantage of the inner city proposed by Porter
(1995), as many of these neighborhoods are close to the central business
districts and regional nodes.

Common knowledge as well as empirical studies suggest that the poorest neighborhoods are underserved by medical doctors, yet at first glance,
this premise does not seem to hold in Ohio central cities. There is virtually as much employment in medical services per 1,000 population in se-
vere- and extreme-poverty neighborhoods as elsewhere. This finding re-
quires closer examination because medical services contain several
distinct industries, and the aggregation may have covered some important variations. Medical services are composed of eight three-digit SIC industries: offices and clinics of medical doctors (SIC 801), offices and clinics of dentists (SIC 802), offices of osteopathic physicians (SIC 803),
offices and clinics of other health practitioners (SIC 804), nursing and
personal care facilities (SIC 805), medical and dental laboratories (SIC
807), home health care services (SIC 808), and miscellaneous health and
allied services (SIC 809). The employment distribution across each category of urban neighborhoods is presented in Table 4.7.

Clearly, offices and clinics of dentists (SIC 802), offices and clinics of
other health practitioners (SIC 804), and home health care services (SIC
808) are middle- and working- class neighborhood industries. They have
only a minimal presence in severe- and extreme-poverty neighborhoods.
It is also clear that the higher than expected representation of other med-

TABLE 4.7   Medical Services Employment Distribution by Neighborhood Type

Service/ Neighborhood	*Establishments (1st quarter 1993)*	*Employment (1st quarter 1993)*	*Employment per 1,000 Residents*	*Number of Neighborhoods*
Offices and clinics of medical doctors (SIC 801)				
Middle-class	760	6,302.7	8.94	25
Working-class	340	2,412.3	3.44	27
Moderate-poverty	226	1,783.0	3.68	16
Severe-poverty	198	1,500.0	5.08	11
Extreme-poverty	156	1,678.3	7.81	13
Offices and clinics of dentists (SIC 802)				
Middle-class	456	2,574.7	3.65	25
Working-class	207	1,259.3	1.79	26
Moderate-poverty	91	427.3	0.88	18
Severe-poverty	34	178.3	0.60	10
Extreme-poverty	22	102.3	0.48	7
Offices of osteopathic physicians (SIC 803)				
Middle-class	45	302.0	0.43	14
Working-class	70	631.7	0.90	15
Moderate-poverty	18	116.0	0.24	10
Severe-poverty	16	110.3	0.37	5
Extreme-poverty	17	210.7	0.98	5
Offices and clinics of other health practitioners (SIC 804)				
Middle-class	266	1,603.3	2.27	24
Working-class	145	570.3	0.81	26
Moderate-poverty	52	206.7	0.43	16
Severe-poverty	43	173.0	0.60	8
Extreme-poverty	19	128.0	0.61	6

(continues)

ical services employment in severe-poverty and extreme-poverty neighborhoods was caused by the heavy presence of offices and clinics of medical doctors (SIC 801) and nursing and personal care facilities (SIC 805), both of which are related to the locational pattern of hospitals previously discussed. However, once the poverty neighborhoods containing the major hospitals are removed from the analysis, the poorest neighborhoods are indeed underserved. After excluding these few poverty neighborhoods, there are only 13.4 employees and 15.8 employees per 1,000 in medical services in severe-poverty and extreme-poverty neighborhoods respectively. It is evident that medical services are a high-income industry more frequently found in middle-class neighborhoods than in any other neighborhood type.

TABLE 4.7   (Continued)

Service/ Neighborhood	Establishments (1st quarter 1993)	Employment (1st quarter 1993)	Employment per 1,000 Residents	Number of Neighborhoods
Nursing and personal care facilities (SIC 805)				
Middle-class	46	5,499.3	7.80	20
Working-class	33	2,994.3	4.27	17
Moderate-poverty	17	1,719.7	3.55	10
Severe-poverty	35	3,535.7	11.97	8
Extreme-poverty	14	1,285.0	5.98	7
Medical and dental laboratories (SIC 807)				
Middle-class	58	383.3	0.54	22
Working-class	27	240.3	0.34	15
Moderate-poverty	27	155.7	0.32	14
Severe-poverty	13	465.3	1.57	8
Extreme-poverty	11	146.3	0.68	9
Home health care services (SIC 808)				
Middle-class	24	871.3	1.24	13
Working-class	19	663.7	0.95	12
Moderate-poverty	5	54.7	0.11	4
Severe-poverty	5	130.0	0.44	3
Extreme-poverty	2	16.7	0.08	2
Health and allied services, not elsewhere classified (SIC 809)				
Middle-class	32	544.3	0.77	12
Working-class	25	800.0	1.14	13
Moderate-poverty	18	941.7	1.94	10
Severe-poverty	12	185.7	0.63	8
Extreme-poverty	14	1075.7	5.01	6

Personal Services.   Finally, personal services have a significant presence in all neighborhood categories but particularly in middle- and working-class neighborhoods (Part J). This is largely due to the presence of one income-dependent industry in better-off areas—eating and drinking establishments.

Conclusion

This descriptive analysis of the demographic, socioeconomic, labor market, and housing characteristics associated with poverty neighborhoods produced few surprises. With rare exceptions, the characteristics associated with neighborhood poverty were expected. If there was any surprise, it was in labor market characteristics. A significantly higher percentage of extreme-poverty residents (of those working) than expected were in professional, management, technical, and administrative occupations. In addition, more extreme-poverty residents than expected were either college graduates or had some college.

The major surprise came from the data for job location. With the exception of the retail, producer services, and personal services sectors, poorer neighborhoods are not particularly disadvantaged. In fact, poverty neighborhoods showed unexpected strength in the relative number of jobs in manufacturing, wholesaling, information services, and social services. The characteristics of neighborhoods associated with particular types of employment are discussed in Chapters 5 through 7.

References

Blair, John P. 1995. *Local Economic Development: Analysis and Practice.* Thousand Oaks, CA: Sage Publications.

Porter, Michael E. 1995. "The Competitive Advantage of the Inner City." *Harvard Business Review* 73(3): 55–71.

5

Minor
(Producer-Oriented) Employers

The next task is to examine the relationships between neighborhood characteristics and neighborhood employment. In Chapter 3 we hypothesized that the characteristics of the community would shape the opportunities for neighborhood employment. These characteristics affect both the supply side and demand side of employment. On the supply side, we expected the labor market characteristics of the population to affect the kinds of jobs, and thus industries, that locate in the neighborhoods. On the demand side, we expected the demographic and socioeconomic characteristics of the neighborhood (e.g., wealth) to affect the industrial composition of the neighborhood.

To test these hypotheses, we selected four classes of independent variables as representative of the neighborhoods: demographic characteristics, socioeconomic characteristics, labor market characteristics, and housing characteristics. The details of the selection of these variables were explained in Chapter 3. The twenty-two variables representing the four classes were then factor analyzed to produce four factors empirically descriptive of the socioeconomic groupings of variables of the urban neighborhoods under study: *poverty neighborhoods, working-class neighborhoods, high-crime neighborhoods,* and *ethnic neighborhoods.*

Also in Chapter 3 we presented the scheme we used for classifying industries in the study. The major industrial classifications are construction, manufacturing, transportation services, wholesale services, retail services, information services, producer services, social services, and personal services. This classification of industries has been useful in past studies (Bingham and Kimble 1995; Bingham et al. 1997).

Analysis here and in the two subsequent chapters is performed for these nine major industrial classifications plus selected two- and three-digit (SIC) industries. We chose these particular breakdowns and combinations of SICs because the data show that these industries are major neighborhood job sources and because the literature indicates that they are important to the viability of urban neighborhoods (Bingham and Zhang 1997).

Adding specific two- and three-digit SIC industries to the study makes it cumbersome to present all of the analysis in one chapter. Thus, for ease of presentation, the nine major industrial classifications have been divided into two groups based upon their overall contributions to neighborhood employment. The industries are classified as *major neighborhood employers* if they contribute a total of more than 50,000 jobs to Ohio's central-city neighborhoods and *minor neighborhood employers* if they contribute fewer than 50,000 jobs. However, the category *major neighborhood employers* encompasses too many industries to analyze in a single chapter, so we have broken it into two subcategories—producer-oriented industries and consumer-oriented industries.

This chapter presents the results of the analysis for the minor neighborhood employers. The major neighborhood employers are discussed in Chapters 6 (producer-oriented industries) and 7 (consumer-oriented industries). This subdivision is also theoretically appealing because employment in producer-oriented industries has been hypothesized as supply-side-driven and consumer-oriented industries as demand-driven. It should be noted that the four industries constituting minor neighborhood employers, discussed in this chapter, are also producer-oriented; they are construction, transportation, wholesale, and information services. Industries covered in Chapter 6 are manufacturing and producer services; analyzed in Chapter 7 are retail, social services, and personal services.

To examine the relationships between neighborhood characteristics and neighborhood employment, we took two steps. First, factor scores from the four factors plus a vector of dummy variables for the Ohio central cities were entered into multiple regression equations with the neighborhood-employment dependent variables. The city dummy variables were included to capture any intercity variation of industry employment in specific industries. Youngstown was omitted from the dummy vector, since it is captured in the intercept.

Second, zero-order correlation coefficients were produced between the individual variables having high loadings on each of the factors and the dependent variables. The purpose of this measure was merely descriptive—to attempt to isolate the factor component(s) that might be important in the causal links the models are suggesting.

All Industries

Although it was not strictly necessary to examine the relationships between the neighborhood factors and overall neighborhood employment because the factors are not all expected to impact similarly on each of the industries, such analysis does provide a useful place to start. As the data in the chart show, there are 786,242 jobs with 42,226 employers located in Ohio's central-city neighborhoods. Note, however, that most of these jobs are located in the better-off neighborhoods. The disparity is partially, but only partially, due to the fact that more people live in the better-off neighborhoods than in the poor neighborhoods.

Type of Neighborhood	Number of Establishments, All Industries	Number of Employees	Number of Neighborhoods
Middle-class	16,680	269,073	26
Working-class	12,437	225,406	27
Moderate-poverty	6,461	114,101	18
Severe-poverty	3,892	95,398	13
Extreme-poverty	2,756	82,264	14
Total	42,226	786,242	98

Table 5.1a shows the regression results. Three of the four factors are significantly related to employment in various neighborhoods when we control for all other variables in the model. (It should be kept in mind that this analysis gives relative employment as neighborhood size is controlled—the variable is employment per 1,000 residents.) *Working-class neighborhoods* and *high-crime neighborhoods* were likely to have significantly fewer jobs per 1,000 residents, whereas *ethnic neighborhoods* were likely to have more. Curiously, *poverty neighborhoods* had no independent impact on job location.

Neighborhoods in one city, Dayton, were also somewhat more likely to have higher employment levels. The independent variables explain about one-quarter of the variance in employment (adjusted R^2).

Table 5.1b shows the zero-order correlations. Thirteen of the twenty-two independent variables composing the factors are significantly related to neighborhood employment.

As might have been expected, only a few (four) of the ten variables with high loadings on *poverty neighborhood* had statistically significant correla-

TABLE 5.1a   Ordinary Least Square Estimates of the Regression Model: All
Industries

	Estimated Coefficient	Standardized Coefficient	t Value
Constant	275.1		2.906**
Factors			
Poverty	−19.9	−0.072	−0.799
Working-class	−55.0	−0.200	−2.020*
High-crime	−144.2	−0.525	−3.393***
Ethnicity	114.1	0.416	4.213***
City dummies			
Akron	108.4	0.102	0.833
Cincinnati	125.1	0.181	1.118
Cleveland	37.1	0.049	0.335
Columbus	−24.2	−0.039	−0.184
Dayton	242.3	0.280	2.055*
Toledo	123.9	0.154	1.081

NOTES: Dependent variable: all industry employment per 1,000 population
$R^2 = 0.332$
Adjusted $R^2 = 0.256$
DF = 87
*0.05 level of significance
**0.01 level of significance
***0.001 level of significance

tions with overall neighborhood employment, none of the relationships
was particularly strong, and all were negative. Percent nonwhite, percent
owner-occupied housing units, percent households with public assistance, and percent female-headed households were all negatively related
to employment.

The correlation coefficients of the variables with high loadings on
working-class neighborhoods also support the regression results. Five of the
seven variables were significantly related to neighborhood employment.
Recall that the factor *working-class neighborhoods* was negatively related to
employment. Within this factor, percent with less than high school education and percent in labor occupations were negatively related to employment. The other three variables were positively related: median value of
owner-occupied housing, percent with a college education, and percent
managers and professionals in the labor force.

Most of the variable loading on *high-crime neighborhoods* and *ethnic
neighborhoods* was also statistically significant and in the expected direc-

TABLE 5.1b   Zero-Order Relationships Between Independent Variables and Population-Weighted Employment in All Industries (n = 98)

	All Industries
Poverty neighborhoods	
Percent population below poverty	–0.016
Percent nonwhite population	–0.218*
Percent owner-occupied housing units	–0.277**
Percent vacant housing units	–0.070
Percent households with public assistance	–0.236*
Percent female-headed households	–0.306**
Percent service occupation	–0.153
Civilian labor force participation rate	0.030
Employment rate	0.175
Percent federally subsidized housing units	–0.120
Working-class neighborhoods	
Median value of owner-occupied housing	0.285**
Per capita income	0.140
Percent less than high school education	–0.313**
Percent high school education	–0.188
Percent college and above education	0.271**
Percent management and professionals	0.253*
Percent labor occupation	–0.284**
High-crime neighborhoods	
Percent housing built before 1950	–0.257*
Violent-crime index (U.S. average = 100)	–0.263**
Nonviolent-crime index (U.S. average = 100)	–0.297**
Ethnic neighborhoods	
Percent Hispanic population	–0.099
Percent foreign-born population	0.512***

NOTES: *0.05 level of significance
  **0.01 level of significance
  ***0.001 level of significance

tions. Both crime measures were negatively related to employment, and percent foreign-born was positively related. Percent Hispanic, however, was not significantly related to neighborhood employment.

From a technical modeling viewpoint, the results of this examination of total neighborhood employment are encouraging. Three of the factors explained about one-fourth of the variance in neighborhood employment with more upper-class, low-crime, and ethnic neighborhoods seemingly having an employment advantage. Furthermore, the zero-order correlations generally substantiated the regression results (except that a few of the important *poverty neighborhoods* variables were also negatively related to neighborhood employment, although the factor itself was not).

Construction Industry

The first of the minor industrial employers examined was the construction industry. This SIC division includes not only new construction work but also additions, alterations, renovations, and repairs. Construction activities are generally administered and managed from one fixed place of business, although the actual construction activity occurs at one or more different sites. Three broad types of construction activity are included in this division: building construction by general contractors, heavy construction, and construction activities by special trade contractors. Building-construction general contractors are primarily engaged in the construction of dwellings, office buildings, stores, and other similar building projects. Contractors in heavy construction are engaged in activities such as building highways, pipelines, power lines, sewer and water mains, and other heavy construction projects. Special trade contractors are primarily involved in specialized construction activities, such as plumbing, painting, electrical work, and work for general contractors under subcontract (Office of Management and Budget 1987, 53–54).

Some of these firms are very large and, in fact, are international in scale, but most are much smaller, usually having fewer than ten employees. Many of these businesses are operated out of the owners' homes, and if not, they are usually located in the neighborhood.

We thus expected that those variables associated with working- and middle-class neighborhoods (see Chapter 4) would be associated with employment in the construction industry. But this does not seem to be strictly the case, as shown by the figures in the chart. About 36 percent of the construction jobs are located in poverty neighborhoods, and these firms are small—they average only eight employees.

Type of Neighborhood	Number of Construction Establishments	Number of Employees	Number of Neighborhoods
Middle-class	1,410	9,256	26
Working-class	1,199	10,713	27
Moderate-poverty	677	5,922	18
Severe-poverty	317	2,385	13
Extreme-poverty	237	2,783	14
Total	3,840	31,059	98

TABLE 5.2a   Ordinary Least Square Estimates of the Regression Model:
Construction

	Estimated Coefficient	*Standardized Coefficient*	*t Value*
Constant	13.5		2.355**
Factors			
Poverty	–1.0	–0.068	–0.635
Working-class	1.7	0.121	1.036
High-crime	0.3	0.020	0.108
Ethnicity	–1.7	–0.116	–1.005
City dummies			
Akron	–1.9	–0.034	–0.235
Cincinnati	7.7	0.216	1.138
Cleveland	0.7	0.018	0.102
Columbus	5.3	0.167	0.669
Dayton	3.8	0.084	0.528
Toledo	–3.3	–0.080	–0.476

NOTES: Dependent variable: construction employment per 1,000 population
$R^2 = 0.081$
Adjusted $R^2 = -0.025$
DF = 87
*0.05 level of significance
**0.01 level of significance
***0.001 level of significance

Table 5.2a shows the regression results for the construction division. The model explains only 8 percent of the variance in neighborhood employment in construction, and none of the factors has a statistically significant relationship with the dependent variable. The zero-order correlation coefficients (Table 5.2b) mirror the regression results. That is, none of the zero-order relationships between the variables with high loadings on the four factors is statistically significant. It thus appears that the characteristics of central-city neighborhoods (even poverty) have little to do with the location of the home offices of construction companies.

To explore further the possible reasons for location, we broke down the construction industry by type of firm: general contractors and operative builders (SIC 15), heavy construction (SIC 16), and special trade contractors (SIC 17). Table 5.2b also shows the zero-order relationships between the individual variables composing the factors and neighborhood employment in the three construction subcategories per 1,000 residents. As with contracting in general, the characteristics of central-city neighbor-

TABLE 5.2b   Zero-Order Relationships Between Independent Variables and Population-Weighted Employment in the Construction Industry (n = 98)

	Construction	General Contractors (SIC 15)	Heavy Construction (SIC 16)	Special Trades (SIC 17)
Poverty neighborhoods				
Percent population below poverty	−0.013	−0.072	−0.061	0.023
Percent nonwhite population	−0.126	−0.041	−0.162	−0.107
Percent owner-occupied housing units	0.018	−0.098	0.138	0.015
Percent vacant housing units	−0.040	−0.064	−0.080	−0.010
Percent households with public assistance	0.034	−0.074	−0.004	0.069
Percent female-headed households	0.003	−0.058	−0.092	0.049
Percent service occupation	−0.148	−0.121	−0.105	−0.126
Civilian labor force participation rate	0.056	0.116	−0.004	0.038
Employment rate	0.108	0.198*	0.120	0.044
Percent federally subsidized housing units	−0.049	−0.092	−0.063	−0.017
Working-class neighborhoods				
Median value of owner-occupied housing	0.146	0.184	0.115	0.101
Per capita income	0.052	0.155	0.074	−0.002
Percent less than high school education	0.136	−0.088	0.066	0.188
Percent high school education	0.074	−0.060	0.103	0.087
Percent college and above education	0.007	0.198*	−0.001	−0.053
Percent management and professionals	−0.010	0.182	−0.024	−0.065
Percent labor occupation	0.098	−0.171	0.087	0.158
High-crime neighborhoods				
Percent housing built before 1950	−0.026	−0.059	−0.028	−0.008
Violent-crime index (U.S. average = 100)	−0.088	−0.091	−0.131	−0.049
Nonviolent-crime index (U.S. average = 100)	−0.120	−0.076	−0.150	−0.091
Ethnic neighborhoods				
Percent Hispanic population	−0.165	−0.196	−0.107	−0.124
Percent foreign-born population	−0.172	−0.097	−0.017	−0.190

NOTES: *0.05 level of significance
**0.01 level of significance
***0.001 level of significance

hoods have little to do with neighborhood employment for the three types of contractors. In fact, only one variable was significantly (but weakly) related to employment—the relationship between neighborhood employment rate and employment in general contracting. This finding obviously has little significance.

Transportation Services

Type of Neighborhood	Number of Transportation Establishments	Number of Employees	Number of Neighborhoods
Middle-class	330	6,019	26
Working-class	341	9,328	27
Moderate-poverty	204	6,200	17
Severe-poverty	117	1,886	12
Extreme-poverty	80	1,570	12
Total	1,072	25,003	94

Transportation services includes the big three—air, rail, and trucking—as well as taxis, buses, water transportation, travel agencies, and pipelines. Employment in these services extends throughout all urban neighborhoods, although most is concentrated in areas with less than 30 percent poverty (see chart). Of all industry divisions considered here and in the next two chapters, transportation services have the fewest employees. However, employers, on average, are fairly large. The average establishment in the transportation sector has 25 employees. Of course, the employment level varies considerably depending on the type of business.

The regression model (Table 5.3a) was only slightly more successful in explaining employment in transportation than it was with construction. The independent variables explained only 7 percent of the variance in neighborhood employment in transportation, and only the factor *working-class neighborhoods* was significantly related to employment. With the correlations, in contrast, it was the violent-crime index (negative) that was related to local transportation employment. Not much should be made of this finding, however, as the correlation was quite weak (Table 5.3b).

In Table 5.3b we also examined the zero-order relationships between the factor variables and a major subdivision of the transportation sector—trucking and warehousing. The zero-order correlations did a little to explain the significance of *working-class neighborhoods* in the regression model.

TABLE 5.3a   Ordinary Least Square Estimates of the Regression Model: Transportation

	Estimated Coefficient	Standardized Coefficient	t Value
Constant	0.1		0.012
Factors			
Poverty	−2.9	−0.115	−1.138
Working-class	6.3	0.251	2.261*
High-crime	−5.5	−0.217	−1.256
Ethnicity	−3.5	−0.138	−1.249
City dummies			
Akron	7.0	0.072	0.528
Cincinnati	18.5	0.292	1.614
Cleveland	12.7	0.183	1.121
Columbus	11.5	0.202	0.852
Dayton	22.5	0.283	1.861*
Toledo	6.4	0.086	0.542

NOTES: Dependent variable: transportation employment per 1,000 population
$R^2 = 0.167$
Adjusted $R^2 = 0.072$
DF = 87
*0.05 level of significance
**0.01 level of significance
***0.001 level of significance

Neighborhoods with a larger percentage of the labor force in labor occupations and a higher percentage of high school (only) graduates seem more likely to have higher levels of employment in trucking and warehousing.

Wholesale Trade

Wholesale trade includes establishments engaged in selling merchandise to retailers as well as those that sell to contractors or other business users. As has been the case with the other minor employers, wholesaling is

Type of Neighborhood	Number of Wholesale Establishments	Number of Employees	Number of Neighborhoods
Middle-class	1,198	13,151	26
Working-class	1,171	14,833	27
Moderate-poverty	577	8,665	18
Severe-poverty	333	4,179	13
Extreme-poverty	249	4,518	13
Total	3,528	45,346	97

TABLE 5.3b   Zero-Order Relationships Between Independent Variables and
Population-Weighted Employment in the Transportation Industry (n = 98)

	Transportation	Trucking and Warehousing (SIC 42)
Poverty neighborhoods		
Percent population below poverty	−0.047	−0.042
Percent nonwhite population	−0.144	−0.154
Percent owner-occupied housing units	0.060	0.074
Percent vacant housing units	−0.078	−0.027
Percent households with public assistance	0.008	−0.009
Percent female-headed households	−0.014	−0.007
Percent service occupation	−0.063	−0.137
Civilian labor force participation rate	0.061	0.107
Employment rate	0.066	0.043
Percent federally subsidized housing units	−0.011	0.042
Working-class neighborhoods		
Median value of owner-occupied housing	−0.042	−0.122
Per capita income	−0.031	−0.051
Percent less than high school education	0.162	0.177
Percent high school education	0.193	0.209*
Percent college and above education	−0.171	−0.195
Percent management and professionals	−0.157	−0.197
Percent labor occupation	0.158	0.255**
High-crime neighborhoods		
Percent housing built before 1950	−0.137	−0.098
Violent-crime index (U.S. average = 100)	−0.206*	−0.127
Nonviolent-crime index (U.S. average = 100)	−0.181	−0.157
Ethnic neighborhoods		
Percent Hispanic population	−0.141	−0.113
Percent foreign-born population	−0.169	−0.145

NOTES: *0.05 level of significance
        **0.01 level of significance
        ***0.001 level of significance

spread throughout all types of urban neighborhoods (see chart). But the
size of these establishments tends to be smaller than might be expected.
The average wholesaling establishment has only 13 employees.

Table 5.4a shows the regression results between the independent variables and neighborhood employment in wholesaling. The model explains
almost none of the variance in neighborhood wholesale employment, and

TABLE 5.4a   Ordinary Least Square Estimates of the Regression Model: Wholesale Trade

	Estimated Coefficient	Standardized Coefficients	t Value
Constant	13.5		1.770*
Factors			
Poverty	0.2	0.009	0.080
Working-class	1.8	0.094	0.805
High-crime	−3.5	−0.184	−1.009
Ethnicity	−1.2	−0.065	−0.560
City dummies			
Akron	7.1	0.098	0.678
Cincinnati	11.6	0.245	1.282
Cleveland	8.6	0.166	0.968
Columbus	6.3	0.148	0.592
Dayton	6.1	0.102	0.637
Toledo	0.7	0.013	0.078

NOTES: Dependent variable: wholesale trade employment per 1,000 population
$R^2 = 0.075$
Adjusted $R^2 = -0.031$
DF = 87
*0.05 level of significance
**0.01 level of significance
***0.001 level of significance

none of the factors has statistically significant relationships with wholesale employment when all other variables in the model are controlled. Further, only one of the zero-order correlations was statistically significant (Table 5.4b).

Information Services

Information services are the final group of industries in the minor-employer category. These include printing and publishing, communications (telephone communications, radio and TV broadcasting, and beeper and paging services), advertising, credit reporting and collections, motion pictures, and engineering and management services. There are nearly 43,500 employees in 2,500 firms in information services in Ohio central-city neighborhoods—an average of 17 employees per establishment.

Type of Neighborhood	Number of Information Services Establishments	Number of Employees	Number of Neighborhoods
Middle-class	1,232	20,037	26
. Working-class	681	11,531	27
Moderate-poverty	281	3,435	18
Severe-poverty	167	1,487	13
Extreme-poverty	139	7,004	12
Total	2,500	43,494	96

Employment in the industry is concentrated in the wealthier neighborhoods (see chart) with the exception of the 7,000 employees in information services working in extreme-poverty neighborhoods. This is explained by the presence of one large printing and publishing firm in a Columbus extreme-poverty neighborhood (employing well over 1,000 workers) and a few printing and publishing establishments in two Dayton neighborhoods (employing almost 2,000 workers). When this group is excluded, only 1,298 workers are employed in the information services sector in extreme-poverty neighborhoods. The large Columbus firm engages in periodicals printing and publishing, and the Dayton firms print business forms or engage in general commercial printing.

Note that printing and publishing firms are also heavily represented in middle-class and working-class neighborhoods. However, these firms are a different type: There are two greeting card manufacturers, one located in a Cleveland middle-class neighborhood and the other in a Cincinnati working-class neighborhood, employing about 5,000 workers.

Table 5.5a shows the results of the regression model for information services. For all of information services, the independent variables again explain virtually none of the variation in information services employment. However, one of the regression coefficients is statistically significant—*high-crime neighborhoods*. It appears that these neighborhoods are somewhat less likely to have employment in information services. The zero-order relationships add little to our understanding of information services neighborhood employment (Table 5.5b). At the zero-order level, the two crime measures are unrelated to information services employment. Only percent foreign-born is significantly related to neighborhood

TABLE 5.4b   Zero-Order Relationships Between Independent Variables and Population-Weighted Employment in the Wholesale Trade Industry (n = 98)

	Wholesale Trade
Poverty neighborhoods	
Percent population below poverty	0.042
Percent nonwhite population	−0.107
Percent owner-occupied housing units	−0.085
Percent vacant housing units	0.070
Percent households with public assistance	0.075
Percent female-headed households	0.077
Percent service occupation	−0.111
Civilian labor force participation rate	0.073
Employment rate	0.072
Percent federally subsidized housing units	0.066
Working-class neighborhoods	
Median value of owner-occupied housing	0.107
Per capita income	0.009
Percent less than high school education	0.138
Percent high school education	0.030
Percent college and above education	0.012
Percent management and professionals	−0.045
Percent labor occupation	0.127
High-crime neighborhoods	
Percent housing built before 1950	−0.111
Violent-crime index (U.S. average = 100)	−0.174
Nonviolent-crime index (U.S. average = 100)	−0.211*
Ethnic neighborhoods	
Percent Hispanic population	−0.101
Percent foreign-born population	−0.102

NOTES: *0.05 level of significance
        **0.01 level of significance
        ***0.001 level of significance

employment (positively). Possibly the lack of relationship among Hispanic neighborhoods caused *ethnic neighborhoods* to wash out in the regression equation.

Curiously, some of the zero-order relationships between the factor component variables and employment in some of the information services industries are significant. Thus, these are highlighted in the following discussion.

TABLE 5.5a   Ordinary Least Square Estimates of the Regression Model: Information Services

	Estimated Coefficient	Standardized Coefficient	t Value
Constant	6.4		0.556
Factors			
Poverty	−2.3	−0.082	−0.775
Working-class	−1.4	−0.050	−0.437
High-crime	−9.9	−0.346	−1.926*
Ethnicity	3.7	0.129	1.129
City dummies			
Akron	4.1	0.037	0.261
Cincinnati	16.3	0.226	1.202
Cleveland	14.8	0.188	1.107
Columbus	−4.1	−0.063	−0.255
Dayton	20.7	0.229	1.447
Toledo	5.7	0.068	0.413

NOTES: Dependent variable: information employment per 1,000 population
$R^2 = 0.101$
Adjusted $R^2 = -0.002$
DF = 87

Printing, Publishing, and Allied Industries (SIC 27)

The first such major industrial group is printing and publishing. As Table 5.5b shows, only one of the independent variables, percent foreign-born, is significantly related to the location of printing and publishing firms in urban neighborhoods. The higher the percentage of foreign-born in the neighborhood, the more likely the neighborhood is to have relatively higher levels of employment in the industry.

Communications (SIC 48)

The second information services group examined is communications. Variables expressed in the *working-class neighborhoods* factor appear to hold much of the key to neighborhood employment in communications (see Table 5.5b). But they are expressed in the opposite direction from the variable loadings on the factor. They thus seem to represent middle-class, not working-class, neighborhoods. Employment in communications seems to be centered in neighborhoods with higher individual incomes,

TABLE 5.5b Zero-Order Relationships Between Independent Variables and Population-Weighted Employment in the Information Services Industry (n = 98)

	Information	Printing and Publishing	Communications	Advertising	Credit Reporting and Collection	Motion Picture and Allied Services
Poverty neighborhoods						
Percent population below poverty	-0.054	0.035	-0.236*	-0.169	-0.352***	-0.105
Percent nonwhite population	-0.028	0.012	-0.075	-0.182	-0.227*	-0.229*
Percent owner-occupied housing units	-0.077	-0.136	0.170	0.063	0.075	0.002
Percent vacant housing units	-0.103	-0.068	-0.100	-0.090	-0.140	-0.119
Percent households with public assistance	-0.159	-0.085	-0.202*	-0.160	-0.325**	-0.178
Percent female-headed households	-0.120	-0.065	-0.128	-0.197*	-0.298**	-0.218*
Percent service occupation	0.019	0.103	-0.174	-0.297**	-0.381***	-0.201*
Civilian labor force participation rate	-0.057	-0.163	0.262**	0.199*	0.415***	0.123
Employment rate	0.085	0.008	0.191	0.207*	0.319**	0.227*
Percent federally subsidized housing units	-0.035	0.016	-0.133	-0.147	-0.155	-0.116
Working-class neighborhoods						
Median value of owner-occupied housing	0.141	0.001	0.368***	0.479***	0.296**	0.193
Per capita income	0.036	-0.077	0.268**	0.365***	0.391***	0.159
Percent less than high school education	-0.137	-0.053	-0.229*	-0.159	-0.374***	-0.169
Percent high school education	-0.018	0.022	-0.090	-0.203*	-0.030	-0.111
Percent college and above education	0.057	-0.059	0.295**	0.334**	0.335**	0.179
Percent management and professionals	0.055	-0.052	0.264**	0.338**	0.330**	0.193
Percent labor occupation	-0.145	-0.058	-0.231*	-0.231*	-0.317**	-0.180
High-crime neighborhoods						
Percent housing built before 1950	-0.143	-0.046	-0.287**	-0.063	-0.487***	-0.067
Violent-crime index (U.S. average = 100)	-0.088	-0.037	-0.167	0.072	-0.306**	-0.059
Nonviolent-crime index (U.S. average = 100)	-0.081	-0.051	-0.088	0.010	-0.246*	-0.080
Ethnic neighborhoods						
Percent Hispanic population	-0.087	-0.058	-0.079	-0.107	-0.098	-0.073
Percent foreign-born population	0.333**	0.326**	0.069	0.017	0.100	-0.065

NOTES: *0.05 level of significance; **0.01 level of significance; ***0.001 level of significance

higher housing values, higher educated populations, and a management and professionals workforce.

Advertising (SIC 731)

Advertising is composed mostly of advertising agencies, but the industry group also includes billboard advertising and advertising contract representatives. As Table 5.5b shows, advertising has a significant presence in middle-class neighborhoods. Advertising employment, like communications employment, seems to be located in neighborhoods with higher individual incomes, higher housing values, and more educated and white-collar workforces.

Consumer Credit Reporting and Collection Agencies (SIC 732)

The credit reporting and collection group consists mainly of establishments providing mercantile and consumer credit reporting services, but it also includes establishments engaged in the collection or adjustment of claims (other than insurance). As was the case with communications and advertising, credit reporting employment is strongly related to middle-class neighborhoods (Table 5.5b). Credit reporting employment is also found in higher income neighborhoods with higher housing values and educated and white-collar workers. But many of the variables with high loadings on the *poverty neighborhoods* factor are also related (negatively) to credit reporting. Credit reporting neighborhoods tend to be lower-poverty neighborhoods with higher rates of employment and smaller nonwhite populations. In addition, the variables loading on *high-crime neighborhoods* all have significant negative relationships with credit reporting employment. Credit reporting firms are located in lower-crime neighborhoods with newer housing.

Motion Picture Production and Allied Services (SIC 781)

The grouping of motion picture production and allied services is represented in only twenty-six urban neighborhoods, probably accounting for the fact that only four factor variables are related to neighborhood employment in this field. The variables are percent nonwhite (negative), percent female-headed households (negative), the employment rate (positive), and percent in service occupations (negative).

Conclusion

Our examination of the relationships between neighborhood characteristics and neighborhood employment in producer-oriented minor-employer industries met with only modest success. For three of the four industrial classifications—construction, transportation, wholesale trade—the independent variables did little to explain neighborhood employment. We thus must conclude that neighborhood characteristics have little influence on the location of construction, transportation, or wholesale establishments. These industries are simply not connected to the neighborhoods in which they are located.

Information services, however, is different. For information services overall, crime level is a factor in firm location, particularly for credit reporting firms. These industries tend to locate in neighborhoods where there is less crime. In addition, credit reporting firms and firms in communications and advertising all seem to locate in middle-class neighborhoods. Why? At this point, we can only guess. It may be that these firms are geared toward middle-class clients and thus locate in middle-class neighborhoods.

Also, why are information services the only category of the smaller producer-oriented service industries where the model had some explanatory success? The first possible explanation might be size. There are 45,000 people in the urban neighborhoods employed in information services. Thus, the industry is almost in the major-employer category. It may be that the model is successful in explaining employment in large industries with many jobs, but not successful with smaller industries. The second explanation may be location. Information services are located virtually everywhere. It may be that the model does a better job explaining the location of employment where employment is spread out (as opposed to industries where there may be no employment in about half of the neighborhoods). Finally, it may be that the model is more effective in explaining neighborhood employment for industries that are consumer-oriented. Although information services serve the business community, many of the industries in this category also serve consumers. In the next two chapters, we examine these alternative explanations.

References

Bingham, Richard D., William M. Bowen, Yosra A. Amara, Lynn W. Bachelor, Jane Dockery, Jack Dustin, Deborah Kimble, Thomas Maraffa, David L. McKee, Kent P. Schwirian,

Gail Gordon Sommers, and Howard A. Stafford. 1997. *Beyond Edge Cities.* New York: Garland.

Bingham, Richard D., and Deborah Kimble, 1995. "The Industrial Composition of Edge Cities: The New Urban Reality." *Economic Development Quarterly* 9 (August): 259–272.

Bingham, Richard D., and Zhongcai Zhang. 1997. "Poverty and Economic Morphology of Ohio Central-City Neighborhoods." *Urban Affairs Review* 32(6): 766–796.

Office of Management and Budget. *Standard Industrial Classification Manual, 1987.* 1987. Springfield, VA: National Technical Information Service.

6

Major Neighborhood Employers: Producer-Oriented Industries

Only two industries among the major neighborhood employers are classified as producer-oriented: manufacturing and producer services. In the urban neighborhoods studied, these industries have a pervasive presence.

Manufacturing

Type of Neighborhood	Number of Manufacturing Establishments	Number of Employees	Number of Neighborhoods
Durable goods			
Middle-class	492	18,385	26
Working-class	710	34,278	27
Moderate-poverty	561	16,111	18
Severe-poverty	297	15,013	13
Extreme-poverty	220	11,390	14
Total	2,280	95,390	98
Nondurable goods			
Middle-class	144	6,675	26
Working-class	237	13,956	27
Moderate-poverty	117	4,891	18
Severe-poverty	86	5,393	13
Extreme-poverty	76	4,649	14
Total	660	35,564	98
Total durable and nondurable	2,940	130,741	98

Compared with the other industries studied thus far, manufacturing accounts for a huge number of jobs—more than 130,000 (see the chart,

TABLE 6.1a   Ordinary Least Square Estimates of the Regression Model: Manufacturing Industries

Independent Variables	Estimated Coefficient	Standardized Coefficient	t Value
Constant	19.37		0.517
Factors			
Poverty	-1.56	-0.016	-0.158
Working-class	30.80	0.318	2.856**
High–crime	6.33	0.065	0.376
Ethnicity	-3.70	-0.038	-0.345
City dummies			
Akron	12.10	0.032	0.235
Cincinnati	67.44	0.276	1.522
Cleveland	75.23	0.281	1.716
Columbus	39.75	0.182	0.764
Dayton	72.68	0.238	1.557
Toledo	-1.78	-0.006	-0.039

NOTES: Dependent variable: manufacturing employment per 1,000 population
$R^2 = 0.161$
Adjusted $R^2 = 0.065$
DF = 87
*0.05 level of significance
**0.01 level of significance
***0.001 level of significance

which shows employment for both durable and nondurable manufactured goods). These firms are large, with the average manufacturing firm in Ohio's central-city neighborhood employing 45. Furthermore, the jobs are not restricted to certain types of neighborhoods—they are everywhere.

As is shown by Table 6.1a, manufacturing firms tend to be located in *working-class neighborhoods,* although the amount of explained variance is quite small. The same is true when manufacturing is broken into durable goods and nondurable goods. The factor *working-class neighborhoods* has a positive impact on location of both durable and nondurable manufacturing industries, and such effect is statistically significant (Tables 6.1b and 6.1c). In nondurable manufacturing, Cincinnati is the aberrant case in that it has more nondurable manufacturing than might be expected. Recall from Chapter 2 that Cincinnati is home to many nondurable manufacturing firms, such as Procter and Gamble, Avon Products, Kroger, U.S. Shoe Corporation, and Gibson Greetings.

TABLE 6.1b   Ordinary Least Square Estimates of the Regression Model: Durable Manufacturing Industries

Independent Variables	Estimated Coefficient	Standardized Coefficient	t Value
Constant	12.23		0.349
Factors			
Poverty	−3.25	−0.037	−0.353
Working-class	24.71	0.278	2.452*
High-crime	11.15	0.126	0.709
Ethnicity	−1.93	−0.022	−0.192
City dummies			
Akron	1.17	0.003	0.024
Cincinnati	40.93	0.183	0.988
Cleveland	65.16	0.266	1.590
Columbus	41.87	0.209	0.861
Dayton	52.27	0.187	1.198
Toledo	−3.38	−0.013	−0.080

NOTES: Dependent variable: durable manufacturing employment per 1,000 population
$R^2 = 0.126$
Adjusted $R^2 = 0.026$
DF = 87
*0.05 level of significance
**0.01 level of significance
***0.001 level of significance

The correlation coefficients in the first three columns of Table 6.1d support the regression results. For manufacturing in general, jobs tend to be located in neighborhoods that have fewer college graduates and more people with less than high school educations. They are also in areas with a higher percentage of the workforce in labor occupations and a lower percentage in management and the professions. The relationships seem to show that manufacturing workers live near manufacturing jobs, regardless of other neighborhood characteristics. In general, similar results hold for durable goods. With nondurable goods, however, more of the individual factor variables in *working-class neighborhoods* are significantly related to neighborhood employment in nondurables. Also, employment seems to be centered in areas with more female-headed households and with low levels of foreign-born people.

Given the importance of manufacturing jobs to urban neighborhoods, it is useful to study some of the major industry groups in more detail. We

TABLE 6.1c   Ordinary Least Square Estimates of the Regression Model:
Nondurable Manufacturing Industries

Independent Variables	Estimated Coefficient	Standardized Coefficient	t Value
Constant	7.14		0.840
Factors			
Poverty	1.69	0.073	0.757
Working-class	6.09	0.264	2.488*
High-crime	−4.82	−0.209	−1.264
Ethnicity	−1.77	−0.077	−0.729
City dummies			
Akron	10.93	0.123	0.935
Cincinnati	26.51	0.457	2.639**
Cleveland	10.06	0.158	1.012
Columbus	−2.12	−0.041	−0.180
Dayton	20.42	0.281	1.928
Toledo	1.60	0.024	0.156

NOTES: Dependent variable: nondurable manufacturing employment per 1,000
population
$R^2 = 0.238$
Adjusted $R^2 = 0.151$
DF = 87
*0.05 level of significance
**0.01 level of significance
***0.001 level of significance

thus examined simple correlation coefficients for twenty individual manufacturing major groups—ten durable-goods industries and ten nondurable-goods industries (Table 6.1d). We did not, however, compute regression models for these individual industries because we are trying to
use the models to gain insight into the broader picture.

Durable Goods

Following are the ten durable-goods categories, set off in list form and accompanied by pertinent remarks:

Lumber and wood products, except furniture (SIC 24)

This major group includes sawmills; manufacturers of wood flooring,
wood kitchen cabinets, and wood containers; and establishments engaged

TABLE 6.1d   Zero-Order Relationships Between Independent Variables and Population-Weighted Employment in Manufacturing (n = 98)

	Manufac- turing	Durable Manufac- turing	Lumber and Wood Products	Furniture and Fixtures
Poverty neighborhoods				
Percent population below poverty	0.142	0.114	−0.026	0.138
Percent nonwhite population	−0.050	−0.067	−0.088	0.039
Percent owner-occupied housing units	−0.046	−0.033	−0.050	−0.178
Percent vacant housing units	0.071	0.061	−0.058	0.027
Percent households with public assistance	0.172	0.138	0.013	0.180
Percent female-headed households	0.156	0.101	0.001	0.174
Percent service occupation	0.058	0.040	−0.069	0.062
Civilian labor force participation rate	−0.103	−0.082	0.055	−0.040
Employment rate	−0.109	−0.092	0.083	−0.116
Percent federally subsidized housing units	0.082	0.065	0.040	0.185
Working-class neighborhoods				
Median value of owner-occupied housing	−0.154	−0.133	0.077	0.021
Per capita income	−0.196	−0.161	0.004	−0.101
Percent less than high school education	0.338***	0.290**	0.068	0.159
Percent high school education	0.109	0.090	0.036	0.030
Percent college and above education	−0.227*	−0.189	−0.007	−0.044
Percent management and professionals	−0.271**	−0.232*	−0.018	−0.081
Percent labor occupation	0.412***	0.375***	0.041	0.147
High-crime neighborhoods				
Percent housing built before 1950	0.140	0.151	−0.066	−0.020
Violent-crime index (U.S. average = 100)	0.126	0.125	−0.171	−0.165
Nonviolent-crime index (U.S. average = 100)	0.084	0.077	−0.166	−0.171
Ethnic neighborhoods				
Percent hispanic population (PTHISPAN)	−0.007	0.014	−0.110	−0.045
Percent foreign-born population	−0.100	−0.041	−0.169	−0.140

NOTES: *0.05 level of significance
       **0.01 level of significance
       ***0.001 level of significance

(continues)

TABLE 6.1d   *(Continued)*

	Stone, Clay, and Glass Products	Primary Metals	Fabricated Metal Products	Industrial Machinery and Equipment
Poverty Neighborhoods				
Percent population below poverty	−0.042	0.117	0.206*	−0.020
Percent nonwhite population	−0.112	−0.055	−0.048	−0.067
Percent owner-occupied housing units	0.108	−0.015	−0.113	−0.011
Percent vacant housing units	0.002	0.047	0.208*	−0.032
Percent households with public assistance	−0.012	0.149	0.239*	−0.029
Percent female-headed households	−0.065	0.053	0.222*	−0.004
Percent service occupation	−0.107	0.038	0.063	−0.023
Civilian labor force participation rate	0.025	−0.108	−0.113	0.037
Employment rate	0.063	−0.132	−0.140	0.057
Percent federally subsidized housing units	−0.088	−0.004	0.060	0.051
Working-class neighborhoods				
Median value of owner-occupied housing	0.011	−0.081	−0.226*	−0.082
Per capita income	0.022	−0.123	−0.262**	−0.039
Percent less than high school education	0.021	0.263**	0.373***	0.076
Percent high school education	0.011	0.031	0.093	0.046
Percent college and above education	0.040	−0.133	−0.280**	−0.063
Percent management and professionals	0.006	−0.168	−0.329***	−0.071
Percent labor occupation	0.041	0.347***	0.430***	0.066
High-crime neighborhoods				
Percent housing built before 1950	−0.095	0.184	0.151	0.087
Violent-crime index (U.S. average = 100)	−0.134	0.073	0.095	0.166
Nonviolent-crime index (U.S. average = 100)	−0.146	0.045	0.053	0.151
Ethnic neighborhoods				
Percent Hispanic population (PTHISPAN)	−0.010	0.079	0.075	−0.096
Percent foreign-born population	−0.003	0.062	−0.082	−0.106

NOTES: *0.05 level of significance
    **0.01 level of significance
    ***0.001 level of significance

TABLE 6.1d *(Continued)*

	Electronic and Other Electronic	Transpor-tation Equip-ment	Instruments and Related Products	Miscel-laneous Manufac-turing
Poverty neighborhoods				
Percent population below poverty	−0.079	0.095	−0.146	0.170
Percent nonwhite population	−0.087	0.110	−0.174	0.047
Percent owner-occupied housing units	−0.049	0.039	−0.104	−0.084
Percent vacant housing units	0.036	−0.003	−0.043	0.171
Percent households with public assistance	−0.085	0.090	−0.178	0.179
Percent female-headed households	−0.059	0.176	−0.181	0.123
Percent service occupation	−0.089	0.141	−0.154	0.056
Civilian labor force participation rate	0.116	−0.130	0.293**	−0.138
Employment rate	0.081	−0.073	0.175	−0.100
Percent federally subsidized housing units	−0.065	0.210*	−0.123	0.101
Working-class neighborhoods				
Median value of owner-occupied housing	0.058	−0.111	0.060	−0.195
Per capita income	0.053	−0.115	0.077	−0.225*
Percent less than high school education	−0.042	0.107	−0.150	0.277**
Percent high school education	0.057	0.101	−0.117	0.077
Percent college and above education	0.001	−0.136	0.179	−0.260**
Percent management and professionals	−0.006	−0.132	0.097	−0.306**
Percent labor occupation	−0.018	0.138	−0.095	0.338***
High-crime neighborhoods				
Percent housing built before 1950	−0.118	0.005	0.056	0.040
Violent-crime index (U.S. average = 100)	−0.056	0.140	−0.088	−0.109
Nonviolent-crime index (U.S. average = 100)	−0.010	0.057	−0.096	−0.163
Ethnic neighborhoods				
Percent Hispanic population (PTHISPAN)	−0.024	−0.061	0.025	0.034
Percent foreign-born population	0.020	−0.167	0.178	−0.008

NOTES: *0.05 level of significance
**0.01 level of significance
***0.001 level of significance

(continues)

TABLE 6.1d *(Continued)*

	Non-durable Goods	Food and Kindred Products	Textiles Mills Products	Apparel and Other Textile Products
Poverty neighborhoods				
Percent population below poverty	0.158	0.218*	0.021	−0.035
Percent nonwhite population	0.051	0.008	0.006	−0.146
Percent owner-occupied housing units	−0.067	−0.169	0.083	0.073
Percent vacant housing units	0.062	−0.008	0.250*	0.138
Percent households with public assistance	0.193	0.231*	0.069	−0.008
Percent female-headed households	0.264**	0.252*	0.028	−0.041
Percent service occupation	0.090	0.147	0.000	−0.043
Civilian labor force participation rate	−0.116	−0.119	−0.082	−0.078
Employment rate	−0.103	−0.108	−0.054	0.044
Percent federally subsidized housing units	0.096	0.228*	0.038	−0.023
Working-class neighborhoods				
Median value of owner-occupied housing	−0.133	−0.094	−0.098	−0.069
Per capita income	−0.205*	−0.195	−0.082	−0.067
Percent less than high school education	0.305*	0.259**	0.127	0.192
Percent high school education	0.112	0.076	0.112	0.021
Percent college and above education	−0.229*	−0.145	−0.130	−0.119
Percent management and professionals	−0.246*	−0.166	−0.157	−0.144
Percent labor occupation	0.288**	0.172	0.180	0.218*
High-crime neighborhoods				
Percent housing built before 1950	0.009	−0.014	−0.004	0.146
Violent-crime index (U.S. average = 100)	0.049	−0.033	0.087	0.056
Nonviolent-crime index (U.S. average = 100)	0.056	−0.099	0.033	0.061
Ethnic neighborhoods				
Percent Hispanic population (PTHISPAN)	−0.080	−0.040	0.046	0.106
Percent foreign-born population	−0.259**	−0.238*	0.066	0.044

NOTES: *0.05 level of significance
**0.01 level of significance
***0.001 level of significance

TABLE 6.1d *(Continued)*

	Paper and Allied Products	Chemicals and Allied Products	Petroleum and Coal Products	Rubber and Miscellaneous Plastics
Poverty neighborhoods				
Percent population below poverty	0.170	0.148	0.104	−0.070
Percent nonwhite population	0.030	0.129	−0.029	0.014
Percent owner-occupied housing units	−0.179	−0.111	−0.017	0.142
Percent vacant housing units	0.261**	0.077	0.124	−0.061
Percent households with public assistance	0.175	0.150	0.149	−0.037
Percent female-headed households	0.177	0.229*	0.072	0.007
Percent service occupation	0.013	0.044	0.061	0.000
Civilian labor force participation rate	−0.067	−0.038	−0.111	−0.017
Employment rate	−0.090	−0.092	−0.103	−0.001
Percent federally subsidized housing units	0.133	−0.021	0.019	−0.052
Working-class neighborhoods				
Median value of owner-occupied housing	0.028	−0.049	−0.093	−0.101
Per capita income	−0.091	−0.093	−0.139	−0.055
Percent less than high school education	0.241*	0.118	0.280**	0.053
Percent high school education	−0.084	−0.010	−0.007	0.155
Percent college and above education	−0.113	−0.078	−0.165	−0.137
Percent management and professionals	−0.122	−0.077	−0.218*	−0.131
Percent labor occupation .	0.228*	0.122	0.358***	0.109
High-crime neighborhoods				
Percent housing built before 1950	0.090	0.019	0.191	−0.087
Violent-crime index (U.S. average = 100)	0.155	0.021	0.086	0.030
Nonviolent-crime index (U.S. average = 100)	0.005	0.046	0.061	0.124
Ethnic neighborhoods				
Percent Hispanic population (PTHISPAN)	0.054	−0.107	0.047	−0.058
Percent foreign-born population	−0.106	−0.061	0.078	−0.154

NOTES: *0.05 level of significance
**0.01 level of significance
***0.001 level of significance

(continues)

TABLE 6.1d   *(Continued)*

	Rubber Products	Plastics Products	Leather and Leather Products
Poverty neighborhoods			
Percent population below poverty	−0.024	−0.068	−0.068
Percent nonwhite population	−0.058	0.021	0.014
Percent owner-occupied housing units	0.114	0.129	0.046
Percent vacant housing units	0.028	−0.065	−0.049
Percent households with public assistance	0.017	−0.040	−0.067
Percent female-headed households	0.000	0.007	−0.022
Percent service occupation	0.006	−0.001	−0.030
Civilian labor force participation rate	−0.020	−0.014	0.028
Employment rate	−0.009	0.000	0.044
Percent federally subsidized housing units	−0.014	−0.050	−0.031
Working-class neighborhoods			
Median value of owner-occupied housing	−0.145	−0.084	0.055
Per capita income	−0.107	−0.042	0.034
Percent less than high school education	0.074	0.044	−0.016
Percent high school education	0.172	0.135	−0.021
Percent college and above education	−0.160	−0.118	0.039
Percent management and professionals	−0.186	−0.108	0.037
Percent labor occupation	0.176	0.088	−0.060
High-crime neighborhoods			
Percent housing built before 1950	0.092	−0.099	0.039
Violent-crime index (U.S. average = 100)	0.085	0.019	0.015
Nonviolent-crime index (U.S. average = 100)	0.045	0.119	0.028
Ethnic neighborhoods			
Percent Hispanic population (PTHISPAN)	−0.030	−0.055	−0.037
Percent foreign-born population	−0.043	−0.150	−0.075

NOTES: *0.05 level of significance
  **0.01 level of significance
  ***0.001 level of significance

in wood preserving. The manufacture of lumber and wood products is usually located near the source of raw materials and cannot really be classified as an urban activity. Ohio's central cities have only 1,123 jobs in this industry via 98 employers. As expected, the independent variables did nothing to explain the location of these jobs. None of the zero-order relationships is statistically significant.

Furniture and fixtures (SIC 25)
Stone, clay, glass, and concrete products (SIC 32)

The furniture and fixtures group includes establishments engaged in the manufacture of household, office, and restaurant furniture and office and store fixtures. The stone, clay, glass, and concrete products group includes establishments manufacturing flat glass and other glass products, cement, clay products, pottery, cut stone, and other products from materials taken from the earth in the form of stone, clay, and sand. As with lumber and wood products, there is no reason to believe that these industries are particularly urban or that the model will explain the location of these industries even when they are in central cities (for example, glass manufacturing in Toledo). In fact, the variables have little explanatory power. For both industry groups, none of the factor variables is related to neighborhood employment.

Primary metals (SIC 33)
Fabricated metal products except
    machinery and transportation equipment (SIC 34)

The primary metals group includes factories engaged in smelting and refining metals; in rolling, drawing, and alloying metals; in manufacturing castings and other basic metal products; and in manufacturing nails, spikes, wire, and cable. The fabricated metal products group includes firms engaged in fabricating such products as cans, hand tools, cutlery, and general hardware from primary metals, as well as those engaged in metal forging and stamping and producing a variety of other metal and wire products.

For both of these major industry groups, variables common to *working-class neighborhoods* are correlates of the industries' neighborhood locations. The location of establishments in these two industries is associated with neighborhoods with a substantial pool of laborers and many individuals without high school educations. For fabricated metal products, many of the other *working-class neighborhoods* variables apply. These include lower per capita income, lower-value housing, and small percentages of college graduates in the neighborhoods and fewer managers and professionals.

In addition, neighborhood employment in fabricated metal products also is related to several factor variables associated with *poverty neighborhoods*—high-poverty population, female-headed households, percent receiving public assistance, and vacant housing units.

Industrial and commercial machinery and computer equipment (SIC 35)
Electronic and other electric equipment (SIC 36)
Transportation equipment (SIC 37)
Measuring, analyzing, and controlling instruments;
    photographic, medical, and optical goods; watches and clocks (SIC 38)

These four categories of industries cover the manufacture of almost all other durable goods, including engines and industrial machinery, computers, office equipment, appliances, electrical equipment, vehicles, boats, aircraft, and a variety of measuring instruments.

For all four of these very large industry groups, the correlates were unsuccessful in explaining neighborhood employment. Only two of the independent variables are significantly related to employment: the relationships between federally subsidized housing units in the neighborhood and employment in transportation equipment, and the labor force participation rate and employment in the manufacturing of instruments. These relationships are essentially meaningless and probably occurred by chance.

Miscellaneous manufacturing industries (SIC 39)

Miscellaneous manufacturing industries, the catchall of other manufactured goods, include firms engaged in the manufacture of jewelry, musical instruments, toys, sporting goods, pens and pencils, and other goods not covered by other of the major manufacturing groups. Neighborhood employment in this sector closely mirrors that of primary metals and fabricated metal products (a surprising finding given that the products are so different).

The major correlates for employment in miscellaneous industries are variables associated with *working-class neighborhoods:* low per capita income, high percentages of residents with less than a high school education and of workers in labor occupations, and low percentages of college-educated and of workers in management and the professions.

Summary

Ten major durable-goods manufacturing groups were examined in an attempt to establish a relationship between neighborhood characteristics and neighborhood employment in these industries. In seven cases, no significant relationships were found. In the other three cases (primary metals, fabricated metal products, and miscellaneous manufacturing), however, there was some relationship between *working-class neighborhoods* factor variables and neighborhood employment. Neighborhoods that are home to these industries tend to have fewer college graduates living in the neighborhood, more residents who did not complete high school, and more residents who worked in labor occupations. The zero-order results thus support the regression results.

This finding is not to suggest that firms in these three manufacturing industries located in these particular neighborhoods to take advantage of the local labor force. More likely, the firms have been in the neighborhoods for a long time and, over the years, have tended to draw workers from the neighborhoods to these relatively well-paying factory jobs.

Nondurable Goods

We also examined the location of jobs in ten nondurable manufacturing industries. The relationships between the independent variables and neighborhood jobs were very similar to those found for durable manufacturing industries. There were essentially no substantive relationships for the following industries:

Textile mill products (SIC 22)
Chemicals and allied products (SIC 28)
Rubber and miscellaneous plastics products (SIC 30)
Rubber products (SIC 301–306)
Miscellaneous plastics products (SIC 308)
Leather products (SIC 31)

Firms in the textile mill products group are engaged in the manufacture of yarn, thread, and fabrics; the dyeing, treating, and finishing of fabrics; and the manufacture of finished goods from textiles. Chemicals and allied products establishments manufacture three major classes of products: basic chemicals such as acids, alkalies, and salts; chemical products to be used in further manufacture, such as synthetic fibers and pigments; and finished chemical products for consumption, such as drugs, cosmetics, and soaps. Also included are chemicals supplied to other industries, such as paints, fertilizers, and explosives. In the group rubber and miscellaneous plastics products are establishments that manufacture products made from plastics resins and natural, synthetic, and reclaimed rubber. This group also includes the manufacture of tires. Because this major group is so important to the Akron area, it was also divided into two subgroups of related industries: rubber products and miscellaneous plastic products. Finally, the group leather and leather products includes estab- · lishments involved in tanning and finishing leather and in manufacturing leather products such as shoes, gloves, luggage, and handbags.

For all of these industries, there is essentially no relationship between neighborhood characteristics and neighborhood employment. Neighborhoods apparently have no impact on these industries, nor, conversely, do the industries have any impact on the makeup of the neighborhoods in which they are located.

Food and kindred products (SIC 20)
Apparel and other finished products made from fabrics and similar
    materials (SIC 23)
Paper and allied products (SIC 26)
Petroleum refining and related industries (SIC 29)

The group food and kindred products includes establishments that manufacture processed foods and beverages and related products, such as ice and chewing gum, for human consumption. It also includes firms that produce prepared feeds for animals and birds. The category apparel and other finished products covers the production of clothing for adults and children. The group paper and allied products includes the manufacture not only of pulp and paper but also of containers, such as boxes, bags, and envelopes. The category petroleum refining and related industries includes establishments engaged in petroleum refining; the production of paving and roofing materials; and the compounding of lubricating oils and greases.

As was the case with manufacturing in general and several durable-goods industries in particular, neighborhood employment in these four industries is related to several of the factor variables composing *working-class neighborhoods*—in particular, the percentage of residents with less than a high school education and the percentage in labor occupations. Again, this finding suggests that these manufacturing industries have been in the urban neighborhoods for years and, over time, have attracted workers to the neighborhoods.

Producer Services

The category producer services includes industries that provide services to producers (manufacturers) and others. Typical industries are utilities, banks, real estate, insurance, and law. As is shown in the chart, producer services account for some 70,000 jobs in urban neighborhoods, heavily concentrated in better-off areas (79 percent). Firms in this category of industries are moderate sized, averaging twelve employees.

Type of Neighborhood	Number of Producer Services Establishments	Number of Employees	Number of Neighborhoods
Middle-class	3,086	37,214	26
Working-class	1,582	18,236	27
Moderate-poverty	691	6,724	18
Severe-poverty	436	4,824	13
Extreme-poverty	304	3,251	14
Total	5,829	70,253	98

However, classification schemes are never perfect, and the producer services classification has weaknesses. The problem is that these industries that serve producers also serve consumers. Thus, any explanation regarding the location of producer services may hinge on the fact that they are consumer services.

We attempted to resolve this problem by determining if there was a relationship between manufacturing jobs and producer services jobs. To test this, an industrial variable was added as an additional independent variable in the analysis—manufacturing employment per 1,000 population. If producer services do indeed mostly serve producers, it is logical to expect that producer services jobs will be located near manufacturing jobs. However, when manufacturing was correlated with neighborhood employment in producer services and with the individual industries making up producer services, no significant relationships emerged. Therefore, manufacturing employment was not included in the model.

Table 6.2a shows the regression results between the independent variables and neighborhood employment in producer services. Results for the banking subgroup appear in Table 6.2b. The model in Table 6.2a explains a substantial 43 percent of the variance. Both *poverty neighborhoods* and *working-class neighborhoods* made significant contributions to the explained variance. However, the coefficients are negative, suggesting that producer services firms tend not to locate in neighborhoods with the characteristics of *poverty neighborhoods* or *working-class neighborhoods*. Also, an odd finding is that they tend to locate not in the city of Cincinnati but rather in one of the metropolitan area's edge cities. In fact, Stafford, McKee, and Amara found that the Blue Ash/Kenwood edge city northeast of Cincinnati has proportionally more employees in producer

TABLE 6.2a   Ordinary Least Square Estimates of the Regression Model: Producer Services Industries

Independent Variables	Estimated Coefficient	Standardized Coefficient	t Value
Constant	43.21		3.782***
Factors			
Poverty	−7.69	−0.204	−2.559*
Working-class	−22.94	−0.608	−6.978***
High-crime	−7.97	−0.211	−1.554
Ethnicity	−0.63	−0.017	−0.194
City dummies			
Akron	2.57	0.018	0.163
Cincinnati	−29.01	−0.305	−2.148*
Cleveland	−10.66	−0.102	−0.798
Columbus	−4.19	−0.049	−0.264
Dayton	−12.61	−0.106	−0.886
Toledo	−4.03	−0.036	−0.291

NOTES: Dependent variable: producer services employment per 1,000 population
$R^2 = 0.486$
Adjusted $R^2 = 0.426$
DF = 87
*0.05 level of significance
**0.01 level of significance
***0.001 level of significance

services than downtown Cincinnati (1997, 149). The model in Table 6.2b also clearly indicates that firms in banking industries tend to avoid locations in poverty and working-class neighborhoods.

The zero-order correlations in column one of Table 6.2c clearly show the type of neighborhoods where producer services tend to locate, since nineteen of the correlation coefficients are statistically significant. They indicate the characteristics that the neighborhoods have and do not have. The neighborhoods where most of producer services employment is located tend to be areas of newer, high-value, owner-occupied housing. The people of the neighborhood are more likely to be employed, have relatively high incomes, hold college degrees, and work in management or the professions. There is also a likelihood that more foreign-born people live in the neighborhoods.

The data also reveal which characteristics the neighborhoods do not have. They are not public housing neighborhoods. They do not have a

TABLE 6.2b   Ordinary Least Square Estimates of the Regression Model: Banking Industries

Independent Variables	Estimated Coefficient	Standardized Coefficient	t Value
· Constant	4.12		2.040*
Factors			
Poverty	−1.38	−0.254	−2.605**
Working-class	−1.58	−0.290	−2.726***
High-crime	−1.59	−0.291	−1.754
Ethnicity	−0.48	−0.087	−0.825
City dummies			
Akron	−0.74	−0.035	−0.267
Cincinnati	−2.05	−0.149	−0.857
Cleveland	0.19	0.013	0.082
Columbus	−0.67	−0.055	−0.240
Dayton	0.00	0.000	0.000
Toledo	−1.08	−0.067	−0.441

NOTES: Dependent variable: banking industries employment per 1,000 population
$R^2 = 0.232$
Adjusted $R^2 = 0.143$
DF = 87
*0.05 level of significance
**0.01 level of significance
***0.001 level of significance

high percentage of residents in poverty, receiving public assistance, or in female-headed households. The neighborhoods do not have a high percentage of nonwhite residents. Residents are not likely to have only high school diplomas (or less). Employed residents are not likely to work in service or labor occupations. And finally, the neighborhoods are not likely to have much crime.

Given the clear success of the model in explaining neighborhood location of producer services jobs, we elected to examine the zero-order relationships of fifteen specific producer services industries in detail. We also elected to test the regression model with the banking industry. Banking was selected because the industry is often accused of underserving low-income neighborhoods. Although the model explained only 14 percent of the variance in neighborhood employment in banking, both *poverty neighborhoods* and *working-class neighborhoods* provided significant ex-

TABLE 6.2c   Zero-Order Relationships Between Independent Variables and
Population-Weighted Employment in Producer Services Industries (n = 98)

	Producer Services	Electric, Gas, and Sanitary (SIC 49)	Banking (SIC 60–62)	Depository Institutions (SIC 60)
Poverty neighborhoods				
Percent population below poverty	−0.377***	0.012	−0.326***	−0.191
Percent nonwhite population	−0.314**	0.073	−0.263**	−0.226*
Percent owner-occupied housing units	0.071	−0.033	0.068	0.099
Percent vacant housing units	−0.119	0.107	−0.080	−0.013
Percent households with public assistance	−0.365***	0.064	−0.315**	−0.222*
Percent female-headed households	−0.368***	0.083	−0.278**	−0.192
Percent service occupation	−0.489***	0.003	−0.392***	−0.238*
Civilian labor force participation rate	0.466***	0.094	0.444***	0.179
Employment rate	0.419***	−0.044	0.323***	0.248*
Percent federally subsidized housing units	−0.230*	−0.127	−0.146	−0.134
Working-class neighborhoods				
Median value of owner-occupied housing	0.561***	0.033	0.221*	0.229*
Per capita income	0.610***	0.004	0.347***	0.233*
Percent less than high school education	−0.522***	−0.034	−0.371***	−0.213*
Percent high school education	−0.258**	−0.026	−0.076	−0.164
Percent college and above education	0.648***	0.043	0.328***	0.190
Percent management and professionals	0.602***	0.013	0.304**	0.218*
Percent labor occupation	−0.527***	0.071	−0.296**	−0.180
High-crime neighborhoods				
Percent housing built before 1950	−0.509***	0.047	−0.505***	−0.181
Violent-crime index (U.S. average = 100)	−0.377***	−0.083	−0.317***	−0.057
Nonviolent-crime index (U.S. average = 100)	−0.341***	−0.016	−0.288**	−0.090
Ethnic neighborhoods				
Percent Hispanic population (PTHISPAN)	−0.155	0.034	−0.097	−0.079
Percent foreign-born population	0.228*	−0.047	0.086	0.053

NOTES: *0.05 level of significance
       **0.01 level of significance
       ***0.001 level of significance

TABLE 6.2C   *(Continued)*

	Com-mercial Banks (SIC 602)	Savings Insti-tutions (SIC 603)	Credit Unions (SIC 606)	Functions Closely Related to Banking (SIC 609)
Poverty Neighborhoods				
Percent population below poverty	−0.235*	−0.273**	0.170	0.184
Percent nonwhite population	−0.237*	−0.178	−0.007	0.219*
Percent owner-occupied housing units	0.138	0.186	−0.128	−0.181
Percent vacant housing units	−0.153	0.143	−0.024	0.246*
Percent households with public assistance	−0.220*	−0.225*	0.030	0.253*
Percent female−headed households	−0.204*	−0.223*	0.070	0.225*
Percent service occupation	−0.255*	−0.249*	0.080	0.155
Civilian labor force participation rate	0.232*	0.201*	−0.137	−0.142
Employment rate	0.251*	0.219*	−0.011	−0.217*
Percent federally subsidized housing units	−0.136	−0.229*	0.103	0.246*
Working-class neighborhoods				
Median value of owner-occupied housing	0.130	0.217*	0.103	−0.157
Per capita income	0.223*	0.262**	−0.053	−0.194
Percent less than high school education	−0.205*	−0.131	−0.065	0.242*
Percent high school education	0.063	−0.351***	−0.052	0.033
Percent college and above education	0.190	0.199*	−0.034	−0.190
Percent management and professionals	0.207*	0.177	0.027	−0.200*
Percent labor occupation	−0.169	−0.104	−0.067	0.198
High-crime neighborhoods				
Percent housing built before 1950	−0.255*	−0.024	−0.012	0.077
Violent-crime index (U.S. average = 100)	−0.129	0.046	0.005	0.053
Nonviolent-crime index (U.S. average = 100)	−0.132	0.038	−0.045	0.022
Ethnic neighborhoods				
Percent Hispanic population (PTHISPAN)	−0.121	0.037	−0.033	−0.073
Percent foreign-born population	−0.025	0.195	−0.057	−0.056

NOTES: *0.05 level of significance
 **0.01 level of significance
 ***0.001 level of significance

(continues)

TABLE 6.2c   *(Continued)*

	Non-depository Institutions (SIC 61)	Security and Commodity Brokers (SIC 62)	Insurance (SIC 63–64)	Insurance Agents, Brokers, and Services (SIC 64)
Poverty neighborhoods				
Percent population below poverty	−0.262**	−0.230*	−0.355***	−0.367***
Percent nonwhite population	−0.186	−0.155	−0.272**	−0.312**
Percent owner-occupied housing units	0.031	0.049	0.192	0.106
Percent vacant housing units	−0.104	0.150	−0.138	−0.175
Percent households with public assistance	−0.241*	−0.205*	−0.326***	−0.359***
Percent female−headed households	−0.207*	−0.237* ·	−0.318**	−0.342***
Percent service occupation	−0.307**	−0.324***	−0.416***	−0.459***
Civilian labor force participation rate	0.394***	0.280**	0.371***	0.380***
Employment rate	0.240*	0.206*	0.339***	0.400***
Percent federally subsidized housing units	−0.094	−0.136	−0.174	−0.177
Working-class neighborhoods				
Median value of owner-occupied housing	0.117	0.316**	0.388***	0.553***
Per capita income	0.253*	0.356***	0.516***	0.653***
Percent less than high school education	−0.294**	−0.313**	−0.440***	−0.503***
Percent high school education	0.002	−0.170	−0.178	−0.252*
Percent college and above education	0.243*	0.405***	0.523***	0.636***
Percent management and professionals	0.211*	0.353***	0.490***	0.591***
Percent labor occupation	−0.226*	−0.287**	−0.432***	−0.531***
High-crime neighborhoods				
Percent housing built before 1950	−0.455***	−0.342***	−0.469***	−0.462***
Violent-crime index (U.S. average = 100)	−0.312**	−0.189	−0.249*	−0.225*
Nonviolent-crime index (U.S. average = 100)	−0.266**	−0.187	−0.203*	−0.195
Ethnic neighborhoods				
Percent Hispanic population (PTHISPAN)	−0.072	−0.042	−0.093	−0.140
Percent foreign-born population	0.043	0.250*	0.185	0.246*

NOTES: *0.05 level of significance
**0.01 level of significance
***0.001 level of significance

TABLE 6.2c *(Continued)*

	Real Estate (SIC 65)	Engineering and Management Service (SIC 87)	Engineering and Architecture (SIC 871)	Accounting (SIC 872)
Poverty neighborhoods				
Percent population below poverty	−0.250*	−0.170	−0.275**	−0.334***
Percent nonwhite population	−0.161	−0.274**	−0.220*	−0.231*
Percent owner-occupied housing units	0.044	−0.104	0.043	0.101
Percent vacant housing units	−0.072	−0.112	−0.134	−0.163
Percent households with public assistance	−0.279**	−0.322**	−0.270**	−0.345***
Percent female–headed households	−0.280**	−0.358***	−0.289**	−0.348***
Percent service occupation	−0.334***	−0.378***	−0.396***	−0.380***
Civilian labor force participation rate	0.266**	0.365***	0.305**	0.319**
Employment rate	0.315**	0.368***	0.324***	0.357***
Percent federally subsidized housing units	−0.173	−0.198*	−0.166	−0.211*
Working-class neighborhoods				
Median value of owner-occupied housing	0.539***	0.537***	0.616***	0.339***
Per capita income	0.479***	0.478***	0.572***	0.512***
Percent less than high school education	−0.429***	−0.449***	−0.358***	−0.467***
Percent high school education	−0.212*	−0.367***	−0.271**	−0.238*
Percent college and above education	0.526***	0.567***	0.553***	0.566***
Percent management and professionals	0.523***	0.518***	0.525***	0.517***
Percent labor occupation	−0.476***	−0.476***	−0.427***	−0.462***
High-crime neighborhoods				
Percent housing built before 1950	−0.337***	−0.258**	−0.303**	−0.287**
Violent-crime index (U.S. average = 100)	−0.141	−0.252*	−0.147	−0.224*
Nonviolent-crime index (U.S. average = 100)	−0.154	−0.250*	−0.152	−0.207*
Ethnic neighborhoods				
Percent Hispanic population (PTHISPAN)	−0.140	−0.163	−0.148	−0.134
Percent foreign-born population	0.208*	0.223*	0.143	0.266**

NOTES: *0.05 level of significance
**0.01 level of significance
***0.001 level of significance

(continues)

TABLE 6.2c   *(Continued)*

	Miscellaneous Business	Legal Services (SIC 81)
Poverty neighborhoods		
Percent population below poverty	−0.302**	−0.206*
Percent nonwhite population	−0.309**	−0.125
Percent owner-occupied housing units	0.008	0.083
Percent vacant housing units	−0.109	−0.043
Percent households with public assistance	−0.301**	−0.226*
Percent female-headed households	−0.320***	−0.233*
Percent service occupation	−0.411***	−0.240*
Civilian labor force participation rate	0.391***	0.210*
Employment rate	0.366***	0.248*
Percent federally subsidized housing units	−0.167	−0.137
Working-class neighborhoods		
Median value of owner–occupied housing	0.490***	0.273**
Per capita income	0.506***	0.388***
Percent less than high school education	−0.423***	−0.330***
Percent high school education	−0.233*	−0.142
Percent college and above education	0.554***	0.388***
Percent management and professionals	0.507***	0.398***
Percent labor occupation	−0.459***	−0.364***
High-crime neighborhoods		
Percent housing built before 1950	−0.441***	−0.219*
Violent-crime index (U.S. average = 100)	−0.395***	−0.196
Nonviolent-crime index (U.S. average = 100)	−0.372***	−0.185
Ethnic neighborhoods		
Percent Hispanic population (PTHISPAN)	−0.146	−0.121
Percent foreign-born population	0.217*	0.176

NOTES: *0.05 level of significance
  **0.01 level of significance
  ***0.001 level of significance

planatory power—and in the expected direction (Table 6.2b). Banks, like producer services in general, tend not to locate in these neighborhoods. Banking is discussed in more detail later.

  In terms of the zero-order relationships (Table 6.2c), of the fifteen specific industries examined, only two industries showed no relationships between the independent variables and neighborhood employment: electric, gas, and sanitary services (SIC 49) and credit unions (SIC 606). Firms in the first group are traditional public utilities delivering electricity, gas, water, sewer, and refuse-collection services to homes and businesses. Credit unions are cooperative thrift and loan associations organized for the purpose of financing credit needs of their members. For both industries, none of the factor variables is significantly related to neighborhood employment.

Banking (SICs 60–62)

The banking category includes the following industries:

Depository institutions (SIC 60)
    Commercial banks (SIC 602)
    Savings institutions (SIC 603)
    Functions related to depository banking (SIC 609)

Nondepository credit institutions (SIC 61)
Security and commodity brokers (SIC 62)

As previously stated, we singled out the banking industry for detailed scrutiny because banks are frequently criticized for underserving poorer neighborhoods. We have defined banking as SICs 60–62, although it may be a stretch to include security and commodity brokers in this category. Yet in today's world they clearly perform many overlapping functions. Depository institutions are typical banks. The category includes commercial banks, savings institutions, credit unions, trust companies, and check-cashing stores. Nondepository institutions include credit agencies, consumer finance companies, auto loan companies, and mortgage bankers and brokers. Finally, security and commodity brokers are stockbrokers, investment bankers, agents for mutual funds, and other such services.

The overall banking correlation coefficients mirror producer services in general, except the coefficients are not quite as strong. Neighborhood employment in banking is significantly related to sixteen of the twenty-two factor variables (third column of Table 6.2c). Banking establishments are more often found in neighborhoods that would generally be considered high socioeconomic status (SES) and less often found in poorer and minority neighborhoods.

We next examined the individual components of the banking industry as identified in the preceding list. Surprisingly, the correlation coefficients were less supportive of efforts to explain neighborhood employment in depository institutions. Only eight variables were related to employment at the zero-order level, and none of the coefficients reached .30. However, four of the variables were in the *poverty neighborhoods* factor and four were in the *working-class neighborhoods* factor. Because this weakness seemed odd, we examined four components of the major group depository institutions—commercial banks, savings institutions, credit unions (already discussed), and check-cashing stores.

For commercial banks, there are eleven significant relationships between the factor characteristics and employment in these firms, but the relationships are not particularly strong (Table 6.2c). Seven of the significant factor variables loaded on *poverty neighborhoods;* only three loaded on *working-class neighborhoods.* The final variable loaded on *crime neighborhoods,* but the pertinent relationship was housing built before 1950, not the crime indexes. Again, all of the signs were in the same direction as with banking, so commercial banks, as a component of both banking and nondepository institutions, also tend to be located in better-off neighborhoods and to ignore poorer neighborhoods.

The pattern with savings institutions is much the same (also Table 6.2c). The eleven statistically significant variables are weakly related to neighborhood employment in S&Ls and are in the same direction as the coefficients for commercial banks.

The data also show that, without question, check-cashing stores (in the subgroup functions closely related to banking) replace other depository institutions in the less well-off neighborhoods. These firms are in neighborhoods that tend to be characterized by vacant housing units, public housing, families on public assistance, female-headed households, and a nonwhite population.

Thus, part of what drives the banking model is a combination of institutional location factors. There are significant, but not particularly strong, relationships between employment in commercial banks and S&Ls and neighborhood wealth, and there is a significant negative relationship between the location of check-cashing stores and neighborhood wealth.

Also driving the banking model is the behavior of nondepository institutions and security and commodity brokers. For both of these industries, the pattern of correlation coefficients is similar, but not identical, to those found for depository institutions. For example, in both cases the correlation coefficient between race and employment is not significant. Yet for nondepository institutions, 6 of the 10 coefficients on the *poverty neighborhoods* factor are statistically significant, 5 of the 7 on the *work-*

ing-class neighborhoods factor, and all 3 on the *high-crime neighborhoods* factor. For security and commodity brokers, the pattern was similar—6 of the 10 coefficients on the *poverty neighborhoods* factor were statistically significant, 6 of the 7 on *working-class neighborhoods,* and 1 on *high-crime neighborhoods.*

In sum, with the exception of credit unions, the location of banking industry establishments is influenced by the conditions associated with *poverty neighborhoods* and *working-class neighborhoods.* Traditional financial institutions have at least partially abandoned these neighborhoods, to be replaced by check-cashing stores that perform quasi-banking functions for the residents.

Other Producer Services Industries

The remaining producer services categories we analyzed include the following:

Insurance agents, brokers, and service (SIC 64)
Real estate (SIC 65)
Engineering, architectural, and surveying services (SIC 871)
Accounting, auditing, and bookkeeping services (SIC 872)
Miscellaneous business services (SIC 67, 73 [except 731–732], 892, 899)
Legal services (SIC 81)

There might be debate as to whether the insurance and real estate industry groups are really services to businesses as opposed to consumers. Nevertheless, they have historically been classified as producer services. The major group insurance agents includes not only agents and brokers dealing in insurance but also organizations offering services to insurance companies and to policyholders. Real estate includes not only real estate brokers but also owners and lessors of real property and developers. Self-explanatory categories are legal services; engineering, architectural, and surveying services; and accounting, auditing, and bookkeeping services. The category miscellaneous business services is composed of holding and other investment offices, mailing companies, photocopying, photography, building cleaning, equipment leasing, employment agencies, and services not elsewhere classified. These six industries are considered together because the impact of the factor variables on neighborhood employment is very similar. (See Table 6.2c for the correlation coefficients.)

In all cases the evidence is clear. The demographic, economic, social, and dwelling conditions of neighborhoods at least partly determine the location of neighborhood employment in these six industries. The patterns again mirror those for banking. These six industries have sparse presence in *poverty neighborhoods* or *working-class neighborhoods.*

Conclusion

The first conclusion to be drawn from this examination of larger producer-oriented industries is that neighborhood characteristics have little to do with manufacturing. At the micro level, there are undoubtedly good reasons that explain why manufacturing establishments locate where they do—such as access to transportation or proximity to suppliers—but these factors do not appear to be related to neighborhood. However, for manufacturing in general, and for some specific manufacturing industries as well, factories tend to locate in neighborhoods where potential workers live. This trend is especially apparent in neighborhoods that are home to people working in labor occupations and those with lower education levels, but it does not hold in poor neighborhoods or those with serious housing deterioration. This finding suggests that over the years, local residents have found well-paying factory jobs in the neighborhoods where they grew up and stayed in those neighborhoods as they became adult workers in the factories.

In contrast, for producer services in general, and for most specific producer services industries, neighborhood employment exhibits a strong relationship to neighborhood characteristics. The data do suggest two reasons why producer services locate where they do.

First, some producer services locate not to reach producers but to reach consumers. Check-cashing stores are a clear example. These institutions clearly locate in poorer neighborhoods. Second, most producer services locate in better-off neighborhoods—in areas where the housing stock is good and the population is more affluent. It is difficult to explain this finding. We can only rely on anecdotal evidence that the owners of these businesses want to locate in attractive, low-crime areas to avoid the disadvantages of deteriorating neighborhoods. Perhaps our clustering of businesses and neighborhood characteristics in Chapter 8 will help us explain.

We can also reach some tentative conclusions with regard to our modeling efforts. Models should be parsimonious. Our regression model is, and it seems to explain satisfactorily which neighborhood characteristics drive neighborhood employment—at least in some industries. Yet the zero-order correlations are important too. They add detail as to which neighborhood characteristics seem to be most closely related to neighborhood employment.

References

Stafford, Howard A., David L. McKee, and Yosra A. Amara. 1997. "Information/Producer Services in Edge Cities." In Richard D. Bingham et al., *Beyond Edge Cities*, pp. 142–165. New York: Garland.

7

Major Neighborhood Employers: Consumer-Oriented Industries

Three consumer-oriented industries—retail services, social services, and personal services—are major neighborhood employers, but social services dwarfs them all. There is more employment in social services industries in urban neighborhoods than for any other category of employment—including manufacturing. However, this strong presence should not detract from the importance of retail or personal services, both of which are significant sources of urban jobs. Retail also has the potential advantage, at least theoretically, of being a source of entry-level jobs.

Retail Trade

For the most part, establishments engaged in retail trade sell merchandise to the general public for personal or household consumption. Exceptions to this general rule are retail stores dealing in such items as wallpaper, computers, or lumber that sell to both the general public and to businesses.

Like manufacturing, retail services have a significant presence in Ohio central-city neighborhoods. In terms of employment, the retail sector is second only to manufacturing in providing these neighborhoods with

Type of Neighborhood	Number of Retail Establishments	Number of Employees	Number of Neighborhoods
Middle-class	2,707	46,899	26
Working-class	2,296	38,888	27
Moderate-poverty	956	11,935	18
Severe-poverty	624	6,030	13
Extreme-poverty	364	3,444	14
Total	6,947	107,196	98

TABLE 7.1a   Ordinary Least Square Estimates of the Regression Model: Retail Industries

Independent Variables	Estimated Coefficient	Standardized Coefficient	t Value
Constant	40.45		2.933**
Factors			
Poverty	−15.30	−0.380	−4.219***
Working-class	−7.42	−0.184	−1.870
High-crime	−11.92	−0.296	−1.926
Ethnicity	−9.19	−-0.228	−2.329*
City dummies			
Akron	−1.52	−0.010	−0.080
Cincinnati	0.48	0.005	0.029
Cleveland	4.35	0.039	0.269
Columbus	6.17	0.068	0.322
Dayton	−1.03	−0.008	−0.060
Toledo	4.72	0.040	0.283

NOTES: Dependent variable: retail employment per 1,000 population
$R^2 = 0.341$
Adjusted $R^2 = 0.265$
DF = 87
* 0.05 level of significance
** 0.01 level of significance
*** 0.001 level of significance

jobs (see chart). It also has more establishments in these neighborhoods than any other private-sector industrial division. The number of establishments (nearly 7,000) and total employment (almost 107,200 jobs) are important factors in these neighborhoods. The average size of these firms is 15 employees.

As we did with producer services in the previous chapter, we added manufacturing employment per 1,000 population to the retail trade employment analysis. Our premise was that a significant manufacturing base in an urban neighborhood would be associated with a significant retail presence as workers shopped near their places of employment. This connection did not hold true, however, as the relationship between manufacturing employment and retail employment was not statistically significant, and thus we removed manufacturing from consideration.

Table 7.1a shows the results of the regression equation for the retail industries model. The independent variables explain a respectable 27 percent of neighborhood retail employment. Two of the factors, *poverty*

TABLE 7.1b   Ordinary Least Square Estimates of the Regression Model: Food Stores

Independent Variables	Estimated Coefficient	Standardized Coefficient	t Value
Constant	10.96		2.285*
Factors			
Poverty	−4.05	−0.318	−3.207**
Working-class	−1.96	−0.154	−1.418
High-crime	−1.08	−0.084	−0.500
Ethnicity	0.05	0.004	0.039
City dummies			
Akron	−1.27	−0.026	−0.192
Cincinnati	0.21	0.006	0.036
Cleveland	−3.66	−0.104	−0.652
Columbus	3.38	0.118	0.508
Dayton	3.61	0.090	0.603
Toledo	−0.76	−0.020	−0.130

NOTES: Dependent variable: food stores (SIC 54) employment per 1,000 population
$R^2 = 0.204$
Adjusted $R^2 = 0.113$
DF = 87
* 0.05 level of significance
** 0.01 level of significance
*** 0.001 level of significance

neighborhoods and *ethnic neighborhoods,* are significant explanatory variables, and the signs on the coefficients for both are negative. This finding indicates that retail industries tend to avoid poor and ethnic areas of Ohio's central cities. In addition, negative signs appear for *working-class neighborhoods* and *high-crime neighborhoods,* although not to a statistically significant extent.

Because food stores and, in particular, grocery stores are important to any neighborhood, we applied the regression model to these establishments. (The results are shown in Tables 7.1b and 7.1c.) In both cases, the *poverty neighborhood* factor has a significant negative effect on the neighborhood location of grocery and other food stores, suggesting that grocery establishments, particularly the large chain stores, tend to be averse to poorer urban areas.

The results of the zero-order correlations describing neighborhood characteristics in relation to neighborhood employment in retail are

TABLE 7.1c   Ordinary Least Square Estimates of the Regression Model: Grocery Stores

Independent Variables	Estimated Coefficient	Standardized Coefficient	t Value
Constant	9.10		2.005*
Factors			
Poverty	−3.70	−0.307	−3.098**
Working-class	−1.91	−0.159	−1.465
High-crime	−1.20	−0.099	−0.589
Ethnicity	0.11	0.009	0.081
City dummies			
Akron	−0.50	−0.011	−0.080
Cincinnati	−0.17	−0.006	−0.032
Cleveland	−3.33	−0.100	−0.627
Columbus	3.16	0.116	0.501
Dayton	4.70	0.124	0.831
Toledo	0.17	0.005	0.030

NOTES: Dependent variable: grocery stores (SIC 541) employment per 1,000 population
$R^2 = 0.204$
Adjusted $R^2 = 0.113$
DF = 87
* 0.05 level of significance
** 0.01 level of significance
*** 0.001 level of significance

shown in the first column of Table 7.1d. Retail establishments, like producer services establishments, are less likely to be found in neighborhoods where housing is older, where public housing is located, and where numbers of dwelling units are vacant. Further, they are less likely to be located in neighborhoods that have a high percentage of poor, nonwhite residents, female-headed households, families receiving public assistance, and residents with low educational levels. They also avoid *high-crime neighborhoods*. Conversely, retail services are more likely to be in neighborhoods with high labor force participation rates, low unemployment, high per capita incomes, and educated and white-collar residents.

Given the fact that community characteristics were reasonably successful in explaining neighborhood employment in retail services, and given the importance of a vital retail presence in neighborhoods, we looked closely at employment in various retail industries. Following are the sub-

TABLE 7.1d   Zero-Order Relationships Between Independent Variables and
Population-Weighted Employment in Retail Services (n = 98)

	Retail	Building Materials and Garden Supplies (SIC 52)	General Merchandise Stores (SIC 53)	Variety Stores (SIC 533)
Poverty neighborhoods				
Percent population below poverty	−0.456***	−0.335***	−0.258**	−0.063
Percent nonwhite population	−0.320***	−0.252*	−0.152	−0.072
Percent owner-occupied housing units	0.160	0.229*	0.106	−0.033
Percent vacant housing units	−0.259**	−0.212*	−0.159	−0.056
Percent households with public assistance	−0.446***	−0.273**	−0.227*	−0.056
Percent female-headed households	−0.375***	−0.227*	−0.172	−0.036
Percent service occupation	−0.463***	−0.325***	−0.244*	−0.079
Civilian labor force participation rate	0.522***	0.354***	0.285**	0.135
Employment rate	0.470***	0.310**	0.226*	0.070
Percent federally subsidized housing units	−0.240*	−0.122	−0.107	0.030
Working-class neighborhoods				
Median value of owner-occupied housing	0.187	0.078	−0.026	−0.093
Per capita income	0.382***	0.198	0.161	−0.016
Percent less than high school education	−0.425***	−0.231*	−0.200*	−0.039
Percent high school education	0.117	0.194	0.200*	0.157
Percent college and above education	0.288**	0.141	0.028	−0.061
Percent management and professionals	0.278**	0.103	0.047	−0.074
Percent labor occupation	−0.310**	−0.119	−0.072	0.056
High-crime neighborhoods				
Percent housing built before 1950	−0.553***	−0.335***	−0.418***	−0.229*
Violent-crime index (U.S. average=100)	−0.335***	−0.291**	−0.114	−0.157
Nonviolent-crime index (U.S. average=100)	−0.299**	−0.235*	−0.141	−0.168
Ethnic neighborhoods				
Percent Hispanic population (PTHISPAN)	−0.180	−0.134	−0.101	−0.030
Percent foreign-born population	−0.007	−0.081	−0.059	−0.069

NOTES: * 0.05 level of significance
** 0.01 level of significance
*** 0.001 level of significance

(continues)

TABLE 7.1d   *(Continued)*

	Food Stores (SIC 54)	Grocery Stores (SIC 541)	Meat and Fish Markets (SIC 542)	Dairy Products Stores (SIC 545)
Poverty neighborhoods				
Percent population below poverty	−0.329***	−0.315**	−0.118	−0.161
Percent nonwhite population	−0.390***	−0.376***	−0.096	−0.127
Percent owner-occupied housing units	0.046	0.039	0.137	0.143
Percent vacant housing units	−0.199*	−0.199*	0.164	−0.071
Percent households with public assistance	−0.390***	−0.387***	−0.071	−0.147
Percent female-headed households	−0.394***	−0.385***	−0.105	−0.160
Percent service occupation	−0.371***	−0.361***	−0.131	−0.166
Civilian labor force participation rate	0.390***	0.390***	−0.047	0.060
Employment rate	0.421***	0.401***	0.091	0.150
Percent federally subsidized housing units	−0.235*	−0.229*	−0.111	−0.085
Working-class neighborhoods				
Median value of owner-occupied housing	0.238*	0.242*	0.039	0.162
Per capita income	0.288**	0.275**	0.161	0.292**
Percent less than high school education	−0.373***	−0.386***	−0.067	−0.173
Percent high school education	−0.008	0.003	−0.084	−0.025
Percent college and above education	0.286**	0.277**	0.084	0.178
Percent management and professionals	0.270**	0.266**	0.093	0.168
Percent labor occupation	−0.307**	−0.302**	−0.045	−0.145
High-crime neighborhoods				
Percent housing built before 1950	−0.258**	−0.261**	−0.083	−0.177
Violent-crime index (U.S. average=100)	−0.226*	−0.228*	0.140	0.113
Nonviolent-crime index (U.S. average=100)	−0.176	−0.172	0.024	0.085
Ethnic neighborhoods				
Percent Hispanic population (PTHISPAN)	−0.113	−0.104	−0.024	−0.049
Percent foreign-born population	−0.007	−0.014	0.104	0.068

NOTES: * 0.05 level of significance
** 0.01 level of significance
*** 0.001 level of significance

TABLE 7.1d *(Continued)*

	Retail Bakeries (SIC 546)	Automotive Dealers and Service (SIC 55)	New and Used Car Dealers (SIC 551, SIC 552)	Gasoline Service Stations (SIC 554)
Poverty neighborhoods				
Percent population below poverty	−0.181	−0.340***	−0.313**	−0.405***
Percent nonwhite population	−0.105	−0.283**	−0.233**	−0.409***
Percent owner-occupied housing units	0.086	0.169	0.105	0.302**
Percent vacant housing units	−0.059	−0.166	−0.183	−0.214*
Percent households with public assistance	−0.161	−0.341***	−0.341***	−0.373***
Percent female-headed households	−0.114	−0.284**	−0.282**	−0.339***
Percent service occupation	−0.132	−0.333***	−0.322***	−0.316**
Civilian labor force participation rate	0.167	0.381***	0.395***	0.272**
Employment rate	0.210*	0.341***	0.321***	0.406***
Percent federally subsidized housing units	−0.062	−0.189	−0.200*	−0.238*
Working-class neighborhoods				
Median value of owner-occupied housing	−0.008	0.102	0.180	0.095
Per capita income	0.088	0.231*	0.269**	0.272**
Percent less than high school education	−0.083	−0.274**	−0.332***	−0.211*
Percent high school education	−0.026	0.169	0.070	0.101
Percent college and above education	0.088	0.101	0.176	0.114
Percent management and professionals	0.084	0.126	0.213*	0.083
Percent labor occupation	−0.129	−0.198*	−0.270**	−0.176
High-crime neighborhoods				
Percent housing built before 1950	−0.068	−0.445***	−0.463***	−0.166
Violent-crime index (U.S. average=100)	−0.038	−0.254*	−0.260**	−0.131
Nonviolent-crime index (U.S. average=100)	−0.041	−0.202*	−0.199*	−0.087
Ethnic neighborhoods				
Percent Hispanic population (PTHISPAN)	−0.031	−0.142	−0.118	−0.114
Percent foreign-born population	0.007	−0.008	0.005	0.180

NOTES: * 0.05 level of significance
** 0.01 level of significance
*** 0.001 level of significance

(continues)

TABLE 7.1d   *(Continued)*

	Apparel and Accessory Stores (SIC 56)	Furniture and Home Furnishing Stores (SIC 57)	Miscella- neous Retail (SIC 59)	Drug Stores and Pro- prietary Stores (SIC 591)
Poverty neighborhoods				
Percent population below poverty	−0.236*	−0.335***	−0.334***	−0.412***
Percent nonwhite population	−0.078	−0.192	−0.142	−0.304***
Percent owner-occupied housing units	0.131	0.102	0.096	0.136
Percent vacant housing units	−0.131	−0.095	−0.203*	−0.165
Percent households with public assistance	−0.212*	−0.316**	−0.305**	−0.409***
Percent female-headed households	−0.151	−0.276**	−0.226*	−0.386***
Percent service occupation	−0.198*	−0.394***	−0.341***	−0.390***
Civilian labor force participation rate	0.194	0.406***	0.426***	0.374***
Employment rate	0.187	0.357***	0.345***	0.411***
Percent federally subsidized housing units	−0.105	−0.232*	−0.147	−0.257*
Working-class neighborhoods				
Median value of owner-occupied housing	0.130	0.331***	0.142	0.266**
Per capita income	0.207*	0.459***	0.323***	0.437***
Percent less than high school education	−0.172	−0.389***	−0.337***	−0.386***
Percent high school education	0.004	−0.098	0.047	−0.100
Percent college and above education	0.164	0.426***	0.291**	0.437***
Percent management and professionals	0.149	0.403***	0.264**	0.408***
Percent labor occupation	−0.170	−0.316**	−0.266**	−0.363***
High-crime neighborhoods				
Percent housing built before 1950	−0.187	−0.385***	−0.484***	−0.190
Violent-crime index (U.S. average=100)	−0.073	−0.253*	−0.377***	−0.135
Nonviolent-crime index (U.S. average=100)	−0.057	−0.248*	−0.338***	−0.063
Ethnic neighborhoods				
Percent Hispanic population (PTHISPAN)	−0.069	−0.153	−0.152	−0.056
Percent foreign-born population	−0.032	0.133	0.050	0.164

NOTES: * 0.05 level of significance
** 0.01 level of significance
*** 0.001 level of significance

TABLE 7.1d   *(Continued)*

	Liquor Stores (SIC 592)	Used Merchandise Stores (SIC 593)
Poverty neighborhoods		
Percent population below poverty	−0.091	0.057
Percent nonwhite population	−0.119	0.039
Percent owner-occupied housing units	0.062	−0.088
Percent vacant housing units	−0.084	0.248*
Percent households with public assistance	−0.085	0.095
Percent female-headed households	−0.100	0.051
Percent service occupation	−0.113	−0.012
Civilian labor force participation rate	0.101	−0.056
Employment rate	0.114	−0.047
Percent federally subsidized housing units	−0.046	0.017
Working-class neighborhoods		
Median value of owner-occupied housing	−0.001	−0.014
Per capita income	0.054	−0.034
Percent less than high school education	−0.049	0.126
Percent high school education	0.085	0.064
Percent college and above education	0.014	−0.045
Percent management and professionals	0.005	−0.071
Percent labor occupation	−0.009	0.089
High-crime neighborhoods		
Percent housing built before 1950	−0.019	−0.020
Violent-crime index (U.S. average=100)	−0.110	−0.128
Nonviolent-crime index (U.S. average=100)	−0.100	−0.093
Ethnic neighborhoods		
Percent Hispanic population (PTHISPAN)	−0.072	0.022
Percent foreign-born population	−0.044	−0.043

NOTES: * 0.05 level of significance
** 0.01 level of significance
*** 0.001 level of significance

categories, set off in list form and accompanied by brief remarks about our analysis:

Building materials, hardware, and garden supplies (SIC 52)

This major group includes retail establishments selling lumber and other building materials; paint, glass, hardware, and wallpaper stores; retail nurseries; and lawn and garden supply stores. Given the middle-class nature of most of these goods, we expected employment in this group to be associated with the characteristics common to middle-class neighborhoods. To some degree this is true (see Table 7.1d), although the relationships are far weaker than for the all-retail analysis. This industry, like retail services in general, has significant negative correlation coefficients between the factor variables associated with *poverty neighborhoods* and *high-crime neighborhoods* and industry employment. Curiously, this is not the case with *working-class neighborhoods*. Building and garden supply stores are as likely to locate in *working-class neighborhoods* as elsewhere.

General merchandise stores (SIC 53)
    Variety stores (SIC 533)
This major group of retail stores sells a number of lines of merchandise, such as dry goods, apparel, furniture and home furnishings, and small wares. Stores in this group include department stores, variety stores, and general merchandise stores.

There is no reason to hypothesize that these stores as a group will be associated with any one particular type of neighborhood. However, malls and shopping centers containing high-end department stores might well be found in affluent neighborhoods. In contrast, discount stores such as Big Lots and Dollar Stores would probably locate in poorer neighborhoods.

As Table 7.1d shows, only eight of twenty-two factor variables are significantly related to employment in general merchandise stores. Only one variable has a coefficient greater than .30—the relationship between pre-1950 housing units and employment. Apparently general merchandise stores tend to locate in areas of newer housing. Except for that feature, general merchandise stores are not associated with any one particular type of neighborhood.

Variety stores are a subgroup of general merchandise stores that might be located in lower socioeconomic neighborhoods. These five-and-dimes carry a range of merchandise in the low and popular price ranges.

Contrary to our expectations, we found virtually no relationships between neighborhood characteristics and neighborhood employment in variety stores. At the zero-order level, there is a slight tendency for variety stores to be located in neighborhoods with newer housing, but this relationship is quite weak.

Food stores (SIC 54)
    Grocery stores (SIC 541)
    Meat and fish (seafood) markets, including freezer provisioners
      (SIC 542)
    Dairy products stores (SIC 545)
    Retail bakeries (SIC 546)

The major group food stores includes retail stores engaged primarily in selling food for home preparation and consumption. The type, location, and quality of food stores have been of serious concern for residents of low-income neighborhoods for decades. It is commonly believed that food stores leave low-income neighborhoods for reasons other than profitability. For this reason, we examined this major group in depth. Neighborhood characteristics are analyzed not only in relation to the major group but also with regard to employment in one selected subgroup—grocery stores.

The regression model for food stores (Table 7.1b) explains 11.3 percent of the variance in neighborhood employment with one variable—*poverty neighborhoods*—being statistically significant and having a negative sign. Employment in food stores thus tends to be lower in these neighborhoods than elsewhere. The model for grocery stores (Table 7.1c), as might be expected, is a mirror image of that for food stores, right down to the same percent of variance explained.

The zero-order relationships between neighborhood employment in food stores and neighborhood characteristics certainly supports the contention of some observers that poor neighborhoods are underserved (Table 7.1d). Nine of the ten zero-order correlation coefficients between the *poverty neighborhoods* factor variables and neighborhood employment in food stores are statistically significant and in the expected direction. But food stores employment is also significantly related to six of the seven variables of the *working-class neighborhoods* factor—yet all point to locations in middle-class, not working-class, neighborhoods. Finally, as expected, food stores also avoid *high-crime neighborhoods*.

Among the four industry groups that fall under the major group food stores, employment in only one, grocery stores, is significantly related to the independent variables. The other three—meat and fish markets, dairy products stores, and retail bakeries—all had few factor variables related to neighborhood employment. In terms of the zero-order correlations, as with the regression equations, grocery stores mirror food stores. The subgroup grocery stores thus drives the food stores model. In every case, neighborhood variables significantly related to neighborhood employment in food stores are also significantly related to neighborhood employment in grocery stores.

But the grocery stores category is unique in other regards. Not only is total neighborhood employment in the industry related to neighborhood characteristics, but the character of grocery stores changes by neighborhood type as well. Grocery stores vary significantly in terms of their scale (measured by total employment per establishment), and their scale determines the nature of their services and customer base. Grocery stores can be classified into four categories: chain supermarkets (stores with 50 or more employees), local neighborhood grocery stores (10 to 19 employees), convenience stores (5 to 9 employees), and mom-and-pop stores (1 to 4 employees). Our earlier study (Bingham and Zhang 1997) showed that supermarkets are clearly related to middle-class neighborhoods, whereas mom-and pop stores are most frequently found in poverty-stricken neighborhoods.

Automobile dealers and gasoline service stations (SIC 55)
    Motor vehicle dealers (new and used) (SIC 551, 552)
    Gasoline service stations (SIC 554)

The pattern of relationships between the independent variables and retail stores in general and also with food stores continues to hold in the model for automobile dealers and service stations. The establishments in this major group also generate significant neighborhood employment in better-off neighborhoods. The same pattern holds for motor vehicle dealers.

However, gasoline service stations are a bit different. The correlation coefficients between employment in these firms and the factor variables of *poverty neighborhoods* are particularly strong. Also, gasoline service stations appear to be much less likely to locate in nonwhite neighborhoods than any of the other industries examined thus far.

Apparel and accessory stores (SIC 56)

Apparel and accessory stores include retail stores engaged primarily in selling new clothing, shoes, hats, furs, undergarments, and other articles for personal wear. Our hypothesis that this class of retail establishments would have a strong association with neighborhood wealth did not hold up. The zero-order relationships between the neighborhood characteristics and neighborhood employment in this major group are nonexistent or trivial.

Home furniture, furnishings, and equipment stores (SIC 57)

This major group includes retail stores selling home furnishings such as furniture, floor covering, draperies, china, household appliances, TVs, and consumer electronics. Because most of these are high-ticket items, we expected these establishments to be located in better-off neighborhoods (as we did with apparel firms). And they are. Stores in this group avoid locating in *poverty neighborhoods, working-class neighborhoods,* or *high-crime neighborhoods.*

Miscellaneous retail (SIC 59)
  Drug stores and proprietary stores (SIC 591)
  Liquor stores (SIC 592)
  Used merchandise stores (SIC 593)

This major retail group is of interest because it contains some industries that we expected would be located in high-income communities and others that would be in poorer areas. In particular, we expected drug stores to exhibit significant employment in higher-income areas and used merchandise stores to be primarily in low-income areas. The category used merchandise stores includes antique shops, used furniture stores, used clothing stores, and pawnshops. Liquor stores are another case. We hypothesized that they would be in both wealthy and poor neighborhoods.

As Table 7.1d shows, the miscellaneous retail category is driven by drug stores. The subgroup drug stores has fourteen factor variables related to neighborhood employment, and all are typical indicators of neighborhood wealth.

Drug stores drive the miscellaneous retail category because there are virtually no relationships between the factor variables and neighborhood employment in either used merchandise stores or liquor stores. These stores are special cases. With used merchandise stores, the nature of the goods sold ensures that the stores are distributed throughout urban neighborhoods regardless of class. The poorest neighborhoods typically have used clothing stores that sell low-end, inexpensive, used clothing. Salvation Army and church-sponsored stores are often common to these neighborhoods. Used appliance stores are also present—selling used refrigerators, washers, dryers, and other major appliances that are being recycled. The same holds for used furniture stores. These stores typically sell used bedding and other recycled low-end furniture.

Yet also included in this group are antique stores and upscale used clothing stores. Both of these types of retail stores tend to be located in moderate- and higher-income urban areas. The antique stores appeal to a variety of moderate- and upper-income buyers—depending on the age and quality of the antiques. Upscale clothing stores appeal to the same groups. These stores often sell (sometimes on consignment) "out of vogue" designer clothes for men and (mostly) women. Many moderate-income people take great pride in the bargains they pick up at such stores. In a nutshell, because this SIC classification covers a spectrum of establishments, used merchandise stores are found throughout all types of urban neighborhoods.

The fact that liquor stores are unrelated to neighborhood characteristics is a situation peculiar to Ohio. The state long had a system of state liquor stores (a monopoly) designed, in part, to reduce liquor consumption in the state by limiting hours of liquor sales and setting (very) high prices. The state also severely limited the number of liquor stores, not only to restrict competition among stores but also to make it inconvenient for consumers to reach them. This system applied to all areas, rural, urban, poor, and wealthy alike.

Ohio now has privatized liquor sales, but it has not relinquished geographic control of retail liquor. The state auctions off liquor permits but still provides a monopoly by geographic area. (And the state still has some control over price and profits.) For example, an acquaintance of ours was recently the successful bidder on a state franchise on Cleveland's east side limited by East 140th Street to East 185th Street on the west and east and Lake Erie and Interstate 90 on the north and south. Regardless of state involvement and control, the result of this franchise is a reasonably equal geographic distribution of retail liquor outlets in a way that ignores neighborhood characteristics.

Summary

In conclusion, retail industries in Ohio's central-city neighborhoods, with rare exceptions, favor locating in high-SES areas. And for those few exceptions, there are logical explanations for where these retail industries locate. But the real question remains: Is this higher-SES focus the action of an efficient capital marketplace, or is the private sector in some way discriminating against the poor and minorities?

Finally, we were clearly misguided in thinking that retail activity somehow was related to manufacturing employment in urban neighborhoods. These two have no connection. For all of the retail industries discussed here, manufacturing employment was unrelated to retail employment in every case.

Social Services

Type of Neighborhood	Number of Social Services Establishments	Number of Employees	Number of Neighborhoods
Middle-class	2,471	66,264	26
Working-class	1,497	41,936	27
Moderate-poverty	847	37,577	18
Severe-poverty	638	44,850	13
Extreme-poverty	553	39,121	14
Total	6,006	229,748	98

Social services is that category of services designed to provide for the general good. This broad category includes government and education, welfare services, not-for-profit organizations, and health and hospitals. Employment in social services is not only huge, 230,000 jobs, but the jobs also are well distributed (see chart). Total social service employment is more than manufacturing and retail employment combined.

Table 7.2a shows the relationships between the independent variables and social services employment. The explanatory power of the model is very strong. The adjusted R^2 for the overall social services model is a solid .327. Employment in social services is negatively related to both *working-class neighborhoods* and *high-crime neighborhoods*, but it is positively related to *ethnic neighborhoods*.

It should be noted at this point that manufacturing employment (per 1,000 population), as an independent variable, was not considered with social services employment. We had predicted a connection between manufacturing jobs in a neighborhood and a retail presence to serve manufacturing workers, but no such link was hypothesized between manufacturing employment and social services.

The zero-order relationships between neighborhood employment in social services and the factor variables are shown in Table 7.2b. The results are enigmatic. First, as expected, there is a strong relationship between

TABLE 7.2a   Ordinary Least Square Estimates of the Regression Model:
Social Services

Independent Variables	Estimated Coefficient	Standardized Coefficient	t Value
Constant	90.82		1.277
Factors			
Poverty	22.14	0.102	1.183
Working-class	−44.95	−0.207	−2.197*
High-crime	−97.84	−0.451	−3.064**
Ethnicity	127.02	0.586	6.240***
City dummies			
Akron	67.76	0.081	0.693
Cincinnati	44.89	0.082	0.534
Cleveland	−61.91	−0.103	−0.744
Columbus	−69.55	−0.142	−0.705
Dayton	126.24	0.185	1.425
Toledo	112.23	0.176	1.303

NOTES: Dependent variable: social services employment per 1,000 population
$R^2 = 0.397$
Adjusted $R^2 = 0.327$
DF = 87
* 0.05 level of significance
** 0.01 level of significance
*** 0.001 level of significance

percent foreign-born and neighborhood employment, but other findings are more difficult to interpret. In the regression equation, there is a significant negative relationship between *high-crime neighborhoods* and neighborhood employment. But although each of the individual factor variables is negatively related to employment as expected, the correlation coefficients are not statistically significant. The factor variable relationships within *working-class neighborhoods* are even more peculiar. The four significant relationships in the table suggest that social services industries locate in middle-class neighborhoods. But why are there no significant positive relationships for median housing value, per capita income, and percent with a college education and above? And why are there so few significant relationships between the *poverty neighborhoods* factor variables and employment? At this point we have no answer.

We examined in more detail employment in a number of industries that are subcategories of social services—in this case eight individual in-

TABLE 7.2b   Zero-Order Relationships Between Independent Variables and
Population-Weighted Employment in Social Services (n = 98)

	Social Services	Medical Services (SIC 80 except 806)	Hospitals (SIC 806)
Poverty neighborhoods			
Percent population below poverty	0.144	−0.026	0.236*
Percent nonwhite population	−0.035	−0.112	0.053
Percent owner-occupied housing units	−0.374***	−0.166	−0.372***
Percent vacant housing units	−0.002	0.035	0.060
Percent households with public assistance	−0.139	−0.118	−0.024
Percent female-headed households	−0.231*	−0.248*	−0.101
Percent service occupation	0.060	−0.133	0.142
Civilian labor force participation rate	−0.182	−0.044	−0.245*
Employment rate	−0.007	0.170	−0.056
Percent federally subsidized housing units	−0.058	−0.046	0.084
Working-class neighborhoods			
Median value of owner-occupied housing	0.192	0.298**	0.115
Per capita income	−0.009	0.273**	−0.127
Percent less than high school education	−0.308**	−0.287**	−0.163
Percent high school education	−0.262**	−0.216*	−0.256*
Percent college and above education	0.195	0.377***	0.094
Percent management and professionals	0.212*	0.416***	0.137
Percent labor occupation	−0.326***	−0.437***	−0.214*
High-crime neighborhoods			
Percent housing built before 1950	−0.082	−0.072	0.128
Violent-crime index (U.S. average=100)	−0.154	−0.069	0.026
Nonviolent-crime index (U.S. average=100)	−0.191	−0.117	−0.097
Ethnic neighborhoods			
Percent Hispanic population (PTHISPAN)	0.011	−0.151	0.028
Percent foreign-born population	0.600***	0.257*	0.414***

NOTES: * 0.05 level of significance
** 0.01 level of significance
*** 0.001 level of significance

(continues)

TABLE 7.2b   *(Continued)*

	Education (SIC 82)	Welfare (SIC 832)	Child Daycare Services (SIC 835)
Poverty neighborhoods			
Percent population below poverty	0.085	0.063	−0.132
Percent nonwhite population	−0.054	0.113	0.114
Percent owner-occupied housing units	−0.292**	−0.105	−0.066
Percent vacant housing units	−0.045	0.123	0.079
Percent households with public assistance	−0.151	0.087	−0.115
Percent female-headed households	−0.212*	0.049	−0.079
Percent service occupation	0.038	0.028	−0.125
Civilian labor force participation rate	−0.121	0.057	0.193
Employment rate	−0.016	−0.017	0.193
Percent federally subsidized housing units	−0.113	0.050	0.067
Working-class neighborhoods			
Median value of owner-occupied housing	0.140	0.380***	0.305**
Per capita income	0.003	0.095	0.281**
Percent less than high school education	−0.278**	−0.044	−0.245*
Percent high school education	−0.194	−0.106	−0.269**
Percent college and above education	0.144	0.170	0.337***
Percent management and professionals	0.139	0.150	0.344***
Percent labor occupation	−0.249*	−0.103	−0.337***
High-crime neighborhoods			
Percent housing built before 1950	−0.154	−0.100	−0.322**
Violent-crime index (U.S. average=100)	−0.192	−0.260**	−0.211*
Nonviolent-crime index (U.S. average=100)	−0.170	−0.172	−0.172
Ethnic neighborhoods			
Percent Hispanic population (PTHISPAN)	0.025	0.008	−0.191
Percent foreign-born population	0.546***	0.076	0.082

NOTES: * 0.05 level of significance
** 0.01 level of significance
*** 0.001 level of significance

TABLE 7.2b   *(Continued)*

	Nonprofit (SIC 86)	Government (SICs 91–97)	Miscellaneous Social Services
Poverty neighborhoods			
Percent population below poverty	0.004	−0.174	0.114
Percent nonwhite population	−0.098	−0.185	0.120
Percent owner-occupied housing units	−0.048	0.039	-0.126
Percent vacant housing units	0.049	−0.162	0.197
Percent households with public assistance	−0.062	−0.273**	0.105
Percent female-headed households	−0.114	−0.272**	0.046
Percent service occupation	−0.009	−0.163	0.055
Civilian labor force participation rate	−0.053	0.141	−0.156
Employment rate	0.046	0.156	−0.056
Percent federally subsidized housing units	−0.029	−0.129	0.015
Working-class neighborhoods			
Median value of owner-occupied housing	0.042	0.040	0.103
Per capita income	−0.002	0.106	0.007
Percent less than high school education	−0.149	−0.232*	−0.026
Percent high school education	0.044	0.018	−0.079
Percent college and above education	0.043	0.094	0.152
Percent management and professionals	0.088	0.095	0.131
Percent labor occupation	−0.137	−0.179	−0.110
High-crime neighborhoods			
Percent housing built before 1950	−0.130	−0.254*	0.125
Violent-crime index (U.S. average=100)	−0.110	−0.173	−0.047
Nonviolent-crime index (U.S. average=100)	−0.129	−0.151	−0.102
Ethnic neighborhoods			
Percent Hispanic population (PTHISPAN)	−0.009	−0.045	0.014
Percent foreign-born population	0.126	0.350***	0.038

NOTES: * 0.05 level of significance
** 0.01 level of significance
*** 0.001 level of significance

dustries. Three had few zero-order relationships with neighborhood employment—individual and family social services (SIC 832), membership organizations (SIC 86), and miscellaneous social services (SICs 833–839)—and thus are not discussed further. Following are the other five industries, set off in list form accompanied by commentary.

Health services (SIC 80)
  Medical services (SICs 801–805, 807–809)
  Hospitals (SIC 806)

Medical services is a major group that includes establishments engaged primarily in furnishing medical, surgical, and other health services to persons. It includes HMO offices; offices and clinics of doctors, dentists, and other health practitioners; nursing homes; and medical and dental laboratories. Thus, the medical services group is a very broad category.

The clusters of factor variables suggest that there are reasonable explanations for the location of neighborhood employment in medical services. First, the industry appears to avoid *high-crime neighborhoods.* Second, it registers lower levels of employment in *middle-class neighborhoods.* Third, medical services seem to favor upper-income areas. Finally, these establishments do not avoid neighborhoods with the factor characteristics of *poverty neighborhoods,* perhaps because they are located near hospitals, some of which are in *poverty neighborhoods.*

Within the health services group, hospitals provide a major source of employment for urban residents. Most central-city hospitals have been in their urban neighborhoods for some time. But the correlation coefficients indicate little about location patterns of hospitals. Perhaps this is due to their small numbers, or perhaps they are scattered throughout all types of neighborhoods in Ohio central cities. The data do show, however, that there is some tendency for hospitals to be located in ethnic neighborhoods.

Educational services (SIC 82)

The major group educational services is another significant component of social services. It is composed of elementary and secondary schools, both public and private; colleges, universities, and junior colleges; libraries; vocational schools; and specialized schools (e.g., automobile driving instruction). Again, the zero-order coefficients indicate little about the location of employment in educational services, other than that they tend to be located in areas with high percentages of foreign-born residents.

Child day care services (SIC 835)

Child day care services are critical to low-income families, especially single-parent families. These services include day care centers, nursery schools, preschool centers, and Head Start programs (except where connected to schools). Table 7.2b, however, shows that child day care services are unrelated to *poverty neighborhoods*. These services are neither attracted to nor repelled by poor neighborhoods, but they are not located in either *high-crime neighborhoods* or *working-class neighborhoods*. However, the direction of the correlation coefficients of the *working-class* factor variables indicates quite clearly that neighborhood employment in child day care services is in middle-class neighborhoods.

Public administration (SICs 91–97)

This division essentially defines government. It includes the executive, legislative, judicial, administrative, and regulatory activities of federal, state, and local governments. The explanatory power of the public administration factor variables is weak. But, as with other social services institutions, there is some tendency for government employment to be in ethnic neighborhoods.

Summary

The social services model was as effective in explaining neighborhood employment as was the retail trade model. But the zero-order correlations did not lend as much support to the social services model as to the retail model. This finding perhaps should not be surprising. Most social services organizations provide services to residents from a much larger geographic area than the neighborhood where the institutions are located. Accordingly, neighborhood attributes have little impact on social services.

Personal Services

Type of Neighborhood	Number of Personal Services Establishments	Number of Employees	Number of Neighborhoods
Middle-class	3,570	45,075	26
Working-class	2,696	31,642	27
Moderate-poverty	1,539	12,588	18
Severe-poverty	865	9,313	13
Extreme-poverty	530	4,533	14
Total	9,200	103,151	98

TABLE 7.3a   Ordinary Least Square Estimates of the Regression Model:
Personal Services

Independent Variables	Estimated Coefficient	Standardized Coefficient	t Value
Constant	47.76		4.986***
Factors	−11.43	−0.349	−4.538***
Poverty	−18.84	−0.576	−6.837***
Working-class	−14.20	−0.434	−3.304***
High-crime	3.27	0.100	1.192
Ethnicity			
City dummies			
Akron	11.09	0.088	0.842
Cincinnati	−12.79	−0.155	−1.130
Cleveland	−6.84	−0.076	−0.611
Columbus	−15.40	−0.209	−1.158
Dayton	4.07	0.039	0.341
Toledo	3.26	0.034	0.281

NOTES: Dependent variable: personal services employment per 1,000 population
$R^2 = 0.464$
Adjusted $R^2 = 0.519$
DF = 87
* 0.05 level of significance
** 0.01 level of significance
*** 0.001 level of significance

Personal services are those services that are delivered to individuals. They include such services as laundry, beauty, and barber shops; entertainment; domestic services; hotels; and eating and drinking establishments. More than 100,000 jobs in this sector are available in urban neighborhoods (see chart), but the jobs are skewed toward the more affluent end of the spectrum.

As is shown in Table 7.3a, the independent variables explain 52 percent of the variance in neighborhood employment in personal services. Because of the prevalence of eating and drinking establishments, a subgroup of personal services, we applied the regression model to this category separately; the results appear in Table 7.3b and are discussed later.

For personal services overall, three factors are significantly and negatively related to employment—*poverty neighborhoods, working-class neighborhoods,* and *high-crime neighborhoods.* The data indicate that personal services firms want nothing to do with the characteristics of these neighborhoods.

TABLE 7.3b   Ordinary Least Square Estimates of the Regression Model: Eating and Drinking Establishments

Independent Variables	Estimated Coefficient	Standardized Coefficient	t Value
Constant	27.71		3.510***
Factors			
Poverty	−7.61	−0.312	−3.665***
Working-class	−10.70	−0.439	−4.712***
High-crime	−10.01	−0.410	−2.823**
Ethnicity	3.70	0.152	1.637
City dummies			
Akron	13.31	0.141	1.226
Cincinnati	−4.51	−0.073	−0.483
Cleveland	−6.93	−0.103	−0.751
Columbus	−7.69	−0.140	−0.702
Dayton	5.58	0.073	0.567
Toledo	6.43	0.090	0.672

NOTES: Dependent variable: eating and drinking establishments employment per 1,000 population
$R^2 = 0.412$
Adjusted $R^2 = 0.344$
DF = 87
* 0.05 level of significance
** 0.01 level of significance
*** 0.001 level of significance

This conclusion is supported by the zero-order correlation coefficients in the first column of Table 7.3c. Nineteen of the twenty-two coefficients are statistically significant, and some of them are very large indeed. Eight of the coefficients are above r = .50, and another four are between r = .40 and .50. Personal services firms have a strong affinity for white, affluent neighborhoods.

Following is a discussion of the personal services subcategories, set off in list form:

Private households (SIC 88)
The industry group private households includes private households that employ workers in domestic services occupations, such as cooks, laundresses, maids, sitters, gardeners, and the like. Our expectation that this employment group would appear in the wealthiest neighborhoods

TABLE 7.3c   Zero-Order Relationships Between Independent Variables and Population-Weighted Employment in Personal Services (n = 98)

	Personal Services	Private Households (SIC 88)	Hotels (SIC 70)
Poverty neighborhoods			
Percent population below poverty	−0.454***	−0.206*	−0.191
Percent nonwhite population	−0.443***	−0.139	−0.119
Percent owner-occupied housing units	0.073	−0.029	−0.014
Percent vacant housing units	−0.198*	−0.069	0.006
Percent households with public assistance	−0.520***	−0.258**	−0.217*
Percent female-headed households	−0.543***	−0.280**	−0.203*
Percent service occupation	−0.563***	−0.330***	−0.263**
Civilian labor force participation rate	0.515***	0.218*	0.296**
Employment rate	0.558***	0.293**	0.241*
Percent federally subsidized housing units	−0.283**	−0.169	0.011
Working-class neighborhoods			
Median value of owner-occupied housing	0.474***	0.682***	0.201*
Per capita income	0.610***	0.607***	0.256*
Percent less than high school education	−0.604***	−0.382***	−0.312**
Percent high school education	−0.186	−0.427***	−0.053
Percent college and above education	0.626***	0.635***	0.292**
Percent management and professionals	0.588***	0.592***	0.289**
Percent labor occupation	−0.562***	−0.479***	−0.280**
High-crime neighborhoods			
Percent housing built before 1950	−0.456***	−0.009	−0.454***
Violent-crime index (U.S. average=100)	−0.338***	0.106	−0.295**
Nonviolent-crime index (U.S. average=100)	−0.337***	0.045	−0.303**
Ethnic neighborhoods			
Percent Hispanic population (PTHISPAN)	−0.171	−0.118	−0.120
Percent foreign-born population	0.327***	0.211*	0.157

NOTES: * 0.05 level of significance
** 0.01 level of significance
*** 0.001 level of significance

TABLE 7.3c   *(Continued)*

	Eating and Drinking Establishments (SIC 58)	Repair (SICs 725, 753, and 76)	Laundry (SIC 721)
Poverty neighborhoods			
Percent population below poverty	−0.381***	−0.069	−0.284**
Percent nonwhite population	−0.421***	−0.347***	−0.134
Percent owner-occupied housing units	0.018	0.196	0.154
Percent vacant housing units	−0.240*	−0.081	0.030
Percent households with public assistance	−0.479***	−0.012	−0.237*
Percent female-headed households	−0.499***	−0.102	−0.231*
Percent service occupation	−0.466***	−0.105	−0.369***
Civilian labor force participation rate	0.470***	−0.040	0.266**
Employment rate	0.498***	0.102	0.270**
Percent federally subsidized housing units	−0.300**	−0.087	−0.204*
Working-class neighborhoods			
Median value of owner-occupied housing	0.346***	−0.111	0.461***
Per capita income	0.477***	−0.070	0.500***
Percent less than high school education	−0.543***	0.188	−0.290**
Percent high school education	−0.145	0.287**	−0.274**
Percent college and above education	0.507***	−0.198*	0.463***
Percent management and professionals	0.472***	−0.223*	0.400***
Percent labor occupation	−0.482***	0.231*	−0.291**
High-crime neighborhoods			
Percent housing built before 1950	−0.356***	0.017	−0.252*
Violent-crime index (U.S. average=100)	−0.304**	−0.109	−0.159
Nonviolent-crime index (U.S. average=100)	−0.321***	−0.100	−0.108
Ethnic neighborhoods			
Percent Hispanic population (PTHISPAN)	−0.167	0.165	−0.125
Percent foreign-born population	0.287**	−0.017	0.159

NOTES: * 0.05 level of significance
** 0.01 level of significance
*** 0.001 level of significance

(continues)

TABLE 7.3c   *(Continued)*

	Barber and Beauty Shops (SICs 723 and 724)	Entertainment (SICs 78, 79, and 84 except 781)	Miscellaneous Personal Services
Poverty neighborhoods			
Percent population below poverty	−0.389***	−0.345***	−0.267**
Percent nonwhite population	−0.270**	−0.216*	−0.163
Percent owner-occupied housing units	0.102	0.084	0.106
Percent vacant housing units	−0.145	0.050	−0.093
Percent households with public assistance	−0.366***	−0.358***	−0.233*
Percent female-headed households	−0.365***	−0.386***	−0.210*
Percent service occupation	−0.445***	−0.446***	−0.293**
Civilian labor force participation rate	0.430***	0.313**	0.233*
Employment rate	0.382***	0.383***	0.284**
Percent federally subsidized housing units	−0.211*	−0.056	−0.023
Working-class neighborhoods			
Median value of owner-occupied housing	0.435***	0.519***	0.197
Per capita income	0.560***	0.547***	0.351***
Percent less than high school education	−0.484***	−0.457***	−0.320***
Percent high school education	−0.226*	−0.209*	−0.021
Percent college and above education	0.608***	0.569***	0.295**
Percent management and professionals	0.550***	0.586***	0.299**
Percent labor occupation	−0.498***	−0.500***	−0.295**
High-crime neighborhoods			
Percent housing built before 1950	−0.450***	−0.316**	−0.426***
Violent-crime index (U.S. average=100)	−0.309**	−0.094	−0.275**
Nonviolent-crime index (U.S. average=100)	−0.266**	−0.078	−0.220*
Ethnic neighborhoods			
Percent Hispanic population (PTHISPAN)	−0.103	−0.078	−0.132
Percent foreign-born population	0.250*	0.286**	0.111

NOTES: * 0.05 level of significance
** 0.01 level of significance
*** 0.001 level of significance

proved correct. There are strong negative relationships between neighborhood employment and the factor variables associated with *poverty neighborhoods* and *working-class neighborhoods.*

Hotels (SIC 70)
Eating and drinking establishments (SIC 58)

Major group 70 covers not only hotels and motels but rooming and boarding houses and camps and recreational-vehicle parks. The category eating and drinking establishments is self-explanatory. Both industries provide services to individuals, but they also provide services to businesses and thus might be considered business services as well.

Hotels and motel neighborhood employment seems to be in moderately affluent neighborhoods. Many of the factor variables of *poverty neighborhoods, working-class neighborhoods,* and *high-crime neighborhoods* are related to hotel employment, although few of the relationships are particularly strong.

The picture is different for eating and drinking establishments. The results of the regression model for this category are shown in Table 7.3b. The independent variables explain almost 45 percent of the variance in neighborhood employment in eating and drinking establishments. Three of the factors—*poverty neighborhoods, working-class neighborhoods,* and *high-crime neighborhoods*—exhibit strong negative relationships to the location of these businesses. In the correlation analysis (Table 7.3c), of the twenty-two factor variables, all but three are significantly related to neighborhood employment in these establishments. Eleven of the correlation coefficients are greater than .400. The correlation coefficients clearly support the regression results that show eating and drinking establishments are located in better-off neighborhoods.

Repair (SICs 725, 753, 76)

We created a class of establishments labeled "repair" by combining shoe repair shops and shoeshine parlors (SIC 725) with automotive repair shops (SIC 753) and miscellaneous repair services (SIC 76). Automotive repair shops do not include dealers but are separate establishments such as shops for transmission replacement, independent auto repair, body work, mufflers, glass replacement, and the like. Miscellaneous repair services cover establishments repairing virtually everything except shoes, clothing, computers, and automobiles.

Very few of the factor variables are related to neighborhood repair employment—perhaps because these shops are located almost everywhere. One exception seems to be in nonwhite neighborhoods. This is another case where nonwhite population has a rather strong negative relationship to neighborhood employment.

Laundry, cleaning, and garment services (SIC 721)

This industry includes typical laundry and dry cleaning establishments plus coin-operated laundries, carpet and upholstery cleaning, and industrial launderers. Many of the independent variables have fairly strong zero-order relationships to the neighborhood locations of jobs in laundry services. Laundries are located in high-SES areas and not *poverty* or *working-class neighborhoods*.

Beauty shops and barber shops (SICs 723 and 724)

Factor variables from all four of the factors are strongly related to the neighborhood location of beauty shops and barber shops. The location of these businesses is as expected—neighborhoods having high income, high SES, and high-value housing. Some of the correlation coefficients are extremely high, such as the relationships between this industry and income, percent college graduates, and percent in management and the professions.

Entertainment (SICs 78–79 [except 781], 84)

The final grouping of industries to be discussed combines the following entertainment industries: motion pictures (SIC 78) (except motion picture and video tape production [SIC 781], which was included in information services); amusement and recreation services (SIC 79); and museums, art galleries, and botanical and zoological gardens (SIC 84). The motion pictures category includes both motion picture theaters and video tape rental stores. The category amusement and recreation services covers dance studios and schools, bowling alleys, commercial sports, fitness centers, and video arcades.

Sixteen of the factor variables are significantly related to employment in entertainment at the zero-order level. There is nothing surprising in the zero-order correlations. Employment in entertainment is related to high SES, quality housing, and college graduate and white-collar neighborhoods. Entertainment industries avoid both *poverty* and *working-class neighborhoods*.

Summary

Analysis of the personal services industry produced no particular surprises. Most of these services are designed to serve people in the neighborhoods, and most do. However, as with the retail industry, most of the employment is in better-off areas.

Are the Poor Underserved?

This book is about neighborhood employment. But given the evidence presented in the last several chapters about the relationships between neighborhood characteristics and the location of employment (and thus businesses), it is useful to digress and address the question of whether the poor are underserved. First, let us review the evidence. We found few relationships between community characteristics and business location in the smaller industries: construction, transportation, information, and wholesale services. We also found few relationships between community characteristics and manufacturing. We found a few more significant relationships in the social services sector, but since most of these services have little to do with neighborhood consumers, we found little cause for alarm.

But when it came to producer services that also deal with consumers, and two of the consumer-oriented industries examined in this chapter—retail and personal services—the results are clear. Yes, the poor are underserved. Of course, we are not the first to make this discovery. All one has to do is drive through low-income neighborhoods in urban America and note the boarded-up storefronts, the dearth of banks, and the poor excuses for grocery stores serving the residents. However, the extent of location bias we have uncovered is disturbing.

The real question is not whether the poor are underserved but rather why they are. Market advocates may simply attribute this observation to the fact that the poor do not present the level of demand that can sustain profitable businesses in their neighborhoods. This line of thinking suggests that if a profit could be made by opening a supermarket, bank, or hardware store in a low-income area, then market forces would assure that one opens.

Others are not so sure, however. After all, many profitable establishments in urban America close or move every day. They do not necessarily close or move solely because they are not profitable. Many retail and service firms did suburbanize as a result of the geographic shift of their markets, but many indeed chose to relocate due to increasing concerns about robbery, shoplifting, vandalism, and other safety issues.

The poverty issue is a tough one, and there are no simple answers. But in some urban neighborhoods in Ohio central cities, government has helped lower the cost of starting and doing business in low-income neighborhoods with apparent success.

The Importance of Race

We close this chapter with a look at the relationships between neighborhood characteristics and employment and race. Race is one characteristic of central cities that is highly correlated with other characteristics. The extent of the connection is shown in a zero-order correlation matrix between percent nonwhite and the other neighborhood characteristics (Table 7.4). As can be seen, there are some very strong relationships.

First, remember that these are neighborhood characteristics, not individual characteristics. Percent nonwhite (in the neighborhood) is strongly correlated with almost all of the other neighborhood characteristics. In fact, the correlation coefficients exceed .50 when percent nonwhite is correlated with the poverty level, households receiving public assistance, female-headed households, service occupations, labor force participation rate (negative), employment rate (negative), federally subsidized housing, and per capita income (negative).

Of course, race is a central fact of life in urban America that people hear and read about every day. But what we have not yet accomplished in this analysis is to determine how much of the location (or lack thereof) of business is determined by the racial makeup of neighborhoods and how much is due to other factors. Table 7.5 shows only the statistically significant zero-order relationships between percent nonwhite and neighborhood employment in various industries. The list is long enough to be of concern.

In an attempt to identify how much independent influence the racial makeup of urban neighborhoods has on the location of neighborhood employment, we computed partial correlation coefficients between percent nonwhite and employment in each industry, controlling for the other variables in the model. A zero-order correlation coefficient is a measure of the degree of linear association between two variables. In multiple regression, a partial correlation coefficient measures the association between two variables that are independent of the influence of other variables. Conceptually, the partial correlation coefficient is similar to the partial regression coefficient (Gujarati 1995). Partial correlation coefficients

TABLE 7.4   Zero-Order Relationships Between Percent Nonwhite Population and Other Neighborhood Characteristics (n = 98)

	Percent Nonwhite Population
Poverty neighborhoods	
Percent population below poverty	0.655***
Percent owner-occupied housing units	−0.376***
Percent vacant housing units	0.369***
Percent households with public assistance	0.718***
Percent female-headed households	0.842***
Percent service occupation	0.781***
Civilian labor force participation rate	−0.584***
Employment rate	−0.711***
Percent federally subsidized housing units	0.552***
Working-class neighborhoods	
Median value of owner-occupied housing	−0.235*
Per capita income	−0.516***
Percent less than high school education	0.485***
Percent high school education	−0.082
Percent college and above education	−0.361***
Percent management and professionals	−0.321**
Percent labor occupation	0.298**
High-crime neighborhoods	
Percent housing built before 1950	0.281**
Violent-crime index (U.S. average=100)	0.137
Nonviolent-crime index (U.S. average=100)	0.163
Ethnic neighborhoods	
Percent Hispanic population (PTHISPAN)	−0.042
Percent foreign-born population	−0.348***

NOTES: * 0.05 level of significance
** 0.01 level of significance
*** 0.001 level of significance

TABLE 7.5   Statistically Significant Zero-Order Relationships Between Percent Nonwhite and Employment in Various Industries (n = 98)

Industry	Zero-Order	Partial Correlation Coefficient
All industries	−0.218*	−0.208
Information services		−0.125
Credit reporting and collection	−0.227*	0.074
Motion picture and allied services	−0.229*	−0.074
Producer services	−0.314**	−0.290*
Banking (SICs 60–62)	−0.263**	−0.193
Deposit institutions (SIC 60)	−0.226*	−0.343**
Commercial banks (SIC 602)	−0.237*	−0.178
Functions closely related to banking (SIC 609)	−0.219*	0.133
Insurance (SICs 63–64)	−0.272**	−0.187
Insurance agents, brokers, and services (SIC 64)	−0.312**	−0.404***
Engineering and management services (SIC 87)	−0.274**	0.030
Engineering and architecture (SIC 871)	−0.220*	−0.041
Accounting (SIC 872)	−0.231*	−0.057
Miscellaneous business services	−0.309**	−0.317**
Retail	−0.320***	−0.003
Building materials and garden supplies (SIC 52)	−0.252*	−0.021
Food stores (SIC 54)	−0.390***	−0.208
Grocery stores (SIC 541)	−0.376***	−0.218
Automotive dealers and services (SIC 55)	−0.283*	−0.085
New and used car dealers (SICs 551 and 552)	−0.233*	−0.053
Gasoline service stations (SIC 554)	−0.409***	−0.282*
Drug stores and proprietary stores	−0.304**	−0.143
Personal services	−0.443***	−0.091
Eating and drinking establishments (SIC 58)	−0.421***	−0.095
Repairs	−0.347***	−0.196
Barber and beauty shops (SICs 723 and 724)	−0.270**	−0.101
Entertainment	−0.216*	0.099

NOTES: * 0.05 level of significance
** 0.01 level of significance
*** 0.001 level of significance

should be interpreted as follows: There is an independent negative (or positive) relationship between percent nonwhite in neighborhoods and neighborhood employment in (industry), all other things being equal.

Table 7.5 also shows the partial correlation coefficients between percent nonwhite when the other independent variables are held constant. It is fairly clear from the data that the racial makeup of urban neighborhoods, by itself, has very little to do with neighborhood employment. The partials do show that there are some industries where employment is still negatively related to percent nonwhite, other things being equal. These industries are producer services in general; depository institutions (institutions that are engaged in deposit banking or closely related functions); insurance agents, brokers, and services; miscellaneous business services; and gasoline service stations. For the other industries where race appears to be a factor when the simple correlation coefficients are examined, the partials suggest that other factors, factors correlated with neighborhood racial makeup, account for the significance of the simple correlation coefficients. This analysis is not to make light of the relationships we did find. Perhaps people can live without having an insurance agent in the neighborhood, but the partials suggest that important producer services—particularly depository institutions (commercial banks, savings institutions, credit unions)—have a reduced presence in some urban neighborhoods simply because they are nonwhite.

References

Bingham, Richard D., and Zhongcai Zhang. 1997. "Poverty and Economic Morphology of Ohio Central-City Neighborhoods." *Urban Affairs Review* 32(6): 766–796.

Gujarati, Damodar N. 1995. *Basic Econometrics*. New York: McGraw-Hill.

8

Explaining Neighborhood Social/Industrial Linkages

In the previous three chapters, we examined the linkages between the socioeconomic characteristics of urban neighborhoods and the various industries located in those neighborhoods. The task here is to take the analysis one step further. First, we describe the industrial structure of central-city neighborhoods. Here we are interested in identifying which industries tend to locate in the same neighborhoods. Factor analysis is used to identify these industry clusters. Second, we look at the relationships between the socioeconomic characteristics and industrial specializations. We can thus examine the social/industrial linkages that exist in central-city neighborhoods. Finally, we examine and explain the social/industrial structures of Ohio central cities. We do this on a neighborhood-by-neighborhood basis.

Industrial Structure of Central-City Neighborhoods

For this part of the investigation, factor analysis with varimax rotation was used. Neighborhood employment per 1,000 residents for seventy-one specific two-digit (major group) and three-digit (industry group) industrial classifications were input into the factor analysis. If the three-digit industry groups composing the major group were included, then the major group was not. For example, the major group food stores was not included in the factor analysis, because its components (grocery stores, meat and fish markets, dairy products stores, and retail bakeries) were included. The number of factors was limited using the standard criteria of eigenvalues greater than one. The factor analysis produced twenty-four factors in the industrial structure analysis—many being useful industrial descriptors of urban neighborhoods, and a number not so useful. We

TABLE 8.1   Significant Factors in Industrial Structure of Central-City Neighborhoods

Industry	SIC	Factor Loading
Factor 1: Producer and personal services		
Drug stores and proprietary stores (SIC 591)	591	0.443
Security and commodity brokers (SIC 62)	62	0.507
Insurance agents, brokers, and services	63	0.857
Real estate (SIC 65)	65	0.423
Engineering and architecture	871	0.736
Accounting	872	0.647
Miscellaneous business services	67, 73 (except 731–732), 892, 899	0.685
Legal services	81	0.454
Eating and drinking establishments	58	0.544
Laundry	721	0.778
Barber and beauty shops	723, 724	0.614
Entertainment	78–79 (except 781), 84	0.402
Miscellaneous personal services	722, 726-729, 751, 752, 754	0.582
Factor 2: Specialized strip shopping		
General merchandise stores (SIC 53)	53	0.516
New and used car dealers (SIC 551 & 552)	551, 552	0.412
Communications	48	0.660
Credit reporting and collection	732	0.506
Nondepository institutions (SIC 61)	61	0.874
Factor 5: Neighborhood retail services		
Electronic and other electronic equipment	36	0.661
Grocery stores (SIC 541)	541	0.559
New and used car dealers (SIC 551 & 552)	551, 552	0.506
Gasoline service stations (SIC 554)	554	0.494
Credit unions (SIC 606)	606	0.763
Factor 7: Primary metals and related industries		
Primary metals	33	0.933
Fabricated metal products	34	0.462
Petroleum and coal products	29	0.962
Factor 13: Public services I		
Printing and publishing	27	0.648
Hospitals	806	0.670
Education	82	0.839
Factor 14: Public services II		
Welfare	832	0.873
Entertainment	78–79 (except 781), 84	0.477
Factor 20: Low-income-area industries		
Used merchandise stores	593	0.788
Functions closely related to banking	609	0.569
Factor 24: Rubber products		
Rubber products	301–306	0.782

used a loading of 0.4 as the cutoff point to consider that the industry had a "high" loading on the factor. The useful individual factors are contained in Table 8.1. The complete factor loadings appear in Appendix A.

In Table 8.1, factor 1 is clearly a cluster of *producer and personal services*. Seven producer services industries load on this factor, as do five of the personal services industries. Furthermore, industries not loading on this factor are manufacturing, construction, transportation services, wholesale services, information services, and social services. This factor clearly shows a measure of high-end services and indicates that these services tend to locate in the same neighborhoods.

Factor 2 is not as distinctive as factor 1, but it seems to capture neighborhoods that have a sort of *specialized strip shopping*. The retail businesses associated with this factor are general merchandise stores and car dealerships. The stores and dealerships are supported by nondepository institutions (loan companies) and credit agencies. Such a neighborhood might have a four-lane highway with auto dealerships, large appliance stores, Kmart, Dollar Store, and perhaps a Wal-Mart. Brookpark Road on Cleveland's west side is this type of neighborhood.

The next two factors (not shown) are industrial agglomerations based on neighborhoods, but they appear to be more accidental than theoretical. For example, factor 4 contains relatively high loadings of the following industries: general contractors; stone, clay, and glass products; real estate; medical services; and miscellaneous social services. Because there is no theoretical connection between these industries, the factors have not been named.

Factor 5 is not particularly clear either, but it does suggest a dimension of *neighborhood retail services*. Loaded on this factor are grocery stores, new and used car dealers, and gasoline service stations.

With the exception of factor 7, factors 6 through 12 are not particularly enlightening with regard to neighborhood economies. Factor 7, however, identifies neighborhoods that specialize in *primary metals and fabricated metal products*. It would be reasonable to assume (and we discuss this later) that some neighborhoods in Cleveland and perhaps Youngstown specialize in these industries.

Factor 13 is interesting, as it is a *public services* factor. Hospitals, educational institutions, and printing and publishing all load on this factor. The link between education and hospitals is understandable—universities and university hospitals. However, there is no particular link between printing and publishing and the other two industries.

The variables with substantial loadings on factor 14 also point to a *public services* factor. The social services group includes establishments providing social or rehabilitation services to the community. Entertainment includes not only movie theaters and playhouses but also museums, art galleries, botanical gardens, and zoos.

Finally, eight of the final ten factors must be dismissed, as there is no theoretical explanation for the clusters of industries loading on the factors. Two of the factors do make sense, however. Factor 20 identifies *low-income-area industries*. The two industries with high loading on this factor are used merchandise stores and check-cashing stores. The final factor, factor 24, has only one variable with a high loading, *rubber products*. This factor probably is a result of the location of the rubber industry in Akron.

Thus, of the twenty-four factors produced by factor analysis, only eight (or one-third) make sense from a neighborhood economy perspective. On first glance, this result does not seem very promising, but in fact it is significant. The literature makes clear that economies are regional, and that these regions are much larger than central-city neighborhoods. Thus, it is remarkable that one-third of the factors uncovered have meaning for central-city neighborhoods.

Industrial and Social Structure of Central-City Neighborhoods

The next step is to determine how these eight neighborhood industrial factors we have uncovered relate to neighborhood socioeconomic characteristics. The analysis is shown in Table 8.2. Here we show the correlation coefficients between factor scores of the neighborhood factors and the factor scores of the industrial factors. In most cases (all but three), the statistically significant correlation coefficients were between the industrial clusters we could recognize and the neighborhood factors.

The first industrial factor, *producer and personal services,* has a strong negative relationship with *working-class neighborhoods.* Recall from Chapters 6 and 7 that a negative sign on *working-class neighborhoods* was actually an indicator of middle-class neighborhoods—that is, areas with good housing and an educated and professional population. Thus this relationship makes intuitive sense. Where else might one expect to find a plethora of the types of producer and personal services shown in Table 8.1 under factor 1?

Specialized strip shopping is negatively related to two of the neighborhood factors—*poverty neighborhoods* and *high-crime neighborhoods.* Recall that

TABLE 8.2   Correlation Between Industry Factors and Neighborhood Factors (n = 98)

Factor Number	Factor Name	Poverty	Working-Class	Crime	Ethnicity
			Neighborhood Factor		
1	Producer and personal services	−0.190	−0.615***	−0.126	0.001
2	Strip shopping	−0.280**	−0.045	−0.297**	−0.164
3		−0.092	−0.118	0.070	−0.031
4		0.151	−0.118	−0.073	0.100
5	Neighborhood retail	−0.057	−0.019	−0.116	0.021
6		−0.114	0.151	−0.135	−0.177
7	Primary metals	0.014	0.192	0.041	0.183
8		−0.103	0.185	−0.231*	−0.102
9		−0.087	−0.028	0.030	−0.073
10		−0.068	0.086	−0.066	0.140
11		0.257*	0.175	−0.119	−0.096
12		−0.136	−0.110	0.168	−0.026
13	Public services I	0.031	−−0.086	−0.211*	0.367***
14	Public services II	0.158	−0.194	−0.066	0.095
15		−0.084	−0.071	−0.050	−0.076
16		−0.184	−0.016	−0.156	0.132
17		0.073	0.012	0.085	−0.038
18		−0.044	−0.125	0.006	−0.028
19	Low-income-area industries	0.276**	−0.026	0.095	−0.054
20		0.149	−0.008	−0.013	0.062
21		0.041	−0.017	−0.090	0.014
22		−0.150	0.006	0.179	0.095
23		−0.302**	0.180	0.047	0.149
24	Rubber products	−0.043	0.218*	0.035	0.031

NOTES: *0.05 level of significance
**0.01 level of significance
***0.001 level of significance

specialized strip shopping is characterized by general merchandise stores (like Kmart) and car dealers. Enterprises like these are unlikely to locate in *poverty neighborhoods* due to the limited buying power of local residents. Nor are they likely to locate in *high-crime neighborhoods*. Automobile dealerships usually have a large inventory of cars left in outdoor parking lots, and the large parking lots associated with general merchandise stores can be fearsome places for some potential customers—especially at night.

Three of the industrial factors—*neighborhood retail services, primary metals and related industries,* and *public services II*—were not significantly related to any of the neighborhood factors. We suspect that these factors emerged from unusual concentrations in a very few neighborhoods in one or two cities. This premise is covered later in the chapter.

Public services I is significantly related to two of the neighborhood factors—*high-crime neighborhoods* (negatively) and *ethnic neighborhoods*. The clients of both hospitals and educational institutions are vulnerable populations. Many of these institutions take public safety very seriously— seriously enough, for example, for them to have their own security forces to deter crime. *Public services I* is also strongly related to *ethnic neighborhoods*. No particular causal relationship is suggested here. Most hospitals and educational institutions are not new and tend to be located in older central-city neighborhoods that also happen to have significant foreign-born populations.

Not surprisingly, the factor *low-income-area industries* is positively correlated with *poverty neighborhoods*. Low-income areas are logical locations for used merchandise stores and check-cashing stores.

Finally, *rubber products* is positively related to *working-class neighborhoods*. Again, we suspect that this relationship is unique to Akron, discussed in the next section.

Urban Neighborhoods

In an effort to merge both the neighborhood and industrial factors with the reality of urban neighborhoods, we generated factor scores for each of the identifiable factors for each zip code for Ohio central cities. These factor scores are contained in Appendix B. High scores are indicative of specialized neighborhoods. We initially thought that a factor might be considered characteristic of a given neighborhood if it had a score of more than 1.5 (or less than −1.5) on the factor. We then looked at the highest loading for that factor among all of the ninety-eight neighborhoods to confirm the specialization. In the following sections, we discuss the distinctive characteristics of the central-city neighborhoods of Ohio's seven central cities.

Akron[1]

As we discussed in Chapter 2, Akron's historical economic claim to fame was rubber. Known as the rubber capital of the world, Akron was once

---

[1]Dr. Jesse Marquette, director of the Institute for Policy Studies and Urban Policy Research of the University of Akron, provided us with information on Akron, June 6, 2000.

home to the nation's leading rubber companies. Today, rubber no longer plays the dominant role in Akron's economy that it once did, but an off-shoot of the industry—polymers—is quietly replacing rubber, and many of the dominant players are the same.

Physically locating Akron's rubber activity was complex because three of Akron's major rubber employers have their own postal zip codes that were not geographically identified. But the physical facilities are so large that locating them was not difficult. Four of Akron's neighborhoods, as defined by our zip codes, show economic specializations in *rubber products*—44301, 44305, 44310, and 44313 (Figure 8.1). This was also true of one CBD zip code, 44311, which is considered in this case analysis with the abutting 44301.

Zip code 44301 is in the south-central part of the city, immediately south of 44311 (part of the CBD). The neighborhood contains the old Bridgestone/Firestone plant along Firestone Parkway. In 1993 there were more than 1,300 workers at Bridgestone/Firestone in the area. Bridge-stone/Firestone no longer produces rubber products here, but this neighborhood is the home of the Bridgestone/Firestone Technical Center (R&D in rubber and polymers).

Zip codes 44305 and 44310 are adjoining zip code neighborhoods, with 44305 located in the far eastern portion of the city and 44310 in the northeast. The neighborhood was the home of production for Goodyear Tire and had more than 5,000 employees in *rubber products* in 1993. The area is home to the Akron/Fulton Municipal Airport, and adjoining it is the Goodyear aviation complex. The area is also home to a defense contractor—the Loral Corporation—a company working in polymers. In addition, there are many small polymer plants in the area.

Finally, there is zip code 44313 in the northwestern corner of the city encompassing Akron's West Akron and Fairlawn Heights neighborhoods. This area not only has a *rubber products* specialization but also has a substantial middle-class population and an economic specialization in *producer and personal services*.

West Akron has long been home to much of Akron's wealth and its professional community. It is an area of stately old homes with beautiful trees and lawns. There are two country clubs in the neighborhood. The commercial area is along Market and Exchange Streets. Many old homes along Market Street have been converted into professional office buildings. Farther out along Market is newer construction housing and more professional services and retail activities.

The *rubber products* specialization in the neighborhood resulted from UniRoyal Goodrich with a moderate employment level of several hun-

156

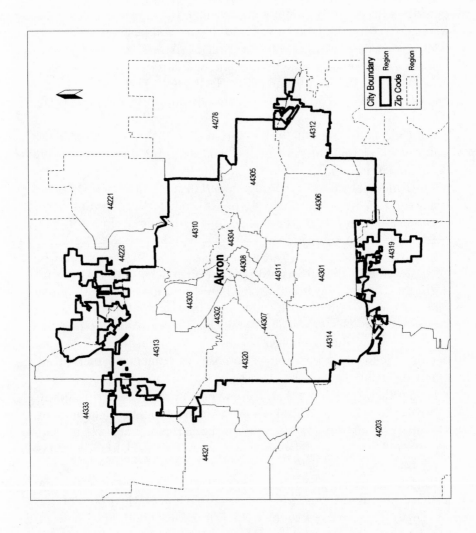

	Poverty	Working-Class	High-Crime	Ethnic	Producer and Personal Services	Strip Shopping	Neighborhood Retail	Primary Metals	Public Services I	Public Services II	Low-Income	Rubber
44301												
44305												1.609
44306												5.770
44310												
44313		-1.778			3.886							3.297
44314												1.517
44320												

FIGURE 8.1 Akron Neighborhood Specializations as Determined by Factor Score

dreds of workers in 1993. General Tire's headquarters function is now in the neighborhood along Gent Road.

Cincinnati[2]

Cincinnati, with a 1990 population of 364,040, is unusual in that none of its neighborhoods seems to have an economic specialization, but this finding is not unduly strange: As we reported in Chapter 2, Cincinnati's economic base is extremely diverse compared with that of other central cities in Ohio (Dockery et al. 1997, 53–56). The city does, however, have neighborhoods with dominant social characteristics as identified by the factor analysis (see Figure 8.2).

Three Cincinnati neighborhoods were identified by the factor analysis as *poverty neighborhoods.* The area of the city known as Camp Washington (zip code 45225) is northwest of the downtown near the Mill Creek Valley. It was formerly the stockyards area. Today it is the poorest neighborhood in Cincinnati with nearly two-thirds of residents in poverty according to the 1990 census. The neighborhood is heavily nonwhite (77 percent) and has a high concentration of renters (81 percent). It has the highest proportion of female-headed households in the city, and the highest school dropout rate, with over half of adult neighborhood residents never receiving a high school diploma. The neighborhood has an unusually high concentration of public housing (31 percent). Economically, Camp Washington is primarily a manufacturing neighborhood; manufacturing firms account for 44 percent of the 4,520 workers in the neighborhood. There is a cluster of food and kindred products firms employing more than 1,000 workers, or about 55 percent of all manufacturing employment.

A second *poverty neighborhood* in Cincinnati is Avondale (zip code 45229), although it is not as poor as Camp Washington. Avondale is located to the north of Cincinnati's CBD. It is really two neighborhoods—South Avondale and North Avondale. South Avondale was a major Jewish settlement in Cincinnati, but the area deteriorated during and after the construction of Interstate 75. Today it is very poor and is largely African American. North Avondale, in contrast, is quite prosperous. It is a racially integrated neighborhood with fine, large, older homes.

---

[2]Professor Howard A. Stafford of the Department of Geography, University of Cincinnati, provided us with information on Cincinnati's neighborhoods, June 7, 2000.

The third *poverty neighborhood* is an area known as Winton Place (zip code 45232). It is also north of but more distant from the CBD. The area is predominantly African American, although some white migrants from Appalachia also reside in the neighborhood. The neighborhood is the second-poorest in Cincinnati, with a poverty rate of 55 percent. It had fewer than 10,000 residents in 1990. Almost three-fourths of its residents are nonwhite; it has 44 percent female-headed households, high unemployment (almost 20 percent), few high school graduates (42 percent dropouts), and a very low per capita income (a little over $6,000 annually). The neighborhood is in Mill Creek Valley and borders an old industrial area. The neighborhood contains one of the city's dump sites.

Two zip code neighborhoods had substantial negative loading on the *working-class neighborhood* factor—45208 and 45220. As expected, both of these neighborhoods are heavily middle-class. The most affluent neighborhood in Cincinnati is Hyde Park (45208), located to the east of the downtown. The Hyde Park neighborhood is an upscale residential area with expensive, large homes. Most of the residents own their own homes, are highly educated, and work in professional occupations. The major commercial street in the area is Erie Avenue, containing high-end small shops and professional offices.

Zip code 45220 is the Clifton neighborhood of Cincinnati and is north of downtown and between two *poverty neighborhoods*—Camp Washington and Avondale. It is also located on the edge of the University of Cincinnati campus, which has more than 33,000 students. Hebrew Union College is also in the neighborhood. The southern half of Clifton is largely a student neighborhood with many apartment buildings and relatively inexpensive single-family dwellings rented to students and younger faculty. The northern half of the neighborhood is much like Hyde Park with large, expensive homes. Many of the university's faculty live in the area, as do a number of professionals working downtown—attorneys, doctors, and managers from Procter and Gamble. The factor analysis showed a substantial foreign-born population in the neighborhood as well. However, this population is foreign students and foreign-born faculty members. It is not what one typically pictures as an *ethnic neighborhood*.

Two of the zip code neighborhoods—45208 (Hyde Park) and 45226—loaded significantly on the *high-crime neighborhood* factor. Our source for Cincinnati information for this chapter, however, is hard pressed to affix that label to these areas.

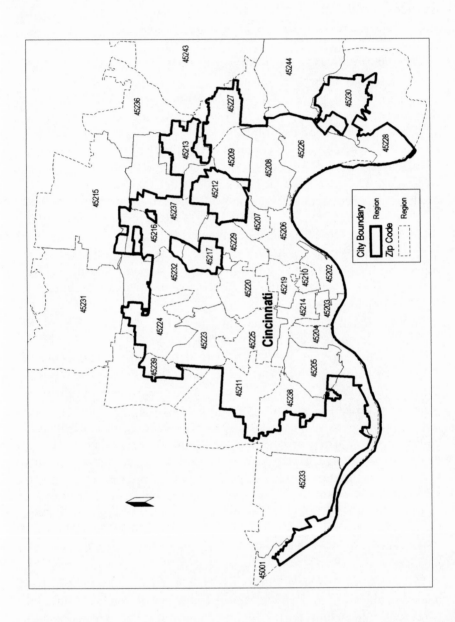

	Poverty	Working-Class	High-Crime	Ethnic	Producer and Personal Services	Strip Shopping	Neighbor-hood Retail	Primary Metals	Public Services I	Public Services II	Low-Income	Rubber
45204												
45207												
45208		-3.114	1.962									
45209												
45211												
45213												
45216				1.669								
45220		-2.126										
45223												
45224												
45225	2.847											
45226			1.786									
45227												
45228												
45229	1.520											
45230												
45232	1.957											
45237												
45238												

FIGURE 8.2   Cincinnati Neighborhood Specializations as Determined by Factor Score

Cleveland

Like most central cities, Cleveland has its poverty neighborhoods, and these are identified by high factor scores on the first factor. As shown in Figure 8.3, most of the poverty neighborhoods are on the east side of the city. Zip codes 44103 and 44108 in the northeast section of the city encompass portions of the Hough, St. Clair/Superior, and Glenville neighborhoods. To the south is zip code 44104, which is also a poverty neighborhood encompassing portions of the Kinsman and Woodland Hills neighborhoods. Zip codes 44103 and 44104 are the poorest neighborhoods in Cleveland and are the only two Cleveland extreme-poverty neighborhoods, with about 49 percent of residents in 44103 below poverty and 53 percent in 44104. Zip code 44108 is the fourth-poorest in Cleveland, with about 35 percent of residents living in poverty, and is one of the two Cleveland severe-poverty neighborhoods. These three neighborhoods are predominantly nonwhite: Zip codes 44103, 44104, and 44108 have 75 percent, 97.9 percent, and 95.9 percent nonwhite population respectively. However, 44103 also has a substantial ethnic population. The St. Clair/Superior neighborhood has historically been the center of Slovenian immigration in Cleveland with its Slovenian churches, restaurants, and retail businesses. Today it is also home to Cleveland's Chinatown, with a growing oriental population and many fine Chinese restaurants and other businesses. St. Clair/Superior is the most ethnically diverse neighborhood in the city.

Also, about half of the adult residents in the three neighborhoods are high school dropouts (53.1 percent, 52.7 percent, and 43.1 percent). In addition, less than one-third of housing units are owned by residents, and median owner-occupied home values were slightly over $50,000 dollars in 1990. A drive through these neighborhoods confirms the factor classification *poverty neighborhoods*.

These three zip codes—44108, 44103, and 44104—surround zip code 44106, University Circle. University Circle is unique in having high factor loading on four factors. It is also a poverty neighborhood. The northern and eastern portions of the neighborhood are parts of the Glenville and Hough communities and are indeed poverty-stricken. The neighborhood had a poverty rate of 37.6 percent in 1990 and was the third-poorest in Cleveland. About two-thirds of the residents in the neighborhood are nonwhite. It also has a higher than average percentage of high school dropouts.

At the same time, the neighborhood has a substantial middle-class population, as indicated by the negative sign on the *working-class neighbor-*

hoods factor. Portions of University Circle are indeed middle-class. Areas close to Case Western Reserve University contain beautiful turn-of-the-century homes and upscale business service and retail firms—all characteristic of middle-class neighborhoods. For example, the median value of owner-occupied housing in the neighborhood is about $81,245 (in 1990 dollars), nearly 20 percent higher than the average of all neighborhoods in the sample.

The University Circle neighborhood also has a substantial ethnic population. Zip code 44106 encompasses the "Little Italy" neighborhood of Cleveland. It is the heart of the Italian community in the city with many Italian businesses. It is now becoming a highly desirable place to live in Cleveland and has many new art galleries and custom shops.

The neighborhood had high factor scores on both of the *public services* factors (but only above 1.5 on *public services II*). That is because the neighborhood includes Case Western and the huge medical complexes of the Cleveland Clinic Foundation, University Hospitals, Rainbow Babies and Children's Hospital, and Mt. Sinai Medical Center (now closed). The hospital cluster provides employment for over 18,000 people. In addition, the area hosts a cluster of medical services establishments with a total employment of nearly 2,000. The high factor score on *public services II* stems from a cluster of entertainment establishments employing nearly 1,300 workers. These facilities include Severance Hall, home of the world-famous Cleveland Symphony Orchestra; the Cleveland Museum of Art, one of the premier small museums in the country; the Cleveland Museum of Natural History; the Cleveland Botanical Garden; and the Western Reserve Historical Society.

Zip code neighborhoods 44127 and 44105 cover the North Broadway, South Broadway, Union-Miles Park, and Corlett neighborhoods. They border Cleveland's Industrial Valley—the area along the Cuyahoga River containing all of the old steel mills that gave Cleveland its manufacturing heritage. It is thus not surprising that the neighborhood specializes in *primary metals and related industries*. The zip code 44127 neighborhood is predominantly a manufacturing complex with the core activities in primary metals and fabricated metal products. Three of every four jobs in the neighborhood are in manufacturing (6,737 manufacturing out of 8,828 jobs, or 76 percent). One cluster of firms specializing in primary metals employs nearly 6,000 workers, and another cluster of firms specializing in fabricated metal products employs more than 500 workers.

The zip code neighborhood 44105 also specializes in manufacturing with about 40 percent of all jobs in the area related to manufacturing. A cluster of

164

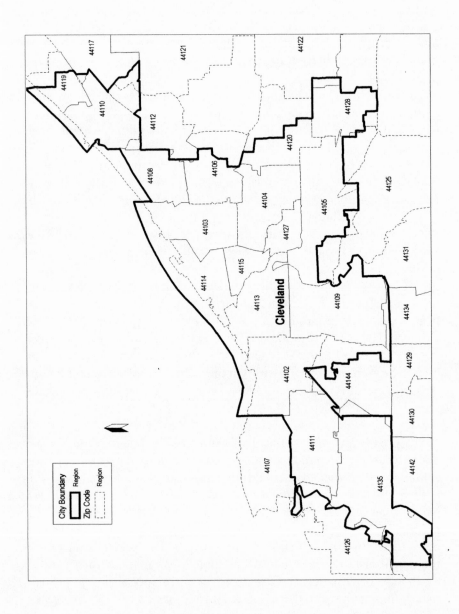

	Poverty	Working-Class	High-Crime	Ethnic	Producer and Personal Services	Strip Shopping	Neighborhood Retail	Primary Metals	Public Services I	Public Services II	Low-Income	Rubber
44102				4.169							2.587	
44103	1.745			1.887								
44104	2.789											
44105				1.527				1.816				
44106	1.925	−1.548		1.513					1.485*	3.063		
44108	1.598											
44109				2.713								
44110												
44111												
44119							2.006					
44120												
44127												
44128												1.821
44135									2.591			
44144												

*Unusual Circumstance

FIGURE 8.3   Cleveland Neighborhood Specializations as Determined by Factor Score

firms in primary metals and fabricated metal products employs about 2,000 workers, 45 percent of all manufacturing employment in the neighborhood. The neighborhood is European ethnic and clearly home to working-class residents. Zip code 44105 is a moderate-poverty neighborhood with a poverty rate of 24.6 percent, and 44127 is a severe-poverty area with a poverty rate over 33 percent. The neighborhood has lower-than-average home values and a higher-than-average percentage of high school dropouts.

Zip code 44104 encompasses the Detroit-Shoreway, Edgewater, and Cudell neighborhoods of Cleveland's west side. It has historically been a European ethnic neighborhood with substantial Italian and Romanian populations. Today, it also has a substantial Hispanic presence and a growing Vietnamese population. It is not classified as a *poverty neighborhood* or a *working-class neighborhood,* yet it has a very high score on the *low-income-area industries* factor. In this case, the designation is not because of check-cashing stores (although there are some) but because of used merchandise stores. For some reason they cluster in the area, between Detroit and Lorain Roads. All kinds of stores sell used furniture and appliances, but there are also many antique stores in the area. It is the center for "antiquing" in Cleveland.

Zip code 44109 is an ethnic neighborhood encompassing the Old Brooklyn, Archwood-Denison, and Clark-Fulton areas of Cleveland. It has an eastern European heritage with many families of Polish and Slovenian backgrounds. There is also a substantial Irish presence in the neighborhood.

In the very northeastern corner of the city is zip code 44119. This neighborhood includes a part of Cleveland's Collinwood neighborhood and part of the city of Euclid. It specializes in *neighborhood retail services* largely because it encompasses a significant part of Euclid's retail strip shopping and the area along Cleveland's East 185th Street known as "Old World Plaza"—and it is a center for grocery stores, new and used car dealers, and gasoline service stations.

Finally, there are zip codes 44144 and 44128. The majority of the area in zip code 44144 is not in Cleveland but in the suburb of Brooklyn, although it does include some of Cleveland's Old Brooklyn neighborhood. The area has an economic specialization in *public services I*. The factor derives not from true public services but from printing and publishing. The industry employs several thousands of workers—almost 50 percent of the employment in the neighborhood. The concentration of employment in printing and publishing is largely due to the presence of American Greetings—one of the largest greeting card companies in America.

Zip code 44128 is the Lee-Miles neighborhood in the southeast corner of the city. The data give the misleading impression that the neighborhood specializes in *rubber products*, but it does not. There are so few establishments in the industry outside of Akron that the presence of a few such firms in a neighborhood gives a statistical indication that it is an important neighborhood employer. The Lee-Miles neighborhood has only a few small rubber firms employing fewer than 100 workers.

Thus, in most cases, the factor analysis is verified through empirical examination. In Cleveland, the factors do capture the characteristics of many of the urban neighborhoods. The neighborhoods not discussed also have all of the activities associated with urban places—they simply do not specialize in any of the dimensions identified by the factor analysis.

Columbus[3]

Columbus is a different case and in fact dominates our study (we explain why later in the chapter). As Figure 8.4 shows, many Columbus neighborhoods have either dominant socioeconomic characteristics or economic specializations, or both. Columbus differs from the other cities we studied because it is spatially huge (it covers 212.6 square miles), because it is the state capital (although we culled most of this impact by excluding downtown employment from the analysis), and because it is the home of Ohio State University with its 55,000 students.

For a large city (population 632,910), Columbus has a very small number of *poverty neighborhoods*—in fact, only two. The two together, known as the Near East Side because of their locational proximity to the Columbus CBD and the fact that they are just east of Interstate 71, are zip codes 43403 and 43205. Both have poverty levels above 40 percent and are characterized as having a worn-out housing stock and numerous boarded-up derelict structures. Another neighborhood somewhat to the north of the Near East Side is Linden (zip code 43211), surrounded on three sides by railroad tracks. Its poverty level is slightly below 40 percent, but it has a very high African American population that gives it a significant negative loading on the *ethnic neighborhood* factor.

Columbus stands out from the other Ohio central cities in the number of neighborhoods classified as middle-class—six neighborhoods. The

---

[3]Our new colleague at the Levin College of Urban Affairs, Cleveland State University, Dr. Brian A. Mikelbank, who received his Ph.D. from Ohio State University, provided us with information on the city of Columbus, June 12, 2000.

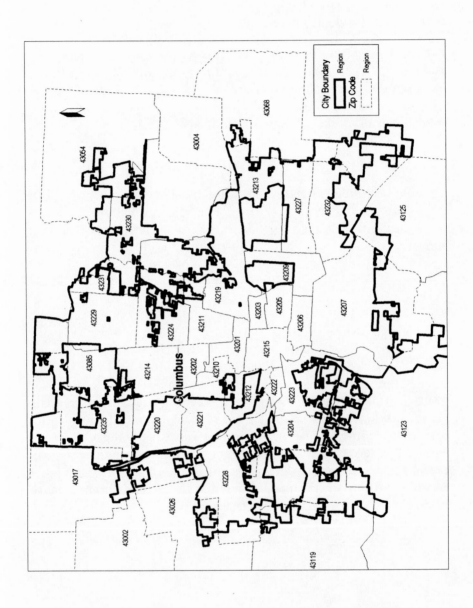

	Poverty	Working-Class	High-Crime	Ethnic	Producer and Personal Services	Strip Shopping	Neighborhood Retail	Primary Metals	Public Services I	Public Services II	Low-Income	Rubber
43017		-2.288			2.115	1.618				6.813		
43085		-1.795			1.401	5.702						
43201			-1.767	1.850								
43202				1.697								
43203	2.319		-1.561									
43204												
43205	1.874											
43206												
43207												
43208												
43209		-1.561										
43210			-2.727	4.107					7.657			
43211				-1.540								
43212		-1.537			1.536							
43213							5.970					
43214		-1.504										
43219												
43220		-2.426			6.199				2.592			
43222												
43223										1.966		
43224			-1.608									
43227												
43228			-1.832			4.166						
43229			-1.679							1.672		
43231			-1.535									
43232			-1.774			4.375						
43235					2.354							

FIGURE 8.4 Columbus Neighborhood Specializations as Determined by Factor Score

first, the Dublin zip code 43017, includes the city of Dublin and a portion of the northwest corner of Columbus. The neighborhood had extremely strong growth during the 1980s. It is a wealthy area with homes ranging from $200,000 to $400,000. The neighborhood had the highest median owner-occupied home value ($208,353) in 1990 among all Ohio central-city neighborhoods under study. In most other cities, this neighborhood would be classified as an "edge city" (Garreau 1991). The area includes a portion of Interstate 270, the beltway around Columbus. It is intensely producer services in terms of the industries that have grown up along the beltway. There is also a *strip shopping* area along Sawmill Road, the main artery running through the neighborhood.

Zip code 43235 is located directly east of Dublin in the extreme northern portion of Columbus and is a neighborhood with population and housing characteristics similar to Dublin's. However, it has an extremely high factor score on *strip shopping*. This is due to the Crosswoods retail area and related developments along Sawmill Road. The strip features stores like Kohl's, Target, Barnes and Noble, Office Max, and a multitude of chain restaurants. A portion of Interstate 270 also runs through the area, bringing accompanying development of producer services industries.

Zip code 43085 is directly east of 43235 but is a much different neighborhood. Known as Worthington, the area is an old-style New England community with its own highly regarded school system. It is a suburban area with older but expensive housing. Worthington Mall provides the neighborhood with commercial activity. The area along High Street is called Old Worthington, which suggests the aura of an old New England town.

Zip code 43209 is directly southeast of Columbus's two poverty neighborhoods. The zip code covers three neighborhoods—Bexley, Eastmore, and Berwick. This near-downtown area is a neighborhood of huge, elegant, old homes and is the city's most prestigious residential neighborhood. Both the governor's mansion and the home of the president of Ohio State University are located in the neighborhood. The Berwick area is an example of one of the city's middle-class racially integrated neighborhoods.

Zip code 43212 is just west of downtown and is an area known as Grandview Heights. It is part of the city but has a separate school system. Homes are of high quality. Grandview Avenue, running through the neighborhood, is a trendy place with a lively restaurant and bar scene. Another shopping area along Fifth Avenue and King Avenue is less trendy with supermarkets and the like.

Zip code 43214 is an area located to the north of the Ohio State University campus (north of the CBD) known as Clintonville. It is a classic close-in suburb—a family-oriented area. A number of OSU faculty and some students live in the area.

Zip code 43220 is Upper Arlington. It is in the northwest area of the city but not as far out as Dublin. Upper Arlington is the city's most elite suburb and has an outstanding school system. The commercial area, located in the northern part of the neighborhood along Henderson Road, has many offices, theaters, and restaurants/bars.

Zip code 43232 in the southeastern corner of Columbus is known as the Brice Road area. It has many large apartment complexes and a huge shopping area. It is home to stores like J.C. Penney, Sears, Target, Best Buy, and numerous car dealerships.

Columbus also has neighborhoods that have significant employment in *public services.* Foremost among these is zip code 43210, which is home to OSU with its student population of almost 55,000 and 31,000 faculty and staff. The area shows up in our statistics as an *ethnic neighborhood* largely because of the international student population.

To the northwest of the university is zip code 43202, which contains enormous apartment complexes supporting Ohio State. This area is also considered an *ethnic neighborhood* because of its large international student population.

Zip code 43229 in the northern portion of Columbus is home to an area known as "The Continent." It is an upscale European-style entertainment center but now losing in popularity. A Budweiser brewery is located in the neighborhood.

Finally, there is one of our favorite neighborhoods—43201. It is south of the university and has many low-cost homes and apartments, usually student rentals. It also contains the neighborhoods of Short North, Victorian Village, and Italian Village. The neighborhood has a high concentration of art galleries and is a busy social place on weekends. Battelle Labs, also located in the neighborhood, was involved with the financing of the renovations in the area.

Dayton[4]

Figure 8.5 shows the concentrations of socioeconomic and industrial clusters for the city of Dayton. Like the other cities in the study, Dayton has its

---

[4]Ms. Jane Dockery of the Center for Urban and Public Affairs, Wright State University, provided us with information on Dayton, May 22, 2000.

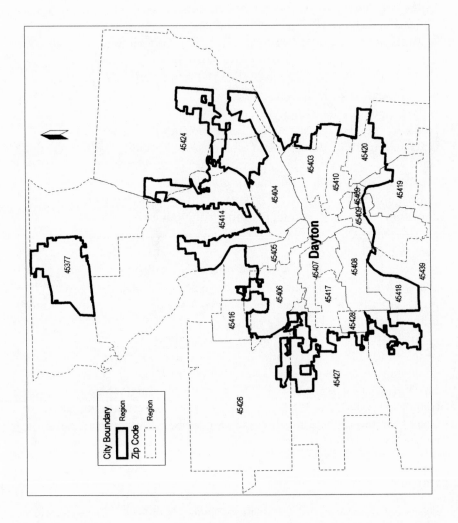

City Boundary

Region

Zip Code

Region

45424
45377
45414
45405
45406
45416
45426
45427
45403
45404
45407
45417
45410
45420
45409 45409
45408
45428
45419
45418
45439

Dayton

	Poverty	Working-Class	High-Crime	Ethnic	Producer and Personal Services	Strip Shopping	Neighbor-hood Retail	Primary Metals	Public Services I	Public Services II	Low-Income	Rubber
45377												
45403												
45404												2.690
45405												
45406												
45407	1.779											
45408	2.085			-1.521							7.714	
45409							5.517					
45410												
45414												
45417												

FIGURE 8.5   Dayton Neighborhood Specializations as Determined by Factor Score

poverty neighborhoods. They are largely contained in zip code neighborhoods 45407 and 45408. Zip code 45407, just west of Dayton's CBD, encompasses the neighborhoods of Five Points, MacFarlane, Wolf Creek, Old Dayton View, Southern Dayton View, and Westwood. The area is extremely poor; in 1990 it had a poverty rate of 41 percent. The area also had a high concentration of nonwhites (95 percent), school dropouts (44 percent), vacant housing (17 percent), and public housing (20 percent). There is very little commercial activity, and many commercial structures are boarded up. In 1990 the area still had some vestiges of its former ethnic population on the western end of the neighborhood. There was a Jewish synagogue in the neighborhood that was at the heart of an eastern European Orthodox Jewish settlement. Several years ago the synagogue was purchased by the Omega Baptist Church. In terms of industry, Reynolds and Reynolds has an automotive forms division in the neighborhood.

The zip code neighborhood 45408, Dayton's other *poverty neighborhood,* is located directly south of 45407. In 1990 it was the poorest neighborhood in the city (46 percent) and had a high concentration of female-headed households (41 percent), high school dropouts (41 percent), and public housing (31 percent). The neighborhoods in this zip code are Carillon, Edgemont, Miami Chapel, Lake View, Madden Hills, Pine View, Highland Hills, and Germantown Meadows. In addition to its poverty identification, 45408 has a strong negative loading on the *ethnic neighborhood* dimension because the neighborhood is heavily African American and nonwhites make up 96 percent of the population. The neighborhood is also different from its 45407 sister in that it has an economic specialization—*low-income-area industries.* Our information source confirmed that the area has economic activity common to poverty neighborhoods, including a number of used merchandise stores (but not antique stores as in Cleveland) and check-cashing stores along the West 3rd Street strip running through the neighborhood. The neighborhood is also home to a major General Motors Delphi Chassis Systems plant and a struggling Franciscan Hospital.

Directly to the east of 45408 is zip code 45409. This neighborhood is located on the south-central border of Dayton and encompasses much of the city of Kettering and a small portion of Oakwood. There are three Dayton neighborhoods in the area—University Park, Shroyer Park, and South Park. University Park is home to the University of Dayton. The commercial activity in the area along Warren/Brown Street is what one would expect in a college neighborhood—bars, fast-food restaurants, and specialty stores. This area is the closest to a middle-income neighborhood in the city.

However, the factor analysis indicates that the area specializes in *neighborhood retail services.* Recall that the establishments with high loadings on this factor are grocery stores, car dealerships, and gasoline stations. These establishments do have a significant presence in the zip code but not in the city of Dayton. They are dominant activities along the South Dixie Highway in Kettering.

As was the case in Cleveland, one Dayton neighborhood, 45404, appears to have a specialization in *rubber products.* But again, there are few rubber product manufacturers in the neighborhood. This is another statistical artifact of the concentration of the industry in Akron.

Toledo[5]

Of Toledo's 13 zip code neighborhoods, four are identified by the factor analysis as having distinguishing neighborhood characteristics (Figure 8.6)—one *poverty neighborhood,* one *working-class neighborhood,* one *high-crime neighborhood,* and one neighborhood with *low-income-area industries.* Zip code 43620 is a neighborhood directly north of Toledo's downtown, abutting the CBD. It is a mixed-income neighborhood with a high poverty level and is known as the Old West End. It was originally Toledo's affluent suburb and the home of the city's major industrialists. Most of the housing is single-family, with structures set well back from the tree-lined streets. The architecture is largely a mix of Victorian through various Greek and Revival styles. The area predates the automobile, and thus there are many carriage houses that have been converted to apartments. The development and growth of Toledo's suburbs in the 1960s and 1970s led to white flight and disinvestment in the community. By 1990 the Old West End was the poorest neighborhood in Toledo with a 43 percent poverty rate and a substantial number of subsidized housing units. In the mid-1980s, however, the gay and arts communities began leading the way toward the rehabilitation of the neighborhood, and the community at large has since begun to reinvest and move back into the area. The National Registry has designated it a historic neighborhood. It has one of the largest collections of Victorian homes in the United States.

[5]Ms. Donna Johnson of the Urban Affairs Center of the University of Toledo provided the information on Toledo's neighborhoods, June 8, 2000.

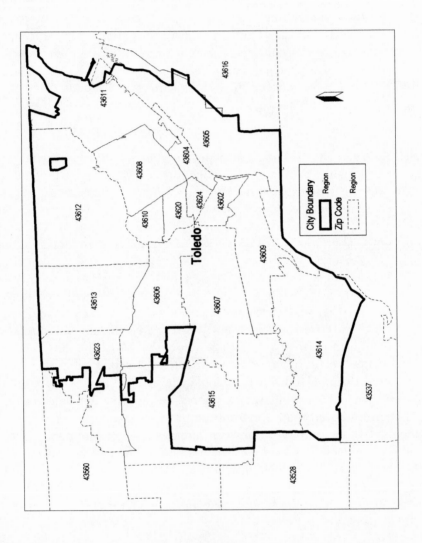

	Poverty	Working-Class	High-Crime	Ethnic	Producer and Personal Services	Strip Shopping	Neighborhood Retail	Primary Metals	Public Services I	Public Services II	Low-Income	Rubber
43605		1.583										
43606												
43607			2.068									
43608												
43609												
43610												
43611												
43612											2.325	
43613												
43614												
43615												
43620	1.823											

FIGURE 8.6   Toledo Neighborhood Specializations as Determined by Factor Score

Zip code 43605 is a *working-class neighborhood* known as the East Side—a reference to its location on the east side of the Maumee River. It is a heavily Catholic, European ethnic neighborhood with French, Irish, German, and Hungarian sections. It also has a growing Hispanic population. It has always been industrial and blue-collar. The East Side is perceived by some as the "poor stepsister" of Toledo by virtue of its blue-collar heritage and its isolation from the rest of Toledo by the Maumee River. Yet it is an interesting place. It is the home of Tony Packo's, a restaurant and bar made famous by Corporal Klinger on the TV show *M.A.S.H.* (anyone who goes to Toledo shouldn't miss it).

Zip code 43607 registers as a *high-crime neighborhood*. It is an inner-city neighborhood extending west from the downtown and encompassing Lenx Hill, originally a German settlement, the Roosevelt and Westmoreland neighborhoods, and the Upton Area and Bancroft Hills. It is a diverse and mostly minority part of town with populations ranging from some of the poorest to affluent middle-class areas. A portion of the area participates in the Department of Justice's Weed and Seed Program.

Finally, one area of Toledo, located in the northern portion of the city, shows a specialization in *low-income-area industries*. The area is known as Washington Township (zip code 43612) and is heavily commercial and industrial. Check-cashing stores are located around the factory areas. Used merchandise stores are part of an old commercial strip in the southern part of the neighborhood along Sylvania Avenue; they include a Goodwill store and several antique and used furniture stores.

Youngstown[6]

Youngstown is different from the other central cities in this study in two ways: It is smaller (1990 population only 95,732), and it has no industrial specializations. The latter feature may be the result of the city's small size, or, as pointed out to us by Dr. Gil Peterson of Youngstown State University, it could be because the city has little industry. Yet two Youngstown neighborhoods are of interest—zip codes 44506 and 44510 (Figure 8.7). Both neighborhoods have a population that is more than 40 percent below the poverty level, both are predominantly African American (69 percent and 81

---

[6]Information on the Youngstown neighborhoods was provided by Dr. Gil Peterson, director of the Public Service Institute, Center for Urban Studies, Youngstown State University, May 25, 2000.

percent respectively), and both are small (neither had even 6,000 residents in 1990), but the factor analysis classifies them very differently. Zip code 44506 is both a *working-class neighborhood* and an *ethnic neighborhood,* and 44510 is a *poverty neighborhood.* Zip code 44510 was the poorest neighborhood in Youngstown in 1990 with 52 percent of residents below the poverty level, followed by zip code 44506 with 47 percent living in poverty.

Zip code 44110 is the neighborhood of Briar Hill, now largely African American but historically one of Youngstown's immigrant stops. It is within walking distance of one of Youngstown's largest steel mills (now closed). One reason for its poverty classification is that Briar Hill contains two large public housing projects (31 percent of all housing in the neighborhood). It is typical of poverty-stricken neighborhoods we have observed in other cities. The neighborhood has the highest school dropout rate (52 percent), the highest percentage of households receiving public assistance (48 percent), and the lowest employment rate (59 percent).

Zip code 44506, the second-poorest neighborhood in Youngstown, encompasses the neighborhoods known as the East Side and Hazelton. The East Side, which is directly east of Youngstown's CBD, is a low-density area with about 20 percent of the land undeveloped. It has a significant and growing Puerto Rican population. Hazelton is an old Slovak neighborhood that still has a significant ethnic presence. Overall, the area has a high concentration of Hispanic residents (20 percent). It also has the lowest median value of owner-occupied housing, the lowest per capita income, the lowest percentage of college graduates, the lowest percentage working in management and the professions, and the highest percentage in labor occupations—all factors contributing to its classification as a *working-class neighborhood.*

Conclusion

Our goals in this chapter were first to describe the industrial structure of central-city neighborhoods, then to study the relationships between the socioeconomic characteristics of urban neighborhoods and their industrial specializations, and finally to conduct a city-by-city examination of neighborhoods with dominant characteristics. Our findings are significant. First, although we recognize that urban economies are regional, we were surprised to find that a substantial number of industries cluster together in central-city neighborhoods in a meaningful way. Our investigation uncovered seven such clusters (eight counting the cluster of a single industry— *rubber products).* Second, we identified a few significant linkages between

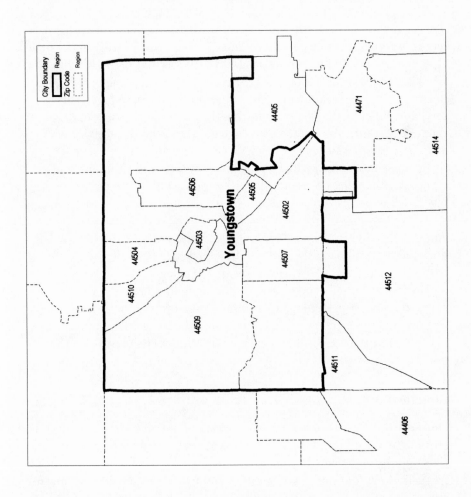

	Poverty	Working-Class	High-Crime	Ethnic	Producer and Personal Services	Strip Shopping	Neighbor-hood Retail	Primary Metals	Public Services I	Public Services II	Low-Income	Rubber
44504												
44505												
44506		2.124		2.001								
44507												
44509												
44510	2.484											
44511												

FIGURE 8.7 Youngstown Neighborhood Specializations as Determined by Factor Score

the socioeconomic characteristics of central-city neighborhoods and industrial clusters. The most important of these in central cities is the strong linkage between *producer and personal services* and *middle-class neighborhoods*.
Finally, through a series of interviews and observations, we were able to
provide a " picture postcard" of urban neighborhoods having dominant socioeconomic characteristics and/or industrial specializations.

Table 8.3 presents a summary of the socioeconomic characteristics and
industrial specializations of our city-by-city analysis (data have been adjusted where required by the case studies, e.g., *rubber products* removed
from Cleveland and Dayton). Overall, some 39 percent of the urban
neighborhoods studied have some sort of strong socioeconomic identity,
and 24 percent have industrial specialization identities. For the most part,
the larger cities have more homogeneous neighborhoods. This is particularly true of Columbus (69 percent) and Cleveland (47 percent). Columbus and Cleveland neighborhoods also rank high in industrial identities—38 and 47 percent respectively. Only Akron was higher (57 percent),
and this is due only to *rubber products.*

Thirteen, also 13 percent, of the urban neighborhoods are classified as
poverty neighborhoods, 10 (10 percent) as *middle-class neighborhoods,* 2 (2
percent) *working-class neighborhoods,* 8 (8 percent) *low-crime neighborhoods,* 3 (3 percent) *high-crime neighborhoods,* and 12 (12 percent) *ethnic
neighborhoods.* Cleveland and Cincinnati have the most *poverty neighborhoods;* Columbus has the majority of *middle-class* and *low-crime neighborhoods.* Columbus is also unique in that it has all of the neighborhoods
with industrial specializations in *strip shopping* and nearly all those in
producer and personal services and *public services* (both *I* and *II*). To some
degree, therefore, Columbus seems to drive the model. But does it?

Columbus is different in several respects. First, with a population of
632,910, it is the largest city in the state and therefore has more neighborhoods. Columbus has 26 zip code neighborhoods, followed by Cincinnati
with 19. But Columbus has 10 neighborhoods with economic specializations, whereas Cincinnati has none. We suggest that this discrepancy is
due to the nature of the cities. Rusk (1993, 1999) has pointed out the
unique nature of Columbus. He calls it an elastic city and compares it
with Cleveland, an inelastic city. Columbus is elastic because it is continu-
ally expanding its boundaries through annexation. For example, Columbus grew from an area of 39 square miles in 1950 to 191 square miles in
1990. In contrast, Cleveland grew from 75 square miles in 1950 to only 77
square miles by 1990 (Rusk 1993, 17). Rusk says it best with the title of his
first book: *Cities Without Suburbs* (1993). Columbus is a city without sub-

TABLE 8.3   Dominant Socioeconomic Characteristics and Industrial Specializations of Ohio Central Cities

	Poverty	Working-class	High-Crime	Ethnic	Producer/Personal Services	Strip Shopping	Neighborhood Retail
Akron	0	1	0	0	1	0	0
Cincinnati	3	2	0	1	0	0	0
Cleveland	4	1	0	5	0	0	1
Columbus	2	6	8	4	5	4	1
Dayton	2	0	0	1	0	0	1
Toledo	1	1	1	0	0	0	0
Youngstown	1	1	0	1	0	0	0
Total	13	12	9	12	6	4	3

	Primary Metals	Public Services I	Public Services II	Low-Income	Rubber	Total Zip Codes
Akron	0	0	0	0	4	7
Cincinnati	0	0	0	0	0	19
Cleveland	2	1	1	1	0	15
Columbus	0	2	3	0	0	26
Dayton	0	0	0	1	0	11
Toledo	0	0	0	1	0	13
Youngstown	0	0	0	0	0	7
Total	2	3	4	3	4	98

	Socioeconomic Identity		Industrial Identity		1990 Population[a]
	n	%	n	%	
Akron	1	14	4	57	165,993
Cincinnati	6	32	0	0	346,092
Cleveland	7	47	7	47	526,778
Columbus	18	69	10	38	725,534
Dayton	2	18	2	18	201,328
Toledo	3	23	1	8	342,671
Youngstown	2	29	0	0	93,098
Total	38	39	24	24	2,401,494

NOTES: [a]Population is aggregated from the zip codes studied in each Ohio central city and does not conform to the population reported for each city in 1990 census, as central business district zip codes were not included and some zip codes studied also encompass portions of adjacent suburbs.

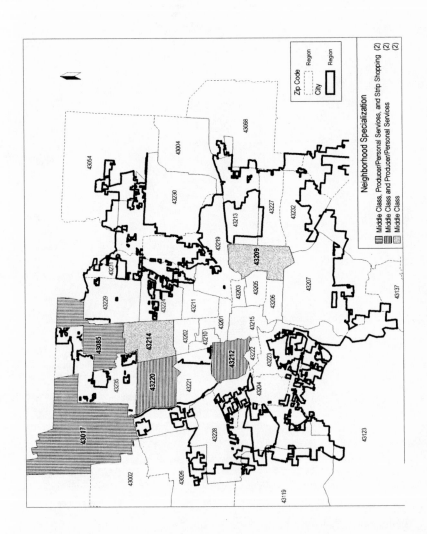

FIGURE 8.8   Columbus Middle-Class, Services, and Strip Shopping Neighborhoods

urbs (not literally). As Columbus's hinterland grew, the city expanded, taking in new population, homes, and economic activity.

Most central cities have one or more middle-class neighborhoods. This is certainly true of the cities studied here, although many of the neighborhoods are not large enough, or wealthy enough, to have been identified in this analysis as *middle-class neighborhoods*. As Figure 8.8 shows, Columbus has six *middle-class neighborhoods*, with four of them being in the extreme northwest area of the city. The map also shows the location of *producer and personal services* and *strip shopping* in the city.

Notice how these neighborhoods overlap, and where they don't overlap, they are in proximity to one another. This connection, of course, is what our correlation coefficients revealed. Thus, Columbus in some ways is different. The sleepy little university-dominated community of the 1950s has grown up—or, more accurately, grown out. In our study, Columbus nicely illustrates the importance of metropolitan integration. Economic functions found in the city of Columbus are certainly present in the other metropolitan areas of the state, but in these inelastic cities, *middle-class neighborhoods* and their accompanying economic activities are found mostly in the suburbs.

It may be that economic activity in areas adjoining neighborhoods may explain the economic activity, or, more accurately, the lack of economic activity, in urban neighborhoods. This is the focus of the next chapter. In Chapter 9 we use simultaneous equation models to examine the impact adjoining neighborhoods have on economic activity.

References

Asher, Herbert B. 1976. *Causal Modeling*. Beverly Hills, CA: Sage Publications.

Davis, James A. 1985. *The Logic of Causal Order*. Beverly Hills, CA: Sage Publications.

Dockery, Jane, Jack Dustin, Gary Gappert, Edward W. Hill, Kent P. Schwirian, Howard A. Stafford, and David Stephens. 1997. "Metropolitan Ohio." In Richard D. Bingham et al., *Beyond Edge Cities*, pp. 45–82. New York: Garland.

Garreau, Joel. 1991. *Edge City: Life on the New Frontier*. New York: Doubleday/Anchor Books.

Rusk, David. 1993. *Cities Without Suburbs*. Washington: Woodrow Wilson Center Press.

_____. 1999. *Inside Game, Outside Game: Winning Strategies for Saving Urban America*. Washington, DC: Brookings Institution Press.

Scott, A. J. 1984. "Industrial Organization and the Logic of Intra-Metropolitan Location III: A Case Study of the Women's Dress Industry in the Greater Los Angeles Region." *Economic Geography* 60: 3–27.

Steed, G.P.F. 1976. "Standardization, Scale, Incubation, and Inertia: Montreal and Toronto Clothing Industries." *Canadian Geographer* 3: 298–309.

9

A Simultaneous Equation Approach for Determining Neighborhood Industry Activity

The distribution of industrial activities across urban neighborhoods is dictated by a host of external and internal factors. Among the external factors are the fluctuation of exogenous demand, technological advances, and increasing interregional and intraregional competition for industry location. Internal factors are those neighborhood-specific variables such as the composition of human capital, the soundness of the housing stock, the socioeconomic well-being of the residents, neighborhood safety, and the like. External forces are important in explaining the changing urban landscape across central cities; internal-specific attributes are more policy-relevant, as they are relatively tangible.

Urban neighborhoods are by no means self-contained economic islands. Rather, they are interwoven in the economic web of a larger unit of the geographic central city, which, together with its suburbs, constitutes the metropolis-based regional economy. Neighborhoods affect and are affected by each other due to pervasive spillover effects. In addition, population-serving industries in one neighborhood are inevitably affecting and affected by those in adjacent neighborhoods, and vice versa. Accordingly, at this point in our study of central-city neighborhoods, it is worthwhile to test a simultaneous model that explores the determinants of neighborhood industry dimensions by incorporating the spatial lag effect.

Model Specification

To examine the effects of neighborhood characteristic dimensions on industry clustering while incorporating spatially lagged industry clustering, we specify a two-stage least square equation as follows. The spatial lagged independent variables (neighborhood socioeconomic dimensions) are used as instruments in the estimation:

Industry factor dimension $_{ij}$ = f (neighborhood socioeconomic dimension$_{ik}$,
spatial lag of industry factor dimension $_{ij}$,
city dummy vector $_n$)   (9.1)

where
i = neighborhood,
j = industry factor (*producer/personal services, strip shopping, neighborhood retail, primary metals, public services I, public services II, low-income-area industries,* and *rubber products*),
k = neighborhood socioeconomic factors (*poverty neighborhood, working-class neighborhood, crime neighborhood,* and *ethnic neighborhood*), and
n = Akron, Cleveland, Cincinnati, Columbus, Dayton, and Toledo. Youngstown is captured in the intercept.

The spatial lag effect may be due to the overall level of industry activities in adjacent neighborhoods. It could also be the result of the concentration of industry activities in a single nearby neighborhood. For example, both the high average level of retailing in adjacent neighborhoods and the presence of heavy concentration of retail shops in one nearby neighborhood may well explain the lower level of retail activities in the primary neighborhood. Consequently, we tested the equation with each of the two specifications of the spatial lagged dependent variable respectively, with the average specification being that the spatial lag is computed as the average value of all adjacent neighborhoods and the maximum specification being that the spatial lag is simply the maximum value among all nearby neighborhoods.

Two-Stage Least Square (2SLS) Results

Equation (9.1) specified above was estimated with the two-stage least square procedure, and the results are summarized in Tables 9.1–9.8 respectively for each of the industry factor dimensions.

Table 9.1 is for the *producer/personal services* factor. In both specifications, the spatially lagged factor has a positive effect on the location of producer and personal services industries in the primary neighborhood, and the effect is statistically significant. Also, the *working-class* factor dimension has a statistically significant negative impact on neighborhood

TABLE 9.1   2SLS Estimates: Producer and Personal Services Industry Factor

Independent Variable	Equation A			Equation B		
	Coefficient	Beta	T	Coefficient	Beta	T
(Constant)	0.158		0.507	0.069		0.213
Spatial lag of dependent variable	0.371	0.272	2.263*	0.247	0.351	2.155*
Neighborhood factor						
Poverty	−0.146	−0.146	−1.786	−0.148	−0.148	−1.724
Working-class	−0.559	−0.559	−5.528***	−0.551	−0.551	−5.088***
Crime	−0.037	−0.037	−0.265	−0.046	−0.046	−0.316
Ethnicity	−0.018	−0.018	−0.204	−0.046	−0.046	−0.490
Intercity dummy						
Akron	0.248	0.064	0.563	0.210	0.054	0.448
Cincinnati	−0.509	−0.202	−1.395	−0.554	−0.220	−1.440
Cleveland	−0.056	−0.020	−0.154	−0.027	−0.010	−0.071
Columbus	−0.133	−0.059	−0.300	−0.312	−0.138	−0.632
Dayton	−0.198	−0.063	−0.516	−0.207	−0.066	−0.512
Toledo	−0.161	−0.055	-0.428	−0.254	−0.087	−0.630
DF	86			86		
Model F	7.692			6.950		
Model significance (p)	0.000			0.000		
R^2	0.496			0.471		
Adjusted R^2	0.431			0.403		

NOTE: Dependent variable: producer and personal services industry factor score

location of industries in producer and personal services, indicating that the location of such industries is favorable to middle-class city neighborhoods. The *poverty* dimension also imposes a negative influence in the neighborhood clustering of producer and personal services industries, but it is not significant at the level we defined in this study. Variations across Ohio central cities are insignificant.

In the neighborhood clustering of *strip shopping* (Table 9.2) and *neighborhood retail* (Table 9.3), no variable on the right side of the equation is statistically significant. However, the spatial lag has positive signs in both specifications for the *strip shopping* model. It is also positive in lag specification of the maximum value of nearby neighborhoods for the *neighborhood retail* model. Both suggest that the location of

TABLE 9.2   2SLS Estimates: Strip Shopping Industry Factor

Independent Variable	Equation A			Equation B		
	Coefficient	Beta	T	Coefficient	Beta	T
(Constant)	0.127		0.311	−0.085		−0.163
Spatial lag of dependent variable	0.977	0.431	1.166	0.562	0.764	1.036
Neighborhood factor						
Poverty	−0.126	−0.126	−0.775	−0.093	−0.093	−0.439
Working-class	−0.017	−0.017	−0.141	0.016	0.016	0.105
Crime	−0.096	−0.096	−0.517	−0.143	−0.143	−0.648
Ethnicity	−0.165	−0.165	−1.310	−0.132	−0.132	−0.800
Intercity dummy						
Akron	−0.233	−0.060	−0.416	−0.050	−0.013	−0.071
Cincinnati	−0.088	−0.035	−0.157	−0.229	−0.091	−0.375
Cleveland	0.078	0.028	0.158	−0.028	−0.010	−0.049
Columbus	0.078	0.035	0.133	−0.593	−0.263	−0.558
Dayton	−0.217	−0.069	−0.403	−0.202	−0.064	−0.313
Toledo	−0.046	−0.016	−0.093	−0.040	−0.014	−0.068
DF	86			86		
Model F	2.096			1.466		
Model significance (p)	0.029			0.159		
R^2	0.216			0.158		
Adjusted R^2	0.111			0.050		

NOTE: Dependent variable: strip shopping industry factor score

nearby *strip shopping* and *neighborhood retail* activities positively influences that of similar industries in the primary neighborhood. Intercity differences are insignificant.

For the *primary metals* factor, the 2SLS result is summarized in Table 9.4. It is noteworthy that the *working-class neighborhood* characteristic dimension has a significant positive impact on the neighborhood location of industries in the *primary metals* factor. Intercity differences are not observed.

Tables 9.5 and 9.6 present the 2SLS estimates for *public services I* and *public services II*. The *public services I* factor is clearly adversely affected by the *crime* dimension of neighborhood characteristics and positively by the *ethnic* factor. Significant cross-city variations are not present. The

TABLE 9.3   2SLS Estimates: Neighborhood Retail Industry Factor

Independent Variable	Equation A			Equation B		
	Coefficient	*Beta*	*T*	*Coefficient*	*Beta*	*T*
(Constant)	−0.824		−1.038	−0.160		−0.335
Spatial lag of						
dependent variable	−1.849	−0.896	−1.003	0.348	0.447	0.385
Neighborhood factor						
Poverty	−0.068	−0.068	−0.495	−0.107	−0.107	−0.755
Working-class	0.008	0.008	0.049	−0.065	−0.065	−0.493
Crime	−0.308	−0.308	-1.319	−0.352	−0.352	−1.360
Ethnicity	0.025	0.025	0.160	0.124	0.124	0.655
Intercity dummy						
Akron	0.731	0.189	0.849	0.135	0.035	0.199
Cincinnati	0.600	0.239	0.831	0.114	0.045	0.192
Cleveland	0.703	0.254	0.977	0.131	0.047	0.186
Columbus	0.206	0.091	0.258	−0.685	−0.304	−0.445
Dayton	2.359	0.748	1.547	0.501	0.159	0.371
Toledo	0.748	0.255	0.986	0.196	0.067	0.310
DF	86			86		
Model F	0.562			0.641		
Model significance (p)	0.854			0.789		
R^2	0.067			0.075		
Adjusted R^2	−0.052			−0.042		

NOTE: Dependent variable: neighborhood retail industry factor score

model was not successful in explaining variations in *public services II* factorial dimension across neighborhoods.

The *low-income-area industries* model estimates are summarized in Table 9.7. The *poverty* factor is the only variable with a significant positive impact on the location of these industries. As presented in Table 9.8, none of the explanatory variables has a significant influence on the neighborhood specialization of *rubber products* industries.

Discussion

This 2SLS estimating with the incorporation of the spatially lagged dependent variable met with moderate success. Several observations can be

TABLE 9.4   2SLS Estimates: Primary Metals Industry Factor

Independent Variable	Equation A			Equation B		
	Coefficient	Beta	T	Coefficient	Beta	T
(Constant)	−0.234		−0.651	1.063		0.312
Spatial lag of						
dependent variable	2.138	0.940	0.825	−3.226	−4.376	−0.407
Neighborhood factor						
Poverty	−0.127	−0.127	−0.889	0.866	0.866	0.383
Working-class	0.207	0.207	1.940*	−0.077	−0.077	−0.099
Crime	0.083	0.083	0.511	0.050	0.050	0.068
Ethnicity	0.033	0.033	0.325	−0.176	−0.176	−0.244
Intercity dummy						
Akron	0.457	0.118	0.473	−1.339	−0.347	−0.380
Cincinnati	0.514	0.204	0.747	−1.247	−0.496	−0.333
Cleveland	−0.444	−0.161	−0.267	6.429	2.327	0.467
Columbus	0.607	0.269	0.836	−0.617	−0.274	−0.208
Dayton	0.404	0.128	0.606	−1.702	−0.540	−0.368
Toledo	0.247	0.084	0.400	−1.095	−0.373	−0.354
DF	86			86		
Model F	1.964			0.100		
Model significance (p)	0.042			0.999		
R^2	0.201			0.012		
Adjusted R^2	0.099			−0.113		

NOTE: Dependent variable: primary metals industry factor score

made from this exercise. First, neighborhood clustering of *producer and personal services* industries is affected not only by characteristics related to middle-class neighborhoods but also by the nearby clustering of the same types of industries. This observation is consistent with the findings presented earlier. This also suggests that industries in *producer and personal services* tend to form larger clusters across urban neighborhoods. Second, *strip shopping* may not be a phenomenon that is confined to neighborhood. Rather, it is more likely that such clustering tends to service multiple neighborhoods. Third, the *primary metals* factorial dimension is found to be significantly determined by *working-class neighborhood* characteristics, another observation that is consistent with our earlier findings. This is largely due to the fact that the host neighborhoods were developed and have evolved over time around this industry specialization.

TABLE 9.5   2SLS Estimates: Public Services I Industry Factor

Independent Variable	Equation A			Equation B		
	Coefficient	Beta	T	Coefficient	Beta	T
(Constant)	0.172		0.344	−0.088		−0.212
Spatial lag of						
dependent variable	1.125	0.476	1.327	0.223	0.324	1.303
Neighborhood factor						
Poverty	0.027	0.027	0.218	0.026	0.026	0.240
Working-class	−0.010	−0.010	−0.062	−0.044	−0.044	−0.334
Crime	−0.543	−0.543	−2.590*	−0.515	−0.515	−2.757**
Ethnicity	0.365	0.365	2.357*	0.370	0.370	2.602*
Intercity dummy						
Akron	0.100	0.026	0.149	0.251	0.065	0.432
Cincinnati	0.159	0.063	0.281	0.265	0.105	0.535
Cleveland	−0.346	−0.125	−0.604	−0.228	−0.082	−0.458
Columbus	−0.803	−0.357	−1.182	−0.799	−0.354	−1.289
Dayton	0.202	0.064	0.310	0.444	0.141	0.833
Toledo	0.259	0.088	0.439	0.366	0.125	0.710
DF	86			86		
Model F	1.905			2.312		
Model significance (p)	0.495			0.016		
R^2	0.196			0.228		
Adjusted R^2	0.093			0.129		

NOTE: Dependent variable: public services I industry factor score

Fourth, *crime* is found to have a significant adverse effect on the location of industries in *public services I*. Firms in this group avoid high-crime areas. However, the cause and effect in this case may also run in the opposite direction: Heightened security measures adopted by firms in the *public services I* factor (typically, large medical complex and educational institutions) may have significantly deterred various crimes. The observation of a positive effect of *ethnic neighborhood* may well be explained by the fact that there are high concentrations of ethnic residents in the neighborhoods as a result of internationals and people of all ethnic backgrounds working and studying in those large medical complexes and universities. Finally, the *low-income-area industries* are significantly associated with neighborhood *poverty*, an observation in accord with our earlier findings and other findings reported in the literature.

TABLE 9.6   2SLS Estimates: Public Services II Industry Factor

Independent Variable	Equation A			Equation B		
	Coefficient	Beta	T	Coefficient	Beta	T
(Constant)	−0.047		−0.061	−0.260		−0.394
Spatial lag of						
dependent variable	0.367	0.160	0.180	0.865	1.035	0.882
Neighborhood factor						
Poverty	0.122	0.122	0.559	0.004	0.004	0.015
Working-class	−0.196	−0.196	−1.074	0.014	0.014	0.042
Crime	−0.104	−0.104	−0.336	−0.195	−0.195	−0.592
Ethnicity	0.104	0.104	0.518	0.169	0.169	0.790
Intercity dummy						
Akron	0.106	0.027	0.167	0.076	0.020	0.085
Cincinnati	−0.063	−0.025	−0.124	0.040	0.016	0.051
Cleveland	0.127	0.046	0.110	−0.499	−0.181	−0.418
Columbus	−0.037	−0.016	−0.028	−1.213	−0.538	−0.670
Dayton	0.234	0.074	0.269	0.147	0.047	0.174
Toledo	0.141	0.048	0.224	−0.060	−0.020	−0.071
DF	86			86		
Model F	0.712			0.387		
Model significance (p)	0.724			0.978		
R^2	0.083			0.047		
Adjusted R^2	−0.034			−0.074		

NOTE: Dependent variable: public services II industry factor score

TABLE 9.7   2SLS Estimates: Low-Income-Area Industries Factor

Independent Variable	Equation A			Equation B		
	Coefficient	Beta	T	Coefficient	Beta	T
(Constant)	−0.296		−0.670	−0.346		−0.831
Spatial lag of						
dependent variable	0.234	0.159	0.486	0.135	0.185	0.598
Neighborhood factor						
Poverty	0.237	0.237	2.056*	0.240	0.240	2.135*
Working-class	−0.017	−0.017	−0.143	−0.022	−0.022	−0.182
Crime	−0.030	−0.030	−0.147	−0.026	−0.026	−0.134
Ethnicity	−0.036	−0.036	−0.305	−0.034	−0.034	−0.286
Intercity dummy						
Akron	0.125	0.032	0.221	0.091	0.024	0.159
Cincinnati	0.292	0.116	0.577	0.274	0.109	0.536
Cleveland	0.396	0.143	0.764	0.368	0.133	0.703
Columbus	0.125	0.055	0.209	0.048	0.021	0.076
Dayton	0.696	0.221	0.922	0.641	0.203	0.857
Toledo	0.357	0.122	0.696	0.281	0.096	0.512
DF	86			86		
Model F	1.224			1.22		
Model significance (p)	0.283			0.286		
R^2	0.135			0.135		
Adjusted R^2	0.025			0.024		

NOTE: Dependent variable: low-income-area industries factor score

TABLE 9.8   2SLS Estimates: Rubber Products Industry Factor

Independent Variable	Equation A			Equation B		
	Coefficient	Beta	T	Coefficient	Beta	T
(Constant)	−0.825		−1.315	−0.551		−1.587
Spatial lag of dependent variable	−1.161	−0.854	−0.574	0.318	0.333	0.376
Neighborhood factor						
Poverty	0.018	0.018	0.165	0.021	0.021	0.234
Working-class	0.135	0.135	1.139	0.178	0.178	1.454
Crime	0.005	0.005	0.028	0.059	0.059	0.358
Ethnicity	0.069	0.069	0.595	0.069	0.069	0.686
Intercity dummy						
Akron	5.117	1.325	1.123	1.517	0.393	0.560
Cincinnati	−0.049	−0.019	−0.072	0.239	0.095	0.580
Cleveland	0.962	0.348	1.219	0.329	0.119	0.400
Columbus	0.496	0.220	0.882	0.310	0.138	0.505
Dayton	0.917	0.291	1.108	0.329	0.104	0.467
Toledo	0.620	0.211	0.991	0.220	0.075	0.351
DF	86			86		
Model F	3.251			4.320		
Model significance (p)	0.001			0.000		
R^2	0.293			0.356		
Adjusted R^2	0.203			0.276		

NOTE: Dependent variable: rubber products industry factor score

10

Poverty, Race,
Industry Location,
and Urban Neighborhoods

We hope this book has provided a comprehensive view of the economies and social structure of certain urban neighborhoods. Of course, it does not pertain to all urban neighborhoods, but rather it deals with the neighborhoods of central cities that are similar to Ohio's—primarily those cities of moderate size located in the Northeast and Midwest.

We believe this book is the first study of its kind; it was made possible only through access to the Ohio Economic Development Database, which provided industrial data at the zip code level. We have thus been able to examine neighborhood economies empirically and relate those economies to other neighborhood characteristics.

A number of observations can be made from this analysis. These observations concern the centrality of poverty neighborhoods, the diversity and specialization of urban neighborhoods, the development of neighborhood economies, and some speculation about how these economies fit into their regions.

The Centrality of Poverty Neighborhoods

Neighborhoods with more than 30 percent of the residents below the poverty level make up almost half of the urban neighborhoods in Ohio's central cities. This characteristic is pervasive. As we found in Chapter 4 in the factor analysis of the independent variables, poverty was the first dimension identified—explaining 32 percent of the variance. Poverty neighborhoods are not just poor neighborhoods; they are neighborhoods that have disproportionate levels of other negative characteristics of urban life. These include female-headed households, joblessness, deteriorating housing stock, low-income housing, low levels of educational attainment, more discouraged workers, and a host of other urban ills. Poverty neighborhoods also have high percentages of nonwhite residents (discussed in more detail later).

Three features stand out about the economies of poverty neighborhoods:

1. There is no particular shortage of jobs in poverty neighborhoods in general (although there is in certain poverty neighborhoods, just as there is in certain middle-class neighborhoods).
2. In some industries, the nature of the establishments in poverty neighborhoods is different from that in other neighborhoods.
3. Some industries are averse to poverty neighborhoods.

In the conduct of this study, we noted that there are plenty of jobs in poverty neighborhoods of Ohio's central cities. But these jobs tend to be in selected industries: Specifically, certain manufacturing (both durable and nondurable goods) and social service industries have a significant presence in poverty neighborhoods.

But this is not because these industries chose to locate in poverty neighborhoods. Most *are* located there because they *were* located there. That is, they were there before the neighborhoods became poverty neighborhoods. For example, a Cleveland poverty neighborhood is home to LTV Steel, the largest steel mill in Cleveland that opened its main production facility at its present location in 1942. Another Cleveland poverty neighborhood hosts the world-famous Cleveland Clinic Foundation, a huge medical complex that has been in its present location since 1924 and has adapted itself to changes in the neighborhood over time. At the time these facilities opened, the neighborhoods were working-class and middle-class respectively. They are no longer so today. But both firms have huge investments in physical structures that cannot realistically be abandoned. After all, a steel mill is hardly an attraction for burglars. And the Cleveland Clinic adapted to neighborhood change by substantially increasing security.

This location factor is called inertia—the tendency to stay put (Blair and Premus 1993; Blair 1995). Inertia is at work in industry location because many forces operate to keep the firm where it is once it is established at a location. Sources of this locational inertia include (1) locational factors that led to the initial selection remain unchanged; (2) the economic and social structures of an area may evolve to reinforce the location; (3) consideration of keeping the firm's workforce intact; and (4) irrelevance of location of a firm that serves the entire region and beyond (e.g., Cleveland Clinic).

Then there are differences in establishments in the same industry between those located in poverty neighborhoods and those located in other neighborhoods. The obvious examples are grocery stores and financial institutions. For both of these industries, there are few differences in the number of establishments between poverty neighborhoods and other neighborhoods, but there are other differences (e.g., size of establishments). In an earlier study, for example, we found that supermarkets were clearly related to middle-class neighborhoods, and mom-and-pop groceries frequently serviced poverty neighborhoods (Bingham and Zhang 1997).

The same sort of pattern exists with financial institutions. Although all urban neighborhoods have traditional banks, they are fewer and smaller in poverty neighborhoods, and they are being replaced by check-cashing stores. Both are depository institutions (SIC 60), but qualitatively, there is a world of difference between them. Whereas traditional financial institutions strengthen neighborhoods through reinvestment—healthy credit flow in the form of home mortgages, equity loans, and so forth—check-cashing outlets provide only cash transactions. Moreover, the cost of these informal transactions varies inversely with the economic status of the area's households (Dymski and Veitch 1996).

Finally, we found that some industries are positively averse to the characteristics associated with poverty neighborhoods. This was shown by the zero-order correlation coefficients in Chapters 5 through 7. Industries particularly averse to poverty neighborhoods (in terms of employment) are

- Credit reporting and collecting
- Banking
- Security and commodity brokers
- Insurance
- Real estate
- Engineering and management services
- Building materials and garden supplies
- General merchandise stores
- Grocery stores
- Automobile dealers
- Gasoline service stations
- Furniture and home furnishing stores
- Drug stores and proprietary stores
- Hotels

- Eating and drinking establishments
- Laundry
- Barber and beauty shops
- Entertainment

Thus, as this list shows, neighborhoods with some or all of the characteristics of poor neighborhoods lack many retail and personal service activities. This deficiency is truly unfortunate because these industries can provide entry-level jobs into the workforce.

Race

Race and poverty are confounding factors in urban neighborhoods for the obvious reason that high-poverty neighborhoods tend to be largely nonwhite. We have tried several different methods to isolate race from poverty to determine if industries avoid nonwhite neighborhoods regardless of economic status. The evidence suggests that they do, but in a limited way.

In Chapter 7 we computed partial correlation coefficients between percent nonwhite and employment in those industries having statistically significant zero-order relationships between percent nonwhite and employment. Very few of the partials were statistically significant. Race (percent nonwhite) was independently and negatively related to only producer services in general, and to depository institutions, insurance agents, miscellaneous business services, and service stations in particular. In these four cases, there were weak but nonetheless significant independent negative relationships between percent nonwhite and neighborhood employment in these producer-oriented and consumer-oriented industries.

Thus the question is, do industries discriminate against neighborhoods because of race (because they are nonwhite)? The answer is yes, but not much. Can we quantify "not much"? No, but all of the evidence we have examined indicates that the racial discrimination, alone, is not very powerful. Of course, any discrimination based on race alone is unacceptable, but the extent to which it exists is quite limited.

Diversity and Specialization of Urban Neighborhoods

Central-city neighborhoods are indeed highly diverse: Healthy neighborhoods coexist with deteriorating ones in all aspects of social and economic well-being. In Chapter 4 we showed some of this diversity in terms of neighborhood social characteristics, and in Chapter 8 we showed it in terms of economic characteristics. Although the bundle of neighborhoods is diverse, a number of individual neighborhoods themselves tend to be quite homogeneous, socially and/or economically. The factor analysis in Chapter 4 clearly illustrates the social diversity. The first factor generated captured an extreme—*poverty neighborhoods*. This factor encompasses many of the negative aspects of urban neighborhoods: low levels of education, high poverty, high concentration of discouraged workers, and the like. What this factor does not capture, because it does not exist in these neighborhoods, is the immediate access to a diversity of businesses and stores. But that is another matter.

The second factor—*working-class neighborhoods*—captured two significant neighborhood characteristics on one dimension. First is the working-class dimension itself that is embodied in the higher percentage of working-age population in labor occupations; second is the characteristic related to a lower proportion of residents in management and professional occupations, a lower-valued housing stock, fewer residents with college degrees, a high percentage of residents with a high school (only) education, and the like. A high negative loading on this dimension indicates middle-class neighborhoods.

Just as some neighborhoods tend to be homogeneous socially, some neighborhoods are homogeneous economically. Economically homogeneous neighborhoods exhibit economic specializations, much in the way many cities do. The industry factors we identified in Ohio central cities are *producer and personal services, specialized strip shopping, neighborhood retail services, primary metals and fabricated metal products, public services I, public services II,* and *rubber products.*

However, as Figures 8.1 through 8.7 show, many urban neighborhoods in Ohio's central cities do not specialize. These neighborhoods exhibit diversity without the extremes. They are ordinary urban neighborhoods, neither rich nor poor, and they have no overall economic specializations. They are heterogeneous neighborhoods.

On the other hand, Ohio central cities have many homogeneous neighborhoods. Some 39 percent of the urban neighborhoods studied had some sort of strong socioeconomic identity, and 24 percent had a generalizable industrial specialization. These numbers are significant. Now when we discuss *poverty neighborhoods,* we are not discussing only the people who live in those neighborhoods but the industrial structure (actually, lack of it) as well. And when we discuss neighborhoods that specialize in *producer and personal services,* we are also talking about the middle-class population residing there. The empirical evidence is compelling.

Development of Neighborhood Economies

How do neighborhood economies become what they are? We cannot definitively answer that question for all neighborhood economies, but our findings allow us to speculate about certain industrial specializations—specifically producer services, retail services, and personal services. Recall that producer services industries include banking, insurance, real estate, accounting, and legal services. Personal services include hotels, eating and drinking establishments, laundry, entertainment, and the like. These industries tend to locate in neighborhoods where the housing stock is sound, the supply of an educated labor force is present, and the demand for services is high. They are "footloose" industries. It is difficult for a hospital to pick up and move, but a law office can easily do so. The same holds true for all retail establishments—they can relocate with relative ease.

Indeed, this is clearly what happens. As a neighborhood begins to change, it is perceived as "going downhill." Then footloose businesses concerned with "image" either move out of the neighborhood to a more desirable one (perhaps in an edge city) or elect not to open an establishment in the neighborhood. And the cycle begins. It is a cycle of disinvestment by the kinds of firms that respond to the changing characteristics of the neighborhoods. Producer service firms want to locate in good neighborhoods to project an image to the clients they serve. And since the clients they serve are not neighborhood-based, these firms can locate anywhere, within reason, in the metropolitan area. The other footloose industries—retail and personal services—are more closely tied to the local economy and are demand-driven. In their search for profits, they will locate in the neighborhood where demand for their products or services is greatest. Like it or not, this is how the market works.

Neighborhood economies in Ohio central cities have evolved over a long time span. The economies of central-city neighborhoods we observe today are the result of a confluence of factors. Central-city neighborhood economies in Midwest and Northeast regions have been losers in most recent rounds of economic competition. At the intraregional level, central-city neighborhoods are collectively victims of suburbanization of population and industries. This result has been well documented in the literature. At the interregional level, central-city neighborhoods are together victims of the sun-belt movement of population and industries. At the industrial structure level, central-city neighborhoods are victims of the economic restructuring that has resulted in the erosion of most of the central-city economic base, which once was centered on relatively high-wage and low-skilled manufacturing industries. The shift of the industrial structure of the U.S. economy away from manufacturing, in which all Ohio central cities were specialized, has also inevitably contributed to the decline in the economies of central-city neighborhoods. Today, the economy is increasingly driven by footloose high-tech industries that put heavy emphasis on such location requirements as the high-skilled labor pool and regional infrastructures that promote localization economies. High-tech-oriented industrial development has ubiquitously favored suburbs across literally all U.S. regional economies in the past several decades. Consequently, strenuous and well-intended efforts to retain and attract industry across central-city neighborhoods have not produced significant results. Although central cities like Cleveland have made remarkable comebacks, these recoveries have been largely confined to the revival of the central business district. Also, although the job market has been tight and the national economy has enjoyed nearly uninterrupted growth in the past decade, many central-city low-skilled workers have been unable to ride with this high-skill and high-wage growth economy. On the contrary, the earnings gap between high-skilled and low-skilled workers has increasingly widened.

Central-City Neighborhoods and the Suburbs

In Chapter 8 we concluded that Columbus was not "like" other Ohio central cities because it was a city without suburbs (Rusk 1993). Thus, when we generalize about central-city neighborhood economies, we are talking not about David Rusk's elastic cities but about the majority of older central cities—inelastic cities.

The economies of suburban neighborhoods are not merely extensions of the central-city neighborhoods they surround. They are very different. Although the suburbs have been studied and speculated about for years (e.g., Fishman 1987), it was Joel Garreau's *Edge City* (1991) that first brought the differences in the economies of suburbs and central cities to the attention of the general public and renewed academic interest in regional economies. This book is a part of that jigsaw puzzle. Garreau offered a five-part definition of an edge city:

- *Has 5 million square feet or more of leasable office space.* This workplace of the information age has more square footage of office space than exists in downtown Memphis.

- *Has 600,000 square feet of leasable retail space.* This is the equivalent of a fair-sized mall containing three department stores and 80 to 100 shops and boutiques.
- *Has more jobs than bedrooms.* Like that of downtowns, the population of edge cities increases during the day.
- *Is perceived by the population as one place.* It has everything from jobs to shopping to entertainment.
- *Was nothing like a "city" as recently as thirty years ago.* The area was probably farm land or suburbs.

Garreau's examples include Tysons Corner, Virginia; the Massachusetts turnpike and Route 128; the Schaumburg area outside Chicago; and the Galleria area of Houston.

A few years ago the Urban University Program (UUP) of the Ohio Board of Regents provided funding for a study of Ohio's edge cities and emerging edge cities using the same data set we have used here (Bingham et al. 1997). Although the statistical methods used were slightly different (cluster analysis versus factor analysis), a comparison of our findings with this study of suburban economies is useful. The UUP study, like ours, combined quantitative analysis with case studies. It identified sixteen edge cities or emerging edge cities surrounding Ohio's seven central cities (studied here). Like some of our urban neighborhoods, the Ohio edge cities tended to be specialized in certain industries. Furthermore, the classification of industries in this study was the same that we initially adopted and described in Chapter 3. The specializations of the edge cities are as follows:

- *Balanced—retail and personal services*   4 edge cities
- *Balanced—wholesale and social services*   3 edge cities
- *Manufacturing*   2 edge cities
- *Services (of all kinds)*   2 edge cities
- *Information/producer services*   2 edge cities
- *Social services*   2 edge cities
- *Retail*   1 edge city

The first two classifications, *balanced*, are fairly representative of all edge cities but with slight specializations—and thus the term *balanced*. (The case studies showed that the edge cities specializing in social services really did not do so.)

Three cases exhibit a close correspondence between the central-city neighborhood specializations we have identified here and the specializations of Ohio's edge cities. In Columbus, the *retail* edge city is referred to as Columbus West. It is zip code 43228 and lies mostly within the western edge of the city of Columbus. Here we identified zip code 43228 as specializing in *strip shopping*.

In our study we found that a number of the neighborhoods in northwest Columbus had industrial specializations in *producer and personal services*. This area of Columbus is called Upper Arlington in the UUP study and is identified as specializing in *services*. Here is another good fit.

Finally, Akron's West Akron and Fairlawn Heights neighborhoods in the northwest corner of the city specialize in *producer and personal services*. This area is adjacent to the emerging edge city of Montrose, which is a *balanced* edge city but has an agglomeration in *personal services*. This comparison is also a good fit.

Public services are also a specialization of the suburbs (termed *social services* in the UUP study), but much of the specialization there is in health and hospitals.

Overall, there is a reasonable correspondence between the two studies in their examination of neighborhood economic specializations. However, almost all of this correlation is due to Columbus with its disproportionate share of neighborhoods having specific economic specializations: Columbus accounts for five of the six neighborhoods with economic specializations in *producer and personal services;* all four with specializations in *strip shopping;* one of the three specializing in *neighborhood retail;* and five of the seven with *public services* specializations.

But Columbus is an elastic city, and the other Ohio central cities are not. Columbus has therefore absorbed the suburban economies in the other regions. For Columbus, the suburbs are a simple extension of the city's neighborhood economies; for the other six central cities they are not. The neighborhood economies of the central-city neighborhoods and the suburban neighborhoods are quite different. The edge-city neighborhoods are vibrant, growing, and technology-based. The neighborhoods in the inelastic central cities are not.

Central-City Economies and Urban Policy

In the past, when we have talked with community development specialists, we always noted how proud they were when they showed us a small strip mall or chain grocery store that they were able to secure for their neighborhoods. Of course, it's normal for people to be proud of their work, but we took these "incidents" with a grain of salt. So someone convinced a grocery chain to open a store in the neighborhood: What's the big deal? We now know it is a big deal. It is a big deal because it runs counter to all of the market forces that keep grocery stores out of *poverty neighborhoods*. It is a big deal because it is an important step in neighborhood development.

If there is one thing this study has shown, it is that communities cannot concentrate neighborhood rehabilitation or development efforts on one or two neighborhood problems. A neighborhood cannot be "fixed," for example, simply by focusing on housing rehabilitation or economic development. We believe the results of our study confirm that this narrow approach is an exercise in futility. Neighborhoods can be improved only by concentrating effort on the whole range of problems that plague inner-city urban neighborhoods. In an economic development sense, market-force factors are simply too great to be overcome to any significant degree by the efforts of community activists. Economic development will come only as neighborhoods are revitalized in their entirety.

The other urban "fact of life" we have confirmed is the economic reality of David Rusk's book *Cities Without Suburbs*. Cities without suburbs are economically healthy because they have the same economic characteristics, and specializations, as their metropolitan region as a whole. Inelastic cities do not have these specializations, nor are they likely to get them. Central-city neighborhoods do not have the advantages of upscale housing, high-tech industries, or significant retail agglomerations. Today, these are suburban functions.

The redevelopment of urban neighborhood economies is by no means hopeless. Many central-city neighborhoods do possess locational advantages such as proximity to the downtown business district and to regional nodes of transportation. Other central-city neighborhoods are situated next to thriving suburban areas. This locational factor contributes to competitive advantages of central-city neighborhoods, a premise that has recently been advocated (Porter 1995). Methods have been developed to help regions identify their competitive advantages (see, for example, the February 2000 issue of *Economic Development Quarterly* for a discussion of industry clusters). Some, but by no means all, urban neighborhoods develop economic specializations. But economic specialization does not necessarily make a healthy neighborhood. Sometimes heterogeneous neighborhoods are the most livable.

Our journey in the study of the economies of central-city neighbor-hoods further allows us to propose at least three perspectives regarding future redevelopment. First, each central-city neighborhood is an integral part of the city's economic base, rather than being a self-contained eco-nomic unit. Neighborhood spillover effects are pervasive, and it is diffi-cult for neighborhood-specific micro redevelopment efforts, no matter how well intended, to reap sustainable results.

Second, central-city neighborhoods are not collectively an economic island. They are an integral part of the metropolitan economy. True, cen-tral cities and their suburbs are competitors for economic resources and population within intra-metropolitan space. However, they are a com-plement to each other beyond the metropolitan space. Their economic fortunes are increasingly interdependent on, rather than independent of, each other because they compete together for economic resources and population with their counterparts in other regions of the national econ-omy and even in other economies of the globe. Central cities and their suburbs collectively contribute to the economic advantage of the metro-politan space they share. With this strategic perspective, the redevelop-ment of central-city neighborhood economies is no longer an isolated, piecemeal effort.

Finally, salient characteristics of any poverty-stricken central-city neighborhood are rampant joblessness, concentration of school dropouts among the working-age population, and a high level of dependency on welfare. Urban neighborhoods literally can be revitalized by renewing and rebuilding a physical housing stock. However, any improvements and de-velopment cannot be sustained if these neighborhoods cannot overcome their human-capital deficit. Welfare benefits and other public capital can revitalize a neighborhood, but this flow of resources cannot produce sus-tainable development if it is not directed at the accumulation of neigh-borhood human capital. Much of urban economic development has fo-cused on bringing low-wage jobs into neighborhoods. It would be difficult for such efforts to generate any long-term improvement in the economic well-being of residents. Although issues such as neighborhood crime and deteriorated housing stock all need to be addressed effectively in central-city neighborhood redevelopment, the most fundamental issue is how to enhance human-capital accumulation. If low-skilled workers do not acquire skills needed for upward mobility on their economic ladder, the chances for them to ride with the mainstream economic prosperity are slim, and neighborhood redevelopment will, at most, merely move people from joblessness to the working poor. We conclude, therefore, that the redevelopment of central-city neighborhoods will come only after the human-capital deficit is effectively addressed.

References

Bingham, Richard D., and Veronica Z. Kalich. 1996. "The Tie That Binds: Downtowns, Suburbs, and the Dependence Hypothesis." *Journal of Urban Affairs* 18(2): 153–171.

Bingham, Richard D., and Deborah Kimble. 1995. "The Industrial Composition of Edge Cities: The New Urban Reality." *Economic Development Quarterly* 9 (August): 259–272.

Bingham, Richard D., and Zhongcai Zhang. 1997. "Poverty and Economic Morphology of Ohio Central-City Neighborhoods." *Urban Affairs Review* 32(6): 766–796.

Bingham, Richard D., William M. Bowen, Yosra A. Amara, Lynn W. Bachelor, Jane Dockery, Jack Dustin, Deborah Kimble, Thomas Maraffa, David L. McKee, Kent P. Schwirian, Gail Gordon Sommers, and Howard A. Stafford. 1997. *Beyond Edge Cities.* New York: Garland.

Blair, John P. 1995. *Local Economic Development: Analysis and Practice.* Thousand Oaks, CA: Sage Publications.

Blair, John P., and Robert Premus. 1993. "Location Theory." In R. D. Bingham and R. Mier (eds.), *Theories of Local Economic Development,* pp. 3–26. Newbury Park, CA: Sage Publications.

Dymski, Gary, and John Veitch. 1996. "Credit Flows to Cities." In Todd Schafer and Jeff Faux (eds.), *Reclaiming Prosperity: A Blueprint for Progressive Economic Reform.* New York: M. E. Sharpe.

Fishman, Robert. 1987. *Bourgeois Utopias: The Rise and Fall of Suburbia.* New York: Basic Books.

Garreau, Joel. 1991. *Edge City: Life on the New Frontier.* New York: Doubleday/Anchor Books.

Porter, Michael. 1995. "The Competitive Advantage of the Inner City." *Harvard Business Review* 73(3) May: 55–71.

Rusk, David. 1993. *Cities Without Suburbs.* Washington: Woodrow Wilson Center Press.

Appendix A

Twenty-four Industry Factors

(NOTE: Bolder scores are those that are either larger than 0.40 in absolute value or the first 10 largest absolute values under each factor.)

Industry	Factor							
	1	2	3	4	5	6	7	8
General contractors	0.169	-0.045	0.116	**0.564**	0.021	0.104	-0.065	0.301
Heavy contractors	0.101	-0.040	**0.557**	0.335	-0.082	0.366	0.212	0.158
Special trades	-0.037	-0.039	**0.674**	0.112	0.022	0.082	0.031	**0.406**
Lumber and wood products	0.045	-0.138	0.143	0.085	0.014	**0.666**	-0.015	0.256
Furniture and fixtures	0.083	0.033	0.007	0.106	0.159	0.061	0.339	-0.027
Stone, clay, and glass products	0.046	0.380	0.118	**0.605**	-0.124	0.079	0.056	-0.141
Primary metals	-0.045	-0.010	0.018	-0.004	-0.027	-0.002	**0.933**	0.007
Fabricated metal products	-0.181	0.109	0.093	0.038	0.017	0.154	**0.462**	0.029
Industrial machinery and equipment	-0.079	-0.024	-0.003	-0.014	-0.005	0.070	0.059	0.011
Electronic and other electrical equipment	0.088	0.040	-0.009	-0.001	**0.661**	-0.021	0.018	0.149
Transportation equipment	-0.020	0.010	-0.052	-0.058	0.068	0.060	-0.044	0.060
Instruments and related products	0.082	-0.015	-0.021	0.004	-0.051	-0.008	0.005	0.052
Miscellaneous manufacturing industries	-0.126	-0.159	0.113	0.084	-0.077	0.090	0.205	**0.647**
Food and kindred products	0.003	0.035	-0.004	-0.005	0.028	0.020	-0.008	0.097
Textiles mills products	-0.022	-0.114	-0.026	0.079	0.045	0.072	-0.006	0.034
Apparel and other textile products	-0.031	-0.035	-0.023	-0.012	-0.036	-0.039	0.021	0.113
Paper and allied products	-0.122	0.104	**0.457**	-0.028	0.051	0.044	0.074	0.014
Chemicals and allied products	-0.022	-0.035	0.111	0.010	0.049	-0.020	-0.025	-0.018
Petroleum and coal products	-0.052	-0.035	0.001	-0.052	-0.029	-0.002	**0.962**	0.032
Rubber products (SIC 301–306)	-0.046	0.023	-0.020	-0.066	-0.007	0.030	0.029	0.126
Plastics products (SIC 308)	-0.025	0.008	-0.066	-0.075	0.009	**0.729**	-0.025	-0.189
Leather and leather products	0.007	-0.068	0.000	0.035	0.019	-0.020	-0.020	-0.026

Transportation services	-0.083	0.123	0.113	0.035	-0.002	**0.832**	0.056	0.117
Wholesale	0.185	0.073	0.323	0.198	0.079	0.089	0.178	0.352
Building materials and garden supplies	0.225	0.296	-0.068	-0.029	-0.038	-0.015	-0.130	**0.724**
General merchandise stores (SIC 53)	-0.050	**0.516**	0.117	-0.121	0.062	0.102	-0.015	0.103
Grocery stores (SIC 541)	0.158	0.266	-0.081	0.070	0.043	0.043	0.031	0.039
Meat and fish markets (SIC 542)	0.082	-0.010	-0.026	0.269	-0.072	-0.115	-0.040	0.022
Dairy products stores (SIC 545)	0.249	0.033	0.016	-0.031	-0.071	-0.046	0.004	0.020
Retail bakeries (SIC 546)	0.032	-0.102	-0.041	0.137	0.159	0.151	0.041	0.253
New and used car dealers (SIC 551–552)	0.102	**0.412**	-0.046	-0.120	**0.506**	0.183	-0.071	-0.017
Gasoline service stations (SIC 554)	0.207	0.154	0.093	-0.087	**0.494**	0.198	-0.089	-0.078
Apparel and accessory stores (SIC 56)	0.137	0.135	0.013	0.019	0.005	-0.024	-0.027	0.039
Furniture and home furnishing stores (SIC 57)	0.363	0.242	0.308	0.066	0.069	-0.112	0.118	0.188
Drug stores and proprietary stores (SIC 591)	**0.443**	0.050	-0.089	0.222	0.105	0.075	0.017	0.133
Liquor stores (SIC 592)	-0.053	-0.024	0.225	-0.002	0.080	-0.041	-0.030	0.339
Used merchandise stores (SIC 593)	-0.085	0.062	0.015	0.089	-0.084	0.052	-0.071	-0.061
Printing and publishing	-0.113	0.042	0.201	-0.095	-0.081	-0.009	0.031	-0.118
Communications	0.215	**0.660**	0.081	0.081	0.028	-0.056	0.000	-0.066
Advertising	0.257	0.098	**0.851**	-0.030	-0.003	-0.029	-0.035	-0.103
Credit reporting and collection	0.338	**0.506**	-0.013	-0.004	0.163	0.111	-0.030	0.079
Motion picture and allied services	0.039	0.013	0.050	0.117	0.214	0.021	-0.050	0.042
Electric, gas, and sanitary	0.080	-0.031	0.018	0.039	-0.019	-0.035	0.021	0.022
Commercial banks (SIC 602)	0.180	0.094	0.131	-0.043	0.036	-0.006	-0.045	-0.023
Savings institutions (SIC 603)	0.256	0.055	-0.009	-0.114	0.029	-0.042	0.304	-0.142

(continues)

(Continued)

Industry				Factor				
	1	2	3	4	5	6	7	8
Credit unions (SIC 606)	-0.001	-0.097	-0.002	0.011	**0.763**	-0.066	-0.038	-0.115
Functions closely related to banking	-0.072	-0.100	-0.055	-0.045	0.303	-0.140	0.087	0.261
Nondepository institutions (SIC 61)	0.146	**0.874**	-0.002	0.050	0.009	0.030	-0.009	0.043
Security and commodity brokers (SIC 62)	**0.507**	0.112	-0.002	0.055	0.040	-0.071	-0.026	0.078
Insurance agents, brokers, and services	**0.857**	0.154	0.061	-0.007	0.082	0.007	-0.015	-0.066
Real estate (SIC 65)	**0.423**	0.219	0.129	**0.542**	0.003	-0.023	-0.065	-0.018
Engineering and architecture	**0.736**	0.033	**0.458**	-0.006	-0.050	0.057	-0.054	0.099
Accounting	**0.647**	-0.032	0.039	0.194	0.038	-0.057	-0.030	-0.143
Miscellaneous business	**0.685**	0.232	0.126	0.217	0.249	-0.042	0.009	0.164
Legal services	**0.454**	0.159	0.050	0.162	0.116	-0.036	-0.028	-0.249
Medical services	0.254	-0.070	-0.052	**0.619**	0.280	-0.039	-0.060	-0.044
Hospitals	-0.116	-0.159	-0.091	0.173	0.274	-0.105	0.037	-0.093
Education	0.208	-0.002	-0.074	-0.054	-0.089	-0.010	-0.036	0.015
Welfare	0.109	0.027	0.051	0.103	-0.041	-0.043	-0.014	0.069
Child daycare services (SIC 835)	0.363	0.244	-0.130	0.087	0.187	-0.012	0.066	0.027
Nonprofit	-0.004	0.280	0.063	0.048	0.321	-0.013	-0.059	0.087
Government	-0.006	0.189	-0.016	-0.081	-0.077	0.076	-0.016	-0.022
Miscellaneous social services	0.032	-0.051	-0.005	**0.838**	-0.054	-0.045	-0.028	0.052
Domestic services	0.383	-0.140	0.385	0.010	-0.122	-0.086	-0.093	-0.174
Hotels	0.292	0.243	0.058	-0.021	0.078	0.099	-0.066	0.131
Eating and drinking establishments	**0.544**	0.083	0.172	-0.009	0.210	0.076	-0.070	0.041
Repair	-0.109	-0.096	0.319	0.058	0.193	0.208	0.092	**0.434**
Laundry	**0.778**	-0.090	-0.003	0.066	-0.169	0.024	-0.026	0.059
Barber and beauty shops	**0.614**	0.166	-0.034	0.001	0.008	-0.114	-0.016	-0.011
Entertainment	**0.402**	0.105	0.063	0.010	0.106	0.067	-0.065	-0.103
Miscellaneous personal services	**0.582**	0.073	-0.113	0.021	0.064	**0.542**	-0.059	0.255

Industry	Factor							
	9	*10*	*11*	*12*	*13*	*14*	*15*	*16*
General contractors	0.089	-0.041	0.016	0.171	-0.044	-0.049	0.292	0.063
Heavy contractors	-0.062	-0.122	-0.044	-0.126	0.118	-0.037	0.084	0.082
Special trades	0.082	0.036	0.277	0.053	-0.061	0.029	0.106	0.016
Lumber and wood products	-0.003	-0.093	0.094	0.142	-0.007	0.013	0.052	-0.095
Furniture and fixtures	0.224	-0.088	**0.506**	0.105	-0.035	-0.191	0.109	0.065
Stone, clay, and glass products	-0.046	0.140	0.164	0.174	-0.085	-0.072	-0.038	-0.171
Primary metals	-0.045	-0.024	0.033	-0.012	-0.012	-0.010	-0.041	0.008
Fabricated metal products	0.076	0.221	0.311	0.187	-0.063	-0.123	-0.003	0.115
Industrial machinery and equipment	0.057	0.068	-0.003	**0.692**	-0.025	-0.018	0.361	0.182
Electronic and other electrical equipment	0.243	0.149	-0.162	0.000	-0.053	-0.131	0.217	-0.133
Transportation equipment	-0.040	-0.065	0.042	0.024	0.070	-0.022	-0.020	-0.037
Instruments and related products	0.119	0.145	-0.050	0.296	-0.076	0.029	0.046	**0.805**
Miscellaneous manufacturing industries	0.002	0.126	-0.010	-0.089	-0.135	0.089	0.037	-0.037
Food and kindred products	0.208	0.006	**0.832**	0.066	-0.068	-0.019	0.055	-0.060
Textiles mills products	-0.040	**0.821**	0.013	-0.007	-0.048	-0.068	-0.024	0.043
Apparel and other textile products	-0.039	0.000	0.077	-0.025	0.012	-0.023	0.021	-0.045
Paper and allied products	0.044	0.003	0.069	0.020	0.022	-0.133	-0.091	0.118
Chemicals and allied products	-0.045	0.068	0.004	-0.076	-0.060	0.025	-0.041	-0.045
Petroleum and coal products	-0.014	-0.020	0.002	-0.017	0.026	0.003	0.017	-0.046
Rubber products (SIC 301–306)	-0.017	-0.049	-0.025	0.030	0.030	-0.048	-0.012	0.058
Plastics products (SIC 308)	-0.026	0.083	-0.042	0.104	-0.055	-0.051	0.051	0.071
Leather and leather products	**0.940**	-0.031	0.133	-0.025	0.037	-0.029	0.027	0.009
Transportation services	-0.007	0.041	0.052	-0.078	-0.034	0.015	-0.032	-0.028

(continues)

(continued)

Industry	Factor							
	9	10	11	12	13	14	15	16
Wholesale	0.022	0.065	**0.525**	0.163	-0.070	-0.005	0.217	0.075
Building materials and garden supplies	-0.015	-0.034	0.205	0.106	0.001	-0.012	0.103	0.116
General merchandise stores (SIC 53)	0.246	-0.131	0.049	-0.141	0.021	-0.096	0.005	0.327
Grocery stores (SIC 541)	0.000	-0.096	0.041	**0.422**	-0.027	0.025	0.064	0.345
Meat and fish markets (SIC 542)	-0.037	-0.005	0.009	-0.050	-0.100	-0.071	0.049	-0.078
Dairy products stores (SIC 545)	0.088	-0.007	-0.087	0.141	-0.059	-0.104	-0.029	-0.072
Retail bakeries (SIC 546)	0.321	0.010	-0.103	0.187	-0.022	-0.076	**0.642**	-0.056
New and used car dealers (SIC 551–552)	0.028	-0.049	-0.009	0.054	-0.098	0.143	0.054	0.036
Gasoline service stations (SIC 554)	0.064	0.095	-0.015	0.169	-0.120	-0.107	0.035	0.098
Apparel and accessory stores (SIC 56)	**0.921**	-0.006	0.105	-0.015	0.022	0.057	0.054	0.114
Furniture and home furnishing stores (SIC 57)	-0.088	0.006	0.029	-0.022	-0.010	0.144	0.307	0.252
Drug stores and proprietary stores (SIC 591)	-0.052	-0.142	-0.045	**0.431**	0.100	-0.181	0.081	0.248
Liquor stores (SIC 592)	0.068	0.083	-0.166	0.130	-0.139	-0.118	-0.299	0.067
Used merchandise stores (SIC 593)	0.105	0.106	0.049	0.035	-0.077	0.052	-0.071	0.093
Printing and publishing	0.257	0.172	-0.077	0.066	**0.648**	-0.028	0.062	-0.026
Communications	0.021	0.126	0.080	0.167	-0.053	0.357	-0.035	-0.134
Advertising	-0.012	0.004	-0.040	0.001	-0.028	0.069	0.015	-0.010
Credit reporting and collection	0.004	-0.058	-0.129	-0.123	-0.010	0.179	0.185	0.089
Motion picture and allied services	-0.075	-0.051	0.160	**0.764**	0.036	0.076	0.051	0.109
Electric, gas, and sanitary	-0.020	0.006	-0.017	0.032	-0.059	0.087	-0.049	0.030
Commercial banks (SIC 602)	-0.045	-0.007	0.172	0.135	-0.037	-0.027	**0.776**	0.090
Savings institutions (SIC 603)	0.167	-0.031	-0.144	0.128	-0.047	0.337	0.161	0.029
Credit unions (SIC 606)	-0.092	-0.063	0.200	0.114	0.080	0.031	-0.016	0.008

Functions closely related to banking	-0.048	0.061	-0.065	-0.074	-0.039	0.114	-0.003	-0.116
Nondepository institutions (SIC 61)	0.009	0.042	0.031	-0.009	0.000	-0.082	0.011	0.033
Security and commodity brokers (SIC 62)	-0.030	**0.639**	0.087	-0.080	-0.025	0.264	0.014	0.207
Insurance agents, brokers, and services	0.055	0.030	0.172	0.067	0.013	0.068	0.033	0.033
Real estate (SIC 65)	0.139	0.095	-0.109	0.030	0.005	0.283	-0.027	0.088
Engineering and architecture	-0.019	-0.062	0.083	0.113	0.187	0.001	-0.028	0.071
Accounting	0.112	0.067	-0.145	-0.154	-0.092	0.050	0.181	0.279
Miscellaneous business	-0.044	0.040	0.185	0.080	0.042	0.154	0.042	0.094
Legal services	-0.016	0.081	-0.047	-0.114	-0.082	0.099	0.046	-0.024
Medical services	-0.066	-0.058	-0.093	0.048	0.135	0.125	-0.043	0.048
Hospitals	-0.097	-0.075	-0.027	-0.052	**0.670**	0.153	-0.003	0.063
Education	-0.023	0.066	-0.017	0.008	**0.839**	-0.072	-0.087	-0.055
Welfare	-0.002	-0.013	0.001	-0.005	-0.022	**0.873**	-0.086	0.024
Child daycare services (SIC 835)	0.061	0.007	-0.274	0.196	-0.073	0.339	0.092	-0.256
Nonprofit	-0.121	0.116	0.303	-0.090	0.254	0.152	0.078	0.007
Government	0.027	**0.769**	-0.064	0.027	0.362	-0.073	0.037	-0.064
Miscellaneous social services	0.048	0.006	0.057	-0.013	-0.030	0.072	-0.004	0.008
Domestic services	0.022	-0.086	-0.150	-0.004	0.017	0.098	0.071	-0.080
Hotels	-0.042	0.358	0.160	-0.116	0.001	0.338	**0.406**	0.263
Eating and drinking establishments	0.035	-0.053	0.037	0.032	0.065	-0.025	0.098	**0.604**
Repair	0.048	0.023	0.151	0.020	-0.090	0.101	0.204	0.032
Laundry	0.082	-0.038	-0.003	0.019	0.042	0.008	-0.090	-0.074
Barber and beauty shops	0.044	0.112	-0.168	0.001	-0.112	0.031	0.122	-0.073
Entertainment	-0.005	-0.065	-0.166	0.048	0.111	**0.477**	0.135	-0.022
Miscellaneous personal services	0.024	0.084	0.074	-0.070	0.101	0.018	0.186	0.050

(continues)

(Continued)

Industry	Factor							
	17	18	19	20	21	22	23	24
General contractors	0.295	0.010	0.131	-0.119	-0.021	-0.047	0.185	-0.100
Heavy contractors	0.037	-0.106	-0.053	0.012	-0.196	-0.012	0.002	0.187
Special trades	0.288	-0.005	0.028	0.036	0.082	-0.086	0.072	0.038
Lumber and wood products	-0.162	-0.051	0.035	0.043	**0.456**	-0.032	-0.026	-0.027
Furniture and fixtures	-0.015	-0.189	-0.078	0.232	**0.431**	0.015	-0.097	-0.113
Stone, clay, and glass products	-0.017	-0.141	-0.086	0.081	-0.136	0.037	0.014	0.127
Primary metals	-0.014	0.018	-0.022	-0.011	0.006	-0.038	-0.010	0.025
Fabricated metal products	**0.525**	-0.028	0.230	0.163	-0.038	0.048	0.067	0.098
Industrial machinery and equipment	0.068	-0.089	0.346	0.018	-0.159	-0.049	-0.008	0.174
Electronic and other electrical equipment	0.061	-0.203	-0.033	0.289	0.046	-0.061	-0.077	-0.042
Transportation equipment	-0.052	-0.059	**0.794**	-0.097	-0.016	-0.008	0.161	-0.026
Instruments and related products	0.016	-0.132	0.054	0.026	0.057	-0.102	-0.044	0.056
Miscellaneous manufacturing industries	-0.061	0.073	0.168	0.161	0.063	0.010	0.078	0.289
Food and kindred products	0.022	-0.043	0.079	-0.030	-0.061	-0.024	0.088	-0.029
Textiles mills products	0.144	-0.042	-0.003	0.211	-0.003	0.097	0.028	0.057
Apparel and other textile products	0.003	-0.031	0.194	0.086	0.025	0.005	**0.823**	-0.074
Paper and allied products	0.318	0.012	**0.648**	0.179	0.073	0.009	0.035	-0.018
Chemicals and allied products	**0.845**	0.009	0.001	-0.086	0.098	0.001	-0.025	0.085
Petroleum and coal products	0.014	-0.017	-0.002	-0.028	0.037	0.012	0.028	-0.005
Rubber products (SIC 301–306)	0.103	-0.024	-0.026	0.062	0.186	0.010	-0.075	**0.782**
Plastics products (SIC 308)	-0.007	-0.080	-0.009	-0.061	-0.036	-0.007	-0.039	-0.029
Leather and leather products	-0.026	-0.046	-0.020	0.018	0.013	-0.040	-0.009	-0.022
Transportation services	0.117	0.038	0.070	0.056	-0.053	-0.089	0.064	0.073

Wholesale	0.284	-0.076	0.068	0.086	0.213	-0.015	0.094	0.068
Building materials and garden supplies	0.045	-0.039	-0.015	-0.060	0.052	-0.008	0.110	0.006
General merchandise stores (SIC 53)	0.223	0.419	0.095	0.128	-0.062	0.189	-0.086	-0.062
Grocery stores (SIC 541)	-0.047	-0.003	-0.040	0.040	0.280	0.018	0.079	-0.118
Meat and fish markets (SIC 542)	-0.013	0.160	0.009	0.022	-0.010	**0.783**	-0.019	0.004
Dairy products stores (SIC 545)	0.017	**0.790**	-0.059	-0.005	0.032	0.135	-0.029	-0.036
Retail bakeries (SIC 546)	-0.037	-0.075	0.008	0.029	-0.075	-0.003	0.000	-0.011
New and used car dealers (SIC 551–552)	0.150	0.224	-0.078	-0.143	-0.004	-0.125	0.148	-0.174
Gasoline service stations (SIC 554)	-0.052	-0.011	-0.221	0.017	-0.076	0.141	0.271	0.356
Apparel and accessory stores (SIC 56)	0.008	0.150	-0.006	0.053	-0.010	0.031	-0.019	0.018
Furniture and homefurnishing stores (SIC 57)	0.139	0.288	-0.137	0.092	0.067	-0.078	0.067	0.122
Drug stores and proprietary stores (SIC 591)	-0.015	-0.017	-0.148	0.031	0.157	0.082	0.189	-0.287
Liquor stores (SIC 592)	-0.266	-0.116	-0.047	-0.280	-0.019	0.143	-0.044	-0.120
Used merchandise stores (SIC 593)	-0.033	0.025	-0.019	**0.788**	0.059	0.054	0.215	0.032
Printing and publishing	-0.032	-0.038	0.223	0.008	0.086	-0.038	0.077	-0.073
Communications	-0.035	-0.142	0.000	-0.078	-0.078	-0.094	0.094	0.161
Advertising	0.002	0.031	0.063	-0.101	0.041	0.012	-0.023	-0.041
Credit reporting and collection	-0.015	-0.057	-0.025	-0.112	0.236	0.244	-0.061	-0.126
Motion picture and allied services	-0.079	0.217	-0.088	-0.038	0.138	-0.026	-0.052	-0.013
Electric, gas and sanitary	0.132	0.038	0.010	-0.021	**0.822**	-0.031	0.021	0.210
Commercial banks (SIC 602)	-0.047	0.007	-0.081	-0.086	0.019	0.103	0.065	-0.025
Savings institutions (SIC 603)	0.151	-0.056	-0.079	-0.189	-0.098	0.428	0.174	0.094
Credit unions (SIC 606)	0.046	0.042	0.290	-0.081	-0.047	-0.036	-0.111	0.027
Functions closely related to banking	-0.066	-0.079	-0.044	**0.569**	-0.118	-0.107	-0.201	0.088
Nondepository institutions (SIC 61)	-0.041	0.082	0.054	0.067	-0.029	-0.024	-0.086	0.003

(continues)

(Continued)

Industry	Factor							
	17	18	19	20	21	22	23	24
Security and commodity brokers (SIC 62)	0.020	0.047	-0.008	0.032	-0.033	0.008	0.005	-0.018
Insurance agents, brokers, and services	-0.028	0.214	-0.057	-0.118	0.043	0.133	-0.018	-0.030
Real estate (SIC 65)	0.246	0.068	-0.028	-0.114	-0.045	0.148	-0.130	-0.149
Engineering and architecture	0.067	0.022	-0.028	-0.019	0.034	-0.011	-0.105	-0.100
Accounting	-0.061	0.183	0.012	-0.175	0.084	0.051	0.072	0.055
Miscellaneous business	0.002	-0.019	-0.149	-0.080	0.116	-0.077	0.025	-0.004
Legal services	-0.238	0.329	0.016	-0.064	-0.030	-0.102	0.045	0.112
Medical services	-0.077	**0.478**	-0.087	-0.091	-0.069	0.071	0.033	-0.005
Hospitals	-0.113	0.145	0.123	-0.115	-0.148	-0.105	-0.059	0.086
Education	0.010	-0.095	-0.097	-0.018	-0.043	0.005	-0.024	0.013
Welfare	0.011	-0.094	-0.067	0.097	0.112	-0.069	0.020	-0.018
Child daycare services (SIC 835)	-0.085	0.079	0.184	0.054	-0.068	-0.258	-0.242	-0.008
Nonprofit	-0.244	0.049	0.006	-0.026	-0.061	0.287	0.126	0.086
Government	-0.060	-0.016	-0.099	-0.119	-0.010	-0.181	-0.021	-0.113
Miscellaneous social services	-0.077	-0.054	-0.044	0.148	0.194	0.161	-0.052	-0.072
Domestic services	-0.070	0.215	-0.011	0.191	-0.027	0.208	-0.002	-0.148
Hotels	-0.015	0.079	0.053	-0.067	0.021	0.090	-0.223	-0.078
Eating and drinking establishments	-0.119	0.209	-0.083	-0.006	-0.097	0.030	-0.015	0.086
Repair	-0.081	0.110	-0.049	0.078	-0.141	-0.009	**0.426**	0.060
Laundry	0.147	-0.190	0.015	0.193	-0.085	0.216	0.010	0.156
Barber and beauty shops	-0.079	0.014	0.018	-0.035	0.147	-0.175	-0.022	-0.133
Entertainment	-0.077	0.147	-0.059	0.093	-0.056	0.252	-0.130	-0.181
Miscellaneous personal services	-0.053	0.132	0.087	-0.074	-0.109	0.009	-0.057	0.032

Appendix B

Factor Loading for Ohio Central-City Neighborhoods

(Note: Numbers in bold are significant factor loadings.)

1. AKRON

a. Neighborhood Factor Loading

Zip Code	Poverty Category	Demographic Factor			
		Poverty	Working-Class	Crime	Ethnicity
44301	10–19.9%	-.540	.810	.164	-.360
44305	10–19.9%	-.731	.898	.190	-.779
44306	30–39.9%	.183	1.017	-.162	-.525
44310	10–19.9%	-.477	.737	-.103	-.116
44313	<10%	-.728	**-1.778**	.302	.169
44314	10–19.9%	-1.058	1.165	.180	-.498
44320	10–19.9%	.280	-.029	.537	-1.020

b. Industry Factor Loading

Industry Factor

Zip	1	2	3	4	5	6	7	8	9	10	11	12
44301	-.337	.214	-.680	-.900	-.589	-.213	-.723	.637	-.491	-.443	.356	-.191
44305	-.113	.048	-.265	-.312	.260	.535	-.616	-.681	.000	-.235	-.724	.415
44306	-.011	-.069	-.351	-.784	-.067	.386	-.518	.294	-.266	-.170	.492	-.332
44310	-.132	.033	.822	-.149	.493	.336	.250	.535	-.067	-1.216	-.388	-1.089
44313	**3.886**	-.313	.870	.203	.275	-.268	.109	-1.770	.534	1.011	-.641	-1.605
44314	-.332	-.178	-.048	-.415	-.395	.100	-.241	-.478	-.290	-.144	.491	-.283
44320	-.211	.513	-.764	-.683	-.271	-.534	-.478	1.249	-.076	-.807	-.191	.849

	13	**14**	**15**	16	17	18	**19**	20	21	22	23	24
44301	.025	-.539	.216	-.385	.769	-.410	-.486	-.729	.212	-.095	-.521	**1.609**
44305	.109	-.835	-.082	-.438	.496	-.528	-.653	-.125	2.685	.214	-.232	**5.770**
44306	-.396	-.440	-.117	-.153	-.426	-.425	.298	-.844	-.222	.044	.445	.447
44310	1.086	.279	.496	2.758	.134	-.113	-1.207	.338	-1.475	-.451	-.287	**3.297**
44313	-.944	.053	1.415	.290	-.425	2.923	.616	-1.267	1.910	1.225	.541	**1.517**
44314	-.404	-.608	.074	-.238	.089	-.447	-.454	-.627	-.432	.238	-.015	.092
44320	.108	.580	-.690	-.485	.044	.239	-.581	.310	-.095	-.675	-.846	1.224

2. CINCINNATI

a. Neighborhood Factor Loading

Zip Code	Poverty Category	Demographic Factor			
		Poverty	Working-Class	Crime	Ethnicity
45204	30–39.9%	.110	.460	.701	.175
45207	20–29.9%	.923	.098	.969	-.824
45208	<10%	-.347	**-3.144**	**1.962**	-.125
45209	10–19.9%	-.558	-.784	1.384	-.029
45211	<10%	-.545	-.075	-.623	-.221
45213	<10%	-.419	-.775	1.036	-.578
45216	10–19.9%	-.538	.717	.785	-.367
45220	20–29.9%	.102	**-2.126**	.773	**1.669**
45223	20–29.9%	.131	.029	.523	-.196
45224	<10%	-.338	-.636	.165	-.620
45225	>=40%	**2.847**	.301	-1.113	-.790
45226	10–19.9%	-.053	-1.490	**1.786**	-.255
45227	10–19.9%	-.205	-.458	.511	-.628
45228	<10%	-1.270	-.539	1.471	-.623
45229	30–39.9%	**1.520**	-.821	.385	-.250
45230	<10%	-.871	-.943	-.010	-.663
45232	>=40%	**1.957**	-.034	-.667	-.259
45237	10–19.9%	.004	-.447	-.025	-.157
45238	<10%	-1.120	-.065	-.318	-.598

b. Industry Factor Loading

Zip						Industry Factor						
	1	2	3	4	5	6	7	8	9	10	11	12
45204	-.686	-.512	.393	-.128	-.443	-.064	-.511	-.792	-.080	.151	2.483	1.499
45207	-.650	.903	.038	-.217	-.582	.429	-.480	-1.163	.149	.033	-.275	.165
45208	**1.400**	-1.195	.900	-.571	-1.297	-.356	-.440	-.860	-.065	-.346	-.665	.704
45209	-.385	-.574	-.855	.054	-.769	.297	.300	-.581	.507	-.012	-1.480	6.803
45211	-.174	.167	.170	-.530	.083	-.393	.219	-.177	.213	-.380	-.722	-.110
45213	.043	-.125	.313	-.739	-.167	-.346	-.339	.007	.044	-.464	-.559	.047
45216	.152	.327	-1.246	-.067	.092	-.529	-.271	.777	-.382	-.671	1.112	.358
45220	-.378	-.785	-.108	.193	.143	-.322	-.070	-.734	-.125	-.676	-.678	-.056
45223	-.338	-.571	-.048	-.097	-.050	.112	.322	.345	.198	-.346	.257	-.055
45224	-.172	-.102	-.411	.372	-.272	-.346	-.364	-.572	-.153	-.292	-.320	-.143
45225	.844	-1.152	-.520	-.708	.758	-.045	.335	-1.206	-.014	-.019	5.882	-.314
45226	.215	-.334	8.197	-.644	-.247	.362	-.320	-.685	-.233	-.688	-.593	-.244
45227	.032	-.659	.002	.298	.174	-.198	-.209	-.295	9.228	-.265	1.257	-.319
45228	-.806	.062	-.210	-.537	-.936	.455	-.307	-.301	-.112	.891	-.195	-.372
45229	-.302	-.781	-.901	1.815	.120	-.288	-.315	.067	-.259	-.644	-.268	-.010
45230	.591	-.169	-.534	-.302	-.028	-.044	-.113	-.801	-.082	-.372	-.818	.120
45232	-.837	-.084	.514	.115	.740	-.288	-.364	-.015	-.310	.042	.240	-.636
45237	.136	-.476	1.060	-.056	.067	-.516	-.350	-.522	-.275	-.248	-.032	-.567
45238	.000	.008	-.490	-.267	-.185	-.340	-.273	.132	.002	-.352	-.471	-.046

	13	14	15	16	17	18	19	20	21	22	23	24
45204	-.693	-.198	-.840	-.997	-.406	.360	-.563	-.778	-.069	.416	-.607	.227
45207	.036	.200	-.765	-.483	-.252	-.713	-.457	.265	-.242	-.583	.492	.665
45208	-.350	-.158	.037	-1.042	-.620	1.386	.013	1.802	.113	2.531	-.234	-1.174
45209	-.387	-.103	1.953	2.288	.670	-.240	1.240	.324	-1.268	-.252	-.021	.337
45211	-.372	.261	.356	.053	-.143	-.274	-.419	-.829	-.090	2.974	.510	.105
45213	-.225	.137	.029	-.262	1.229	-.120	-.759	-.333	-.296	.195	-.037	-.512
45216	.136	-.248	.076	-.127	.722	-.363	1.438	-.860	-.342	-.536	6.340	-1.579
45220	.941	.812	.436	-.061	-.559	.444	-.068	-.104	-.508	.296	-.708	-.597
45223	-.281	-.990	4.142	-1.447	-.054	-.512	-.009	-.430	.546	-.098	.125	-.521
45224	-.414	-.534	-.256	-.095	-.372	-.592	-.532	-.125	-.001	-.058	.033	.074
45225	-.611	-.725	-.298	-.884	-.052	-.466	.503	-.525	.228	.356	-1.123	-.350
45226	.478	-.867	-.918	-.056	.365	-.518	.818	.242	-.286	-.479	-.371	-.952
45227	.355	-.221	.194	.059	-.232	-.397	-.155	.158	-.074	-.369	-.082	-.137
45228	.014	-.554	-.396	-.484	.021	-.052	-.514	-.728	.074	-.923	-.448	-.636
45229	.920	.052	-.138	-.344	.614	.498	.675	-.787	-.512	-1.121	-.240	-.041
45230	-.516	.039	.484	-.132	-.022	-.052	-.349	.216	-.236	.021	.121	-.626
45232	-.277	-.154	-.553	-.365	7.401	.545	.406	-.923	.756	-.907	-.549	-.713
45237	.707	1.096	.651	.278	1.098	.071	-.353	-.029	.428	.199	.116	-.805
45238	-.406	-.403	.248	-.133	-.164	.054	-.231	-.108	-.082	.113	-.098	-.518

3. CLEVELAND

a. Neighborhood Factor Loading

Zip Code	Poverty Category	Demographic Factor			
		Poverty	Working-Class	Crime	Ethnicity
44102	30–39.9%	.136	.779	.916	**4.169**
44103	40% and above	**1.745**	.675	.671	**1.887**
44104	40% and above	**2.789**	.339	-.045	-.989
44105	20–29.9%	.775	.140	1.067	**1.527**
44106	30–39.9%	**1.925**	**-1.548**	.248	**1.513**
44108	30–39.9%	**1.598**	-.316	1.056	.006
44109	20–29.9%	-.631	.762	.890	**2.713**
44110	20–29.9%	.227	.653	.182	.205
44111	<10%	-1.219	.766	.505	.681
44119	<10%	-1.133	.371	.169	1.134
44120	20–29.9%	.791	-1.335	.670	.555
44127	30–39.9%	-.356	1.823	.542	1.335
44128	10–19.9%	.020	.176	.269	-1.256
44135	10–19.9%	-1.022	.905	.315	-.226
44144	<10%	-1.310	.961	-.574	.482

b. Industry Factor Loading

Zip	Industry Factor											
	1	2	3	4	5	6	7	8	9	10	11	12
44102	-.267	-.323	-.067	-.300	-.383	-.178	.139	.229	.019	.128	-.807	-.213
44103	.124	-.939	.096	1.245	.619	-.951	-.084	1.032	-.710	**3.478**	.857	-.642
44104	-.286	-.506	-.534	-.527	.155	-.418	1.427	-.135	-.234	-.297	.931	-.492
44105	.062	-.223	-.759	-.757	-.140	.025	**1.816**	-.681	.399	.077	-.666	.740
44106	-.229	-.626	-.719	.308	-.066	.470	-.247	-.412	-.542	-.381	-.295	-.351
44108	-.325	-.306	-.501	-.351	-.673	-.383	-.252	-.588	-.212	-.188	-.132	-.097
44109	-.441	-.479	-.216	-.622	.345	-.287	.222	-.457	.211	-.178	-.224	-.047
44110	-.692	-.244	-.279	-.391	-.960	-.314	-.138	.171	-.197	.045	-.233	.628
44111	-.368	.085	-.241	-.354	.235	-.240	.046	-.337	.060	-.196	.038	.026
44119	-.045	-.397	-.062	-.166	**2.006**	.142	-.284	-.594	-.161	.070	-.166	.078
44120	.210	-.327	-.262	-.723	.030	-.555	-.084	.144	-.184	-.293	-.749	.230
44127	-.302	-.145	.138	-.092	-.137	.070	**9.094**	.115	-.395	-.268	-.077	-.407
44128	-.319	.260	.521	-.064	-.701	-.757	-.015	**2.083**	.514	.155	-.742	-.269
44135	-.330	-.953	-.428	-.066	.304	1.069	-.071	.216	-.014	**7.412**	-.531	.090
44144	-.851	.377	.635	-.715	-.896	.057	1.086	-.753	.887	1.106	-1.243	.291

(continues)

b. Industry Factor Loading *(continued)*

Zip	Industry Factor											
	13	14	15	16	17	18	19	20	21	22	23	24
44102	-.500	-.181	-.499	.147	-.008	-.136	**2.587**	.464	1.358	.729	1.100	.941
44103	-.374	.138	-.765	-.118	.635	-.015	.919	**4.093**	.322	1.480	1.147	.841
44104	-.278	-.197	-.284	-.515	-.236	-.178	.342	.953	-.008	-.760	-1.351	-.569
44105	-.463	.377	.264	-1.042	**1.814**	-1.116	-.336	-.938	-.697	**2.529**	.366	.468
44106	1.485	**3.063**	1.065	.094	-.453	.520	.122	1.278	-.419	.676	**-1.696**	-1.259
44108	-.379	-.474	-.446	-.074	-.139	-.530	-.053	-.191	-.086	.234	-.479	-.190
44109	.074	.591	-.038	-.293	.254	-.438	-.388	-.438	-.587	.518	.153	.584
44110	-.573	-.040	-.078	.682	.234	-.063	.276	.396	-.315	-.285	-.301	.622
44111	-.404	.009	.079	.195	.218	-.302	-.177	.562	-.623	.002	.121	.133
44119	-.142	-.576	-.753	-.382	-.528	.232	-1.129	-.787	-.798	1.212	**1.968**	1.133
44120	-.416	.361	-.254	-1.145	-.312	-.132	-.015	1.266	-.772	-.407	-1.189	-.286
44127	.016	.070	-.523	.177	-.160	.384	-.232	-.219	.126	-.287	-.164	.203
44128	-.410	.518	.350	.021	.917	1.058	.562	-.634	1.482	-.304	-.396	**1.821**
44135	-.244	-.635	.160	.746	1.064	-.050	-.353	-.512	-.422	.040	-.425	-.662
44144	**2.595**	-.525	.462	-.286	-.171	-.034	.242	-.264	.552	.006	1.543	-.862

4. COLUMBUS

a.   Neighborhood Factor Loading

Zip Code	Poverty Category	Demographic Factor			
		Poverty	Working-Class	Crime	Ethnicity
43017	<10%	-.723	**-2.288**	-.793	.021
43085	<10%	-.740	**-1.795**	-.801	-.113
43201	>=40%	.824	-.547	**-1.767**	**1.850**
43202	10–19.9%	-.259	-.837	-1.282	**1.697**
43203	>=40%	**2.319**	.083	**-1.561**	-.278
43204	10–19.9%	-.733	.858	-1.249	-.516
43205	>=40%	**1.874**	.174	-1.208	-.031
43206	20–29.9%	.049	.037	-.867	.103
43207	10–19.9%	-.521	1.284	-1.304	-.777
43209	10–19.9%	-.335	**-1.561**	-.724	.278
43210	>=40%	.386	.266	**-2.727**	**4.107**
43211	30–39.9%	1.294	.563	-1.483	**-1.540**
43212	<10%	-.380	**-1.537**	-.970	.648
43213	10–19.9%	-.725	.003	-.635	-.331
43214	<10%	-.581	**-1.504**	-.803	.078
43219	20–29.9%	.702	.364	-1.342	-1.202
43220	<10%	-.612	**-2.426**	-.894	.366
43222	>=40%	.950	1.209	-1.406	.655
43223	20–29.9%	-.073	1.274	-1.399	-.390
43224	10–19.9%	-.621	.576	**-1.608**	-.510
43227	<10%	-.795	.531	-1.464	-.649
43228	10–19.9%	-.645	.586	**-1.832**	-.640
43229	<10%	-.703	-.496	**-1.679**	-.183
43231	<10%	-.694	-.489	**-1.535**	-.502
43232	<10%	-.752	.278	**-1.794**	-.530
43235	<10%	.624	-2.082	-1.259	.279

b. Industry Factor Loading

Zip						Industry Factor						
	1	2	3	4	5	6	7	8	9	10	11	12
43017	**2.115**	**1.618**	.453	.190	.241	-.631	.267	-.256	.833	.205	-.303	.556
43085	**1.401**	**5.702**	.807	1.452	-.404	-.507	.172	-.882	-.366	1.730	1.030	2.125
43201	-.469	-.566	.174	.005	-.619	-.452	-.183	.392	-.251	.284	-.279	-.420
43202	.923	-.981	-.548	-.085	-.480	-.568	-.204	-.935	-.155	.229	-.553	-.717
43203	.010	-.160	-.440	-.212	-.387	-.250	-.053	-.502	-.065	-.189	-.112	-.190
43204	-.708	-.114	1.855	-.331	.564	-.384	-.077	3.487	.608	1.002	-1.406	.867
43205	-.861	-.557	-.077	1.979	.690	-.415	-.006	-.323	-.258	-.251	-.107	-.952
43206	.863	-.220	-.116	.053	-.225	-.227	-.116	-1.320	-.255	-.203	.083	-.998
43207	.221	.605	.275	1.458	-.769	1.336	.317	-1.564	.055	.197	1.015	.535
43209	.410	-.394	.487	-.307	-.828	-.186	-.497	-.745	-.307	-.408	-.605	-.382
43210	-1.026	.247	-.272	-.402	-.495	-.596	-.171	-.383	.056	1.408	-.289	-.214
43211	-.409	-.290	-.088	-.471	-.396	-.079	-.244	-.004	-.185	-.254	-.171	-.131
43212	**1.536**	.048	.128	1.793	.873	.323	.411	1.435	-.574	-.938	1.528	2.393
43213	.764	.769	-.293	-.451	.562	-.767	.179	1.133	.611	-.013	-2.592	-.405
43214	.754	-.464	-.023	1.995	**5.970**	-.650	-.015	.285	.109	-.322	-.605	-1.285
43219	.202	-.631	-.319	.948	-1.244	2.295	-.214	4.010	.010	-.587	.399	-1.112
43220	**6.199**	-.830	-.906	-.557	-1.049	.663	-.220	1.499	-.550	-1.192	.099	.587
43222	-.674	-.720	.913	1.930	-.008	1.737	-.003	.981	.021	-.303	.308	-.482
43223	-1.179	-.897	.458	.578	-.503	1.385	-.461	1.704	-.137	-.187	-.161	1.244
43224	-.443	.214	-.346	-.817	-.533	-.551	-.396	.487	-.004	.616	-.221	-.011
43227	-.877	1.487	-.243	-1.069	1.132	.305	-.365	-.351	.043	-.453	-.463	-.537
43228	-1.228	**4.166**	.096	-.068	.397	1.847	.289	-.623	.711	-.681	1.278	-.859
43229	.971	.890	-.113	-1.080	.283	-.319	-.436	1.422	-.109	2.141	1.638	-.679
43231	.642	.254	-.286	-.132	-.309	-.872	-.159	.914	-.564	-.501	.049	-.079
43232	-.651	**4.375**	-.986	-.503	-.528	.073	-.423	1.453	-.071	-1.001	-1.011	-1.469
43235	**2.354**	.685	-.443	-.364	-.749	-1.177	.057	-.321	-.054	1.318	-1.099	-.669

	13	14	15	16	17	18	19	20	21	22	23	24
43017	-.608	**6.831**	-.913	.377	1.177	-2.039	-.189	-1.152	.570	.209	.390	-.543
43085	-.142	.172	-.183	-2.409	-1.555	-.355	-.358	-.805	-1.207	-1.543	.111	1.703
43201	-.269	.469	.336	.110	-.682	.314	.277	-.002	-.050	-.327	-.589	-.019
43202	-.992	-.578	-.512	6.120	-1.078	-.773	.046	-.300	-.460	-1.158	-.082	.255
43203	-.540	.445	-.472	-.847	-.601	.114	.468	-.112	.005	-1.088	-.906	-.014
43204	-1.211	-1.135	-3.043	.467	-2.371	-1.373	-.409	-2.767	-.081	1.415	-.413	-.834
43205	.351	1.870	.333	-.497	-1.479	.655	.225	.422	-.317	-.365	-.503	.160
43206	-.814	-.807	-.680	.395	-.886	.235	.482	.240	-.258	-1.071	.715	.723
43207	-.343	-.611	-.839	-.576	.369	-1.351	-.569	2.663	-.364	.093	.454	.638
43209	-.166	.797	.269	.227	-.023	.265	-.791	2.676	-.078	-.416	2.410	.297
43210	**7.657**	-.560	-.193	-.516	-.301	-.104	-.750	-.631	.537	-.253	.059	.177
43211	-.210	-.240	-.153	-.298	.046	-.459	-.533	-.037	-.223	-.236	-.395	-.322
43212	.662	-1.336	.295	1.684	-.593	-1.220	-1.297	.679	6.087	-.648	-.166	**-2.283**
43213	-.575	-1.463	1.787	-1.593	-.029	-1.864	-.627	2.558	-.184	-.676	-.782	-.461
43214	.504	-.281	1.209	.744	-.201	.877	-.341	-.799	-.253	-.523	1.215	.279
43219	.033	.301	1.869	-.625	-.200	.171	1.145	-.541	-.619	-1.002	-.906	.492
43220	**2.592**	-1.202	-1.776	-.282	1.187	-1.762	-.303	.667	-1.800	.947	-.435	-.080
43222	-.526	.747	-.493	-.534	-.081	.833	-.922	.100	-.972	-1.807	1.329	.458
43223	-.139	**1.966**	-.926	-.826	-1.228	.779	-.543	1.365	2.093	.523	.950	.086
43224	.072	-.319	-.413	-.096	-.423	-.028	-.802	1.793	-.150	-.726	-.124	-.620
43227	-.633	.156	.072	.336	.433	.674	-.854	-.724	.109	-.534	.429	-.866
43228	.055	-1.194	-.979	2.777	1.219	1.293	1.493	2.802	-.201	.633	-.013	-.264
43229	.018	**1.672**	.720	2.195	-.303	.798	-.451	-.495	-.600	-.471	-.879	-1.099
43231	-.087	-.562	-.416	.147	.420	.023	-.954	-.357	.433	-1.321	.446	-.509
43232	.206	-.608	.537	.870	.053	-.293	.438	-.152	.951	1.312	-1.050	-1.291
43235	-1.224	-.699	.867	-1.260	-.657	-.002	1.053	-.546	.481	-2.892	-.649	-.866

5. DAYTON

a.   Neighborhood Factor Loading

Zip Code	Poverty Category	Demographic Factor			
		Poverty	Working-Class	Crime	Ethnicity
45377	<10%	-1.104	.122	-.985	-.969
45403	20–29.9%	-.327	.645	1.283	-.053
45404	20–29.9%	.088	1.072	-.299	-.426
45405	10–19.9%	-.146	-.243	.373	-.018
45406	20–29.9%	.358	-.416	.964	-.746
45407	>=40%	**1.779**	.041	1.024	-.937
45408	>=40%	**2.085**	-.008	.389	**-1.521**
45409	30–39.9%	-.088	-.981	-.332	.664
45410	10–19.9%	-.487	.386	1.254	-.403
45414	10–19.9%	-.706	.493	-.880	-.864

b. Industry Factor Loading

Industry Factor

Zip	1	2	3	4	5	6	7	8	9	10	11	12
45377	.688	-.193	-.669	-.640	.892	7.752	-.175	-.768	-.133	.087	-.828	-.530
45403	-.438	-.551	-.030	-.554	.268	-.353	-.182	.194	-.354	.018	.038	.056
45404	-.271	-.549	.614	.234	.030	.097	.240	3.296	.112	.218	1.988	.431
45405	.264	-.364	.008	.277	.407	.181	-.149	.289	-.034	-.789	-.575	-.595
45406	-.330	-.432	-.586	-.065	-.070	-.542	-.019	-.111	-.268	-.493	-.492	-.262
45407	-.540	-.075	.017	-.340	-.816	-.050	-.212	-.495	.164	-.066	-.735	.295
45408	-.296	-.109	-.255	-.146	.794	-.402	-.247	-.966	-.339	-.236	-.189	.350
45409	-.467	-.922	.053	.662	**5.517**	-.279	-.438	-.959	-.862	-.552	.830	2.085
45410	-.604	-.222	.000	.094	-.220	-.303	-.183	.127	-.088	.276	-.351	-.127
45414	-.466	.300	2.335	.093	-.196	-.081	-.202	-.520	-1.096	.014	1.595	1.336
45417	-.452	-.297	-.478	-.482	-.268	2.218	-.234	-1.570	-.194	.284	-.209	.234

Zip	13	14	15	16	17	18	**19**	20	21	22	23	**24**
45377	-.060	.523	.160	-.674	-.485	.135	.068	-.758	.437	.086	.035	-.610
45403	-.325	-.144	-.529	-.210	.429	-.287	-.259	1.346	-.119	-.150	-.088	.110
45404	.076	.707	.187	-.121	.409	-.142	1.147	.680	-1.072	.350	-.862	**2.169**
45405	-.225	-.270	.070	-.272	.376	.140	.172	-.387	-1.301	-.782	-.299	-.354
45406	.000	.151	-.315	.103	-.190	-.204	-.340	.817	-.350	-.498	-.769	-.546
45407	-.079	.907	-.121	-.635	-.772	.009	.558	2.020	.217	-1.418	-.311	-.360
45408	1.048	-.081	-.073	-.510	-.975	-.398	**7.174**	-.648	.183	-.106	-.699	.029
45409	1.037	.750	-1.714	.602	-.431	1.810	.172	-1.278	-.425	-.468	-.389	.193
45410	-.393	-.273	-.558	-.272	-.737	.095	-.093	-.519	.039	-.434	.002	-.256
45414	-.026	-.164	5.265	.795	.161	-.423	-.844	-.599	-.693	.157	-.327	.097
45417	-.518	-.604	-.483	.237	-.178	-.843	-.419	-.759	-.052	-.154	-.524	-.638

6. TOLEDO

a. Neighborhood Factor Loading

Zip Code	Poverty Category	Demographic Factor			
		Poverty	Working-Class	Crime	Ethnicity
43605	20–29.9%	-.694	**1.583**	.945	.594
43606	10–19.9%	-.215	-.991	.613	.416
43607	20–29.9%	.269	.029	**2.068**	-.531
43608	20–29.9%	-.358	1.444	1.089	.723
43609	20–29.9%	-.795	1.308	1.001	.783
43610	30–39.9%	.836	.494	.902	-.090
43611	10–19.9%	-.938	.949	.455	-.885
43612	<10%	-1.191	.624	.694	-.504
43613	<10%	-1.198	.259	.687	-.637
43614	<10%	-.761	-.833	.363	-.365
43615	10–19.9%	-.766	-.350	.074	-.332
43620	>=40%	**1.823**	-.694	.605	-.427
43623	<10%	-1.064	-.494	.490	-.712

b. Industry Factor Loading

Zip						Industry Factor						
	1	2	3	4	5	6	7	8	9	10	11	12
43605	-.324	.032	-.112	.259	-.091	-.030	-.223	-.575	-.202	-.123	.346	-.150
43606	1.170	-.314	-.020	.544	.170	-.160	-.028	-.638	-.644	.028	.527	-1.061
43607	-.140	-.095	-.379	-.291	-.687	-.422	-.195	.249	-.263	-.345	.218	.071
43608	-.533	-.303	-.579	-.341	-.234	-.116	-.243	-.181	-.172	-.352	-.011	-.135
43609	-.644	-.262	.094	-.374	-.411	-.149	-.211	-.086	-.256	-.231	.058	.316
43610	-.767	-.464	-.426	-.499	-.647	-.524	-.390	-.992	-.117	.077	-.367	-.468
43611	-.425	.098	-.359	-.501	-.515	-.491	-.136	-.440	-.154	-.211	-.159	-.128
43612	.013	.063	.275	-.740	.191	.525	-.114	1.256	.085	-.580	.285	.194
43613	-.012	-.175	-.384	-.592	.453	-.287	-.259	-.159	-.188	-.461	-.096	.125
43614	-.281	1.279	-.336	-.092	.714	-.440	-.365	-.112	-.491	-.032	.511	-.943
43615	.278	.272	.068	-.270	.388	.110	-.149	-.562	-.248	-.306	-.276	-.528
43620	-.750	-.352	-.596	1.210	-.274	-.423	-.306	-.646	-.174	-.215	-.147	-.432
43623	.820	.713	-.377	-.300	-.589	-.291	.094	1.056	.723	-.416	-.522	2.015

(continues)

b. Industry Factor Loading (Continued)

Zip	Industry Factor											
	13	14	15	16	17	18	19	20	21	22	23	24
43605	-.467	-.548	-.465	-.229	-.463	-.672	-.511	-.485	-.487	-.155	-.198	.308
43606	.882	-.182	.193	.715	-.706	1.008	.055	-.246	-.495	-.768	-.244	.556
43607	-.305	-.523	-.416	-.394	.892	-.580	-.207	-.433	-.347	.347	-.302	-.051
43608	.765	-.234	-.595	1.032	-.018	-.310	-.427	-.427	-.237	-.321	.047	.107
43609	-.214	.505	-.356	-.145	-.002	-.199	-.569	-.133	-.330	-.098	.066	-.395
43610	-.306	.754	-.553	-.329	.175	-.014	.167	-.624	3.986	-.453	-.195	.899
43611	-.406	-.564	-.291	-.182	-.244	-.081	.344	.002	.101	1.134	-.338	-.422
43612	-.203	-.156	-.580	.343	.170	-.178	**2.325**	-.411	-.400	.192	.596	-.115
43613	-.332	-.350	-.200	-.055	.001	-.194	-.432	-.205	-.289	.705	.132	-.074
43614	.440	.366	.362	.481	-.950	.103	.183	-.278	.054	4.118	-.676	-.258
43615	-.629	-.006	-.007	-.117	-.073	.779	-.465	-.423	-.102	-.589	.626	-.511
43620	-.076	.346	-.764	.039	-.075	.287	-.214	-.446	.034	-.273	-.495	-.635
43623	-.173	-1.113	-.897	-.679	.461	6.956	-.892	.107	-.489	.436	-.474	-.801

7. YOUNGSTOWN

a. Neighborhood Factor Loading

Zip Code	Poverty Category	Demographic Factor			
		Poverty	Working-Class	Crime	Ethnicity
44504	20–29.9%	.091	-.284	.581	.602
44505	30–39.9%	.460	.412	-.371	-.374
44506	>=40%	.354	**2.124**	.949	**2.001**
44507	30–39.9%	.365	.988	.479	.269
44509	10–19.9%	-.908	1.228	.638	-.120
44510	>=40%	**2.484**	.535	.243	-.505
44511	10–19.9%	-.685	.550	-.066	-.656

b. Industry Factor Loading

	Industry Factor											
Zip	1	2	3	4	5	6	7	8	9	10	11	12
44504	-.327	.213	-.235	7.302	-.903	-.202	-.141	-.603	.030	-.249	-1.090	-.463
44505	-.395	-.108	-.132	.037	-.331	-.271	-.236	.228	-.100	-.016	.152	-.427
44506	-.789	-.360	-.354	-.050	-.642	-.168	-.108	-.321	.117	-.270	-.001	-.123
44507	-.896	.444	.153	-.338	.104	-.606	-.295	.393	-.634	-.179	2.600	-.592
44509	-.492	-.293	.021	-.324	.090	-.250	.454	1.213	-.139	-.004	-.014	-.623
44510	-.480	-.364	-.316	-.120	-.361	-.615	.534	-.449	-.247	-.209	.264	-.667
44511	-.325	-.295	-.337	-.557	-.599	-.438	-.218	-.582	-.022	-.319	-.310	-.120

	13	14	15	16	17	18	19	20	21	22	23	24
44504	-.404	-1.294	-.445	-.111	.866	-.885	.000	-.891	-.739	1.723	-.750	-.727
44505	-.417	-.275	1.440	.004	-.484	.040	-.221	.119	.008	2.567	-.307	.008
44506	-.355	.211	-.188	.044	-.232	-.197	-.543	.467	-.072	-.325	.406	-.932
44507	.307	.308	.509	.063	-.900	.143	-.931	.020	-.265	.303	.896	-.514
44509	-.143	-.169	.805	-.506	-.836	-.089	.013	-.348	-.553	-.003	3.437	.028
44510	-.424	-.463	-.414	-.185	-.411	-.266	-.323	.049	.201	-.634	-.949	-.429
44511	-.373	-.377	.176	-.247	-.041	-.448	-.210	-.412	.280	-.218	-.362	-.195

Index

About the Authors

Richard D. Bingham is professor of public administration and urban studies at the Levin College of Urban Affairs, Cleveland State University, where he is also senior research scholar of the Urban Center. He teaches courses in industrial policy and research methods. His current research interests include the economies of urban neighborhoods and modeling urban systems. He has written widely in the fields of economic development and urban studies. His latest books include *Industrial Policy American Style* (1998); *Beyond Edge Cities*, coauthored with colleagues from the Urban University Program (1997); *Dilemmas of Urban Economic Development*, edited with Robert Mier (1997); and *Global Perspectives on Economic Development*, edited with Edward Hill (1997). He is founding editor of the journal *Economic Development Quarterly* and is past president of the Urban Politics Section of the American Political Science Association.

Zhongcai Zhang is director of database marketing at Ohio Savings Bank. At Ohio Savings, Dr. Zhang manages data-mining activities and performs various analytics and modeling in support of the bank's branch development, marketing campaigns, and other customer relationship management initiatives. He is also an adjunct faculty of data mining at Cardean University. Prior to his current position at Ohio Savings, he was a senior research associate at the Center for Urban Studies, School of Architecture and Planning, at the University at Buffalo. His research interests include urban and regional economic development, metropolitan income and earnings convergence, industry location, and neighborhood economies. He has published in *Economic Development Quarterly*, *Industry Week*, *Journal of the American Planning Association*, and *Urban Affairs Review*. He has also authored or coauthored several research reports for the U.S. Environmental Protection Agency and Department of Housing and Urban Development.